HULLABALOO
In The Kitchen II

**Dallas County
Texas A&M University
Mothers' Club**
Artwork by Benjamin Knox '90

All proceeds from the sale of this cookbook will be returned to Texas A&M University for scholarships and student activities.

Library of Congress Catalogue Card Number 98-86674
ISBN 0-9612446-1-5

Additional copies may be obtained by writing:
HULLABALOO IN THE KITCHEN II
Dallas County A&M University Mothers' Club
P. O. Box 796212
Dallas, Texas 75379-6212

First Printing, November, 1998 - 5000 copies

cookbook
resources.
541 Doubletree Drive
Highland Village, TX 75067
972/317-0245

INTRODUCTION

Aggie Moms are known for their enthusiasm for Texas A&M University, for contributing funds to support campus activities and scholarships, and for being excellent cooks!! They enjoy making their family's favorite meals and sharing their recipes with friends. It is their way of expressing their love, care, and concern. Thus, a second cookbook is being published by the Dallas County A&M Mothers' Club so that you can enjoy some of our favorite foods!!

In 1922, eleven Dallas area mothers journeyed 200 miles southeast in their Model T Fords over bumpy, unpaved roads to bring picnic baskets of home cooked foods to their boys. It was on March 3, 1922, that the very first A&M Mothers' Club was formed with Mrs. H. L. Peoples as President. The idea quickly spread and there are now over 120 Mothers' Clubs in the state and nation.

The Dallas County A&M Mothers' Club was conceived to support its students and the A&M campus. Each year, we combine our efforts to produce Boutique items, sell Christmas trees, attend meetings to hear speakers talk about the campus and its varied activities, and support our spring event. We are proud to support the students and University by annually sending thousands of dollars to the campus for scholarships and many student organizations.

Included in the cookbook are favorite recipes from Aggie Moms, friends, and celebrities to share with you. Also included are beautiful pictures of the A&M campus and some of the outstanding traditions. We hope you will get as much fun and satisfaction preparing these dishes as we have had in compiling them. We think you will agree, Aggie Moms are the best cooks around!!

Gig 'em!!

JaNahn Rodriguez
President 1997-1998

Gloria Gilpin
President 1998-1999

ACKNOWLEDGEMENTS

The Dallas County A&M University Mothers' Club Cookbook Committee wishes to express their grateful appreciation and thanks to the following individuals.

Color Photography
Richard Korczynski, Aggie Dad
(3501 North Navarro, Victoria, Texas 77901)
Michael Blachly, '99
George Bush Library
Circa Antiques, Bryan, Texas

Wine Section
Merrill Bonarrigo, Messina Hof Wine Cellars
(4545 Old Reliance Road, Bryan, Texas 77808)

Legal Advisor
Larry Dwight

Benjamin Knox
The Dallas County A&M Mothers' Club wishes to express our sincere gratitude to Benjamin Knox for his contributions to our cookbook. His consultation on style and advice on publication were invaluable; his artistic talent is incredible.

"With his eloquent artistic style, his admirable work ethic, and unquestionable pride in wearing his Aggie ring, Benjamin Knox and his work are now part of A&M traditions."

Rob Clark
The Bryan-College Station Eagle

Benjamin Knox creates artwork to be treasured by capturing memories and the spirit of Aggieland. His gallery offers distinctive gift ideas for all occasions —birthdays, graduations, weddings, and other special events. Contact the gallery for the latest catalog, newsletter, and gallery exhibit information. Visit us on the web at www.benjaminknox.com

Aggie Moms are very special to me. They form a unique bond because of their love and support for their children at Texas A&M. By unifying individual abilities and talents, the Aggie Moms work countless hours to create scholarships, care packages, and provide encouragement to students. I was one of those students.

I was solely responsible for my education and almost was not able to attend Texas A&M. Scholarships were the determining factor that enabled me to be a Texas Aggie. My hometown Aggie Moms' Club of Lubbock played a significant roll in helping me. Money for college was still scarce, so I began my art career while a sophomore in the Corps of Cadets. As my work as an artist developed, all Aggie Moms supported and encouraged me. I graduated with a degree in Architecture and, soon after, opened College Station's first artist-owned gallery.

I believe strongly in giving back so that more people can experience the same important benefits that I received. I donate art prints to all scholarship fundraising events. Please contact the gallery if we can be of assistance in your next scholarship fundraiser.

In creating the drawings and paintings for this special cookbook, we wanted to express how the Aggie Moms have made a significant difference in the lives of Aggies. We also wanted to focus on how their epicurean expertise has been an important part of Aggie culture throughout history.

I want to extend a special thank you to all Aggie Moms. Your hard work makes a difference in people's lives. I am living proof!

Gig 'em!

Benjamin Knox '90

BK | BENJAMIN KNOX GALLERY

404 University Drive East
(409) 690-5669

College Station, TX 77840
1-800-299-5669

COOKBOOK COMMITTEE

Chairperson

JaNahn Rodriguez

Publication Chairperson

Julie Thedford

Judy Boldt
Patricia Bradfield
Vara Buchanan
Eileen Buis
Marion Crawford
Gloria Gilpin
Janice Myers
Anna Sheffield
Martha Tucker

Assistants

Mary Aasterud
Helen Beasley
Cindie Deasey
Cindy Etier
Pat Hardi
Katherine Thedford
Tillie Vogeli

The cookbook committee wishes to express our appreciation to our members, celebrities, and friends who so generously contributed their favorite recipe. Even though the cookbook committee did not personally test all the recipes, the recipes are "tried and true" recipes of our members and friends.

A sincere thank you also goes to our husbands and families who donated their time and energy to make this cookbook possible. We hope that you will enjoy the many outstanding and treasured recipes on the following pages.

The Dallas County A&M Mothers' Club gratefully acknowledges these generous donors who have made possible the publication of *Hullabaloo in the Kitchen II.*

Aggie Gold Sponsor
The Dixie Chicken
Rother's Bookstore & Americana Collections

Aggie Silver Sponsor
ANCO Insurance
Blue Bell Creameries
First American Bank of Bryan/College Station, Texas

Whoop! Sponsor
Dallas A&M Club
Past Presidents of Dallas County A&M University Mothers' Club
　　Mary Aasterud
　　Helen Beasley
　　Mary Ellen Blankenship
　　Nina Cox
　　Bonner DeShazo
　　Peggy Erickson
　　Opal Jones
　　Mary Lou Laden
　　Wanda Lymenstull
　　Janice Myers
　　JaNahn Rodriguez
　　Carol Smith

Gig'em Sponsor
Julee White
Cafe Eccell

Twelfth Mom Sponsor
Marion Crawford
Gloria Gilpin
Anna Sheffield
Glinn White, Jr.

Table of Contents

College Station 1938

Spirit of
Aggieland

THE SPIRIT OF AGGIELAND

"Some may boast of prowess bold
Of the school they think so grand.
But there's a spirit can ne'er be told.
It's the Spirit of Aggieland."

Bob's wife had never seen him cry. But here he was, a grown man with a family, standing shoulder to shoulder with his old Aggie friends, swallowing hard to hold back the tears. His shivering chest defied heroic efforts to subdue his emotions as they sang "The Spirit of Aggieland."

Since its humble beginning as a public land grant college, Texas A&M University has inspired students far beyond mere school loyalty. What began as a small, all-male, military institution is now recognized as an established leader in education. Yet A&M still provides more commissioned officers to our armed forces than any institution outside the military academies.

Established in 1876, A&M can boast of being the first public institution of higher education in Texas. The main campus includes 5,115 acres and is the largest campus of any major university in the country. A&M also proudly boasts the George Bush Presidential Library and Museum. The University's enrollment now exceeds 40,000 students, but its size has not diminished the value of Aggie Spirit.

Aggies are more inclined to talk about the Spirit of Aggieland than of its many accomplishments. The Spirit is a matter of the heart, steeped in tradition. The intangible Spirit of Aggieland is exemplified in traditions and a sense of camaraderie, manifested in the students and carried through generations of Aggies around the world. Tradition is what makes A&M unique and is the binding link between Aggies of yesterday, today, and tomorrow.

Aggie Spirit can put a lump in your throat and a tear in your eye! If you are not an Aggie, you do not understand it. If you are an Aggie, you cannot explain it.

BONFIRE

Darkness falls on the campus of Texas A&M University as tens of thousands of Aggie supporters begin to gather around the six-level stack of logs. They eagerly find a place in the Aggie family circle—groups of talkative friends—young couples walking hand in hand—dads with young children on their shoulders—curious new Aggie parents—old Ags returning to rekindle the Spirit or proudly accompanying their sons and daughters (the next generation of Aggies).

A muffled drum cadence escalates to heart-pounding rhythm as the band and the Yell Leaders march into the circle and around the stack. The band plays the "Aggie War Hymn" while the exuberant crowd stands arm in arm singing ... "Hullabaloo, Caneck, Caneck...". Torches gleam against the dark night, making a comet-like streak as they are propelled toward the logs. Yell Practice begins. The flames grow brighter. Catch the Spirit! Feel the Heat!

What began as a casual custom of gathering scrap wood in the 1920's has become a tradition of building the world's largest bonfire. The event is always held before the Aggie-Longhorn game, the spiraling flames a symbol of undying Aggie Spirit and the burning desire "to beat the hell outta t.u."

There is more to Bonfire than tradition and symbolism. It is a very organized effort, implemented by student leadership. Students learn quickly what is expected and then do whatever is necessary to get the job done. They learn the benefits of starting at the bottom, by carrying logs and then working their way up to designing the stack. Thousands of students don hard hats and spend countless hours cutting, hauling, and unloading the logs. They build and guard the stack. It is a unique effort of students working together, a synthesis of camaraderie, enthusiasm, hard work, pride in their school, and pride in their accomplishments.

Since the 1920's, Bonfire has been burned every year except 1963. The lighting of the Bonfire was canceled out of respect for President John F. Kennedy, who died a few days earlier. In 1994, excessive rain saturated and softened the ground underneath the stack, causing it to fall two weeks before Bonfire. Students and community volunteers worked around the clock to rebuild the stack, a feat usually requiring two months. And, once again, Bonfire burned brightly, a luminous testimonial to the fierce Aggie pride, spirit, and determination. The 1994 Aggies can boast, "We built it twice!"

Organization, teamwork, leadership! Perhaps these elements, combined with tradition, are why A&M graduates are successful. Leadership skills are ingrained into them - or perhaps strong leaders choose to attend Texas A&M.

14

THE TWELFTH MAN

There is no need for A&M students to bring stadium seats to their football games. Aggies have been standing by their team since the January 1, 1922, Dixie Classic Football game when the tradition began. The underdog Aggies were on the verge of beating the Centre College team which boasted three All-Americans. The A&M team was plagued by injuries. Coach Dana X. Bible watched as, one by one, his players were relegated to the sidelines. Fearful of the possibility of having to finish the game with less than a full team, Coach Bible called into the stands for E. King Gill, a former reserve player. Gill donned the uniform of an injured player and stood by, ready to play, although he was never needed. The Aggies won the game 22-14.

Gill's readiness to play symbolizes the willingness of Aggie fans to support their team. This spirit continues today as the Aggie student body, known as the Twelfth Man, stands throughout the game as a gesture of loyalty and readiness for duty.

HULLABALOO

"Hullabaloo, Caneck, Caneck..." is the beginning of the "Aggie War Hymn", the Texas A&M fight song. Hullabaloo means a lot of commotion and Aggies sure know how to do that!

FISH CAMP

A&M Freshmen are called "Fish" and fish have never been known for their great knowledge. Therefore, fish must go to school to gain Aggie knowledge. After three glorious days at a camp in the East Texas Piney Woods, they know what it means to be an Aggie. They know the yells, the "Aggie War Hymn", and "The Spirit of Aggieland". They know about the Twelfth Man, Bonfire, Reveille, and Silver Taps and they know how to "Gig 'em". They know about senior rings and that it will be a long, long time before they have earned the privilege of wearing one. But, most of all, they know about Aggie friendships and have begun to establish bonds that will last a lifetime. They are now Aggies. And, once an Aggie, always an Aggie!

YELL PRACTICE

Remember this—Aggies do not cheer. They yell! Aggies are lead by Yell Leaders, not cheerleaders. Aggies attend Yell Practice, not pep rallies. There is a difference!

The best times for Yell Practice? Midnight before a football game, immediately after every home game, and at Bonfire.

The first Midnight Yell Practice, conceived on a lark by a small group of enthusiastic Aggies in 1932, has become a tradition now held at Kyle Field the night before every home game. Where else but Aggieland could 15,000 students show up at midnight to support their team by shouting Agge yells with spirit and singing Aggie songs with pride?

No matter who is ahead when the clock runs out, Aggies hold a Yell Practice after every home game to get ready for the next game. If the Aggies prevail, freshmen students carry the yell leaders to the Fish pond and hold Yell Practice there. If the Aggies "run out of time" before achieving the highest score, then fans remain in the stands for yell practice. They may be outscored, but Aggies never lose. They just run out of time.

REVEILLE

Contrary to usual custom, the wife of the President of Texas A&M is not the First Lady of Texas A&M. She willingly relinquishes that distinction to Reveille, the collie mascot. With five stars, she is the highest ranking member of the Corps. Cadets must greet her saying, "Howdy, Miss Reveille, Ma'am." And one must never use the "d" word (dog) in her presence. For many decades, she was the only female member of the Corps.

The first Reveille was a small black and white stray that was unavoidably hit by a car, then rescued by a group of Aggies returning to campus after a football game in 1931. The boys cared for her throughout her recovery. Reveille quickly adapted to Corps life, following cadets during their daily routine, and leading the band during march-in at half-time. She was dubbed "Reveille" to her new friends after she yelped repeatedly as the bugler played the morning reveille call.

Today, Reveille is maintained by one Corps unit, Company E-2, with a sophomore cadet responsible for her care. Reveille spends the summer with her new master for the upcoming year. They travel the state visiting A&M affiliated groups and attending special events. She attends classes with the Mascot Corporal and is always welcomed in the restaurants and businesses in the community — sometimes even garnering a free meal for her keeper!

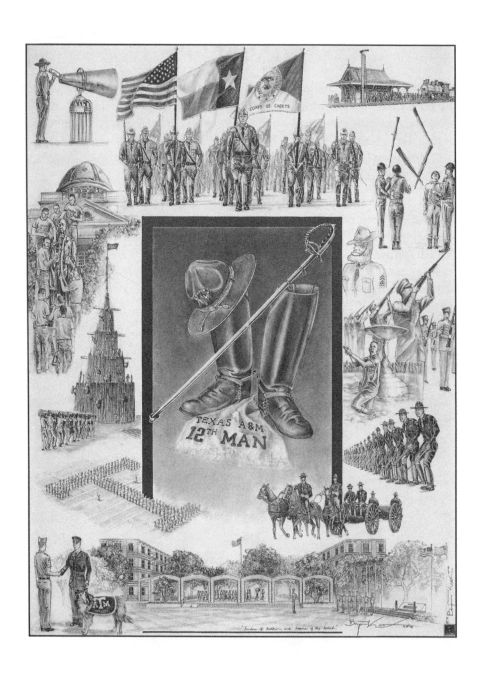

FINAL REVIEW

After the thundering of the Parsons Mounted Cavalry's cannon, the Fightin' Texas Aggie Band loudly proclaims the beginning of Final Review. The Band steps off in precision and leads the Corps onto Simpson's Drill Field where family, friends, and previous Corps members wait in the hot Texas sun.

As the Seniors pass the reviewing stand with the Commandant, University officials, and special guests looking on, they lock their arms together as they leave the field. They realize that this is the final time they will appear with their best buddies as members of the Corps of Cadets at Texas A&M University. The sadness that accompanies this final time is offset by the knowledge that these buddies will probably remain lifelong friends.

On the second pass, each Junior Corps member proudly wears his senior boots for the first time in public. He has been waiting for this day since he first entered the Corps as a lowly "fish". Now it is his turn to strut across the field with his chin held firm, his uniform tucked in to perfection, and his boots shined to the highest possible gloss. He has his spurs firmly secured. He is about to begin his final year as a member of the Corps of Cadets.

The Band continues playing. One by one, each unit with its new commander at the helm, and guidon bearer a few steps behind him, passes in front of the reviewing stand. This is the year that our new Senior Corps member will exercise the leadership skills he has developed in the Corps. It is a great, proud moment for this Corps member and his family!

GIG 'EM!

A closed fist with the thumb up is a sign of approval and of winning just about everywhere. When Aggies give each other this sign (and they frequently do), they accompany it with a hearty "Gig 'Em"! To Aggies, this is encouragement to go out and do your best at whatever you are doing. So, when you see some Aggies, give them a "Gig 'Em!" and they will be proud to give you one right back.

SILVER TAPS

The students know another fellow student's life has ended too soon—perhaps from an automobile accident, or from an illness. Early on the day of Silver Taps notice is posted on the doors of the library, Rudder Tower, and the Memorial Student Center. The flag is placed at half staff.

At 10:30, the chimes from Albritton Tower ring out to announce this ceremony of loyalty and respect. The campus lights are dimmed as students walk silently through the darkness to gather around the flag pole in front of the Academic Building. The Ross Volunteers march in a slow cadence to the statue of Sul Ross and fire three volleys with seven rifles. "Silver Taps" is played three times after the salute. The ceremony of honor is ended and students walk silently and respectfully back to their dorms. An Aggie is gone, but not forgotten. He will be remembered again at Muster.

MUSTER

"Softly call the Muster. Let comrade answer 'Here'!"

Whether in a fox hole, or on the Riviera, Aggies around the world get together every year to remember their college days. "If there is an A&M man within 100 miles of you, you are expected to get together, eat a little, and live over the days you spent at the A&M College of Texas", urged an editorial in the March, 1923, Texas Aggie. Every April 21, the date Texas' independence was won at the Battle of San Jacinto, Aggies gather together wherever they may be. Amid the fellowship and fond memories, homage is also paid to all students and former students who have died during the past year. When roll call for the absent is read, a living comrade answers "here".

Muster in 1942 gained national recognition when it was held at Corregidor Island in the Philippines. Fifteen days before the fall of the island, 25 men, led by General George Moore, Class of 1897, "mustered in the dim recesses of the Rock and answered 'here' for their dead classmates." Another group of Aggies was reported to have held Muster in a submarine.

And, so it has been over the years. That small group started what has become one of the greatest Aggie traditions. The Muster is symbolic of the great loyalty which binds Aggies to their school and to each other.

SENIOR RING

The most exciting day for every student at A&M is the day he receives his senior ring. More than just another piece of gold jewelry, the Aggie Ring is a symbol of countless hours of work and study. Texas A&M class rings may be ordered and worn only by an Aggie in good standing who has at least 95 semester hours with 60 hours at A&M.

Whether traveling around the globe or at a job interview, the distinctive A&M ring is instantly recognized by Aggies everywhere. The ring is worn by students with the writing facing them until they attend their class's Ring Dance, the formal dance that closes a senior's year. While standing inside a giant replica of the ring at the dance, each senior turns his ring around so that it no longer faces the wearer—it faces the world.

The top of the ring shows a shield with 13 stripes and five stars. The shield symbolizes protection of the good reputation of the alma mater. The thirteen stripes represent the original 13 United States and is symbolic of intense patriotism of graduates and undergraduates. The five stars represent phases of development—of mind (or intellect), body, spiritual attainment, emotional poise, and integrity of character.

One side of the ring shows the State Seal. The five-pointed star with olive or laurel leaf wreath represents achievement and a desire for peace. The oak leaves represent the strength to fight. Leaves joined with ribbon represent the necessity of joining these two traits to accomplish one's ambition to serve.

The other side of the ring shows the ancient weapons of saber, rifle, and cannon. These represent the men of Texas who fought for their land and are determined to defend their homeland. The saber symbolizes valor and confidence. The rifle and cannon represent preparedness and defense. The crossed United States and Texas flags represent dual allegiance to nation and state.

THE ASSOCIATION OF FORMER STUDENTS

There are no ex-Aggies. Once an Aggie, always an Aggie! Each year graduates make the automatic transition from the status of students to members of the Association of Former Students. In addition, anyone who has ever attended A&M is an Aggie and may become a member of the Association on request. Friends of the University may also join.

Through the Association, Aggies maintain contact with their old friends as well as make new friends with many generations of Aggies. Former students take pride in their continued support of A&M. Many permanent facilities on campus have been made possible through the Association support.

"We are the Aggies, the Aggies are we.
True to each other as Aggies can be."

MOTHERS' CLUBS

The Mothers' Clubs were established with the purpose to show "by individual effort to contribute in every way to the comfort and welfare of the boys (and now, girls), and to cooperate with the faculty of the college in maintaining a high standard of moral conduct and intellectual attainment." Since the first Mothers' Club was founded in Dallas in 1922, over 120 have been formed in the State of Texas and in other states. Aggie Moms provide scholarships, library endowment funds, and donations to campus organizations. They raise money by selling handmade craft items (and anything that can be Aggie-ized), host receptions for freshmen students and parents, and hold regular meetings to inform and encourage Aggie Moms. The Mothers' Clubs provide moms with an opportunity to know more about Texas A&M and to appreciate the unique honor their children have by being Aggies.

PARENTS' WEEKEND

With the encouragement of Mrs. H. L. Peoples, founder and first president of the Dallas A&M Mothers' Club, A&M officials invited parents to visit their sons on the all-male campus. They anticipated only a handful of parents would travel the great distances across the back roads of the State of Texas, but were surprised when over 600 people came. Students vacated their dorms and slept on the ground to provide space for their parents.

Even today, finding a place to sleep during Parents' Weekend can be a challenge. That first parental visit evolved to honoring mothers on Mothers' Day, then to the designated Parents' Weekend. There are barbecues and picnics, Ol' Army Yell Practice, Awards Ceremonies, Variety Show, Mothers' Club Boutique, Corps of Cadets Military Review, and get-togethers for nearly every student organization.

Students put forth tremendous effort planning and preparing for Parents' Weekend to show their appreciation for their parents. By the time the parents return home, they have come to love A&M nearly as much as their children do.

AN AGGIE PRAYER

God of all men everywhere, we are thankful for your love which penetrates all barriers. Help us to be the men and women we ought to be. Make us deeply aware of the shortness and uncertainty of human life. Forgive us when we seek anything but doing Your will. As we realize our positions of leadership, may our devotion of Your presence in us allow us to stand upright before our fellow men, our leaders, and our loved ones. Instill in mankind a sense of brotherhood and a desire for peace. Amen.

AGGIE CODE OF HONOR

"Aggies do not lie, cheat, or steal, nor do they tolerate those who do."

The Aggie Code of Honor is an effort to unify the aims of Texas A&M university students toward a high code of ethics and personal dignity. For most, living under the code will be no problem, as it asks nothing of a person that is beyond reason. It only calls for honesty and integrity, characteristics which Aggies have always exemplified.

The Aggie Code of Honor functions as a symbol to all Aggies promoting understanding and loyalty to truth and confidence in each other.

Celebrities
and
Friends

To fish Jones
Love, Your Aggie Mom

REVEILLE

"Miss Reveille", the FIRST Lady of Texas A&M, contributed her favorite recipe for Championship Stew, guaranteed to bring HER team victory! "Gig 'em Rev!"

Reveille's Big 12 Championship Stew

1	pound ground LONGHORN	1	bushel TIGER stripes
2	ounces BEAR chops	2	COWBOYS, stewed
½	pound WILDCATS, cubed		Sprinkle of RED RAIDERS
11	JAYHAWK gizzards		

Mix the above ingredients in a large bowl. Stir with the ferocity of a CYCLONE. Dredge all ingredients in ground CORN HUSKS. Stuff the mixture in BUFFALO hide. Roast 60 minutes over preheated roaring AGGIE BONFIRE. Baste with lots of Aggie Spirit. Best if prepared SOONER than needed and reheated on Big 12 Championship Day!

BARBARA BUSH

Former First Lady Barbara Bush sends us one of her family's most popular recipes, along with her best wishes.

Barbecued Chicken

1	large garlic clove, crushed	1	tablespoon oil
1	teaspoon salt	3	tablespoons lemon juice
½	teaspoon pepper	1	(3-pound) fryer chicken, quartered

Put all ingredients in Ziploc bag. Shake to coat well. Refrigerate 24 hours, if possible, turning bag several times. When coals are ready, place chicken on grill, skin side up, basting with marinade. Cook until well-browned before turning. (If baking in oven, bake at 400°, skin side down first.) About 20 minutes before chicken is done, begin using your favorite bottled barbecue sauce.

"LADY BIRD" JOHNSON

Former First Lady Mrs. Lyndon Johnson is another native Texan who wanted to share a favorite recipe enjoyed from the Pedernales River to the Potomac and was featured in our first Hullabaloo in the Kitchen.

Shrimp Squash Casserole

1½ pounds (about 3 cups) yellow squash
¾ cup raw shrimp
2 tablespoons butter
2 tablespoons flour
½ teaspoon salt
⅛ teaspoon pepper
1 cup chicken broth (use bouillon cube)

½ cup whipping cream or 1 small (5.33-ounce) can chilled evaporated milk
1 tablespoon dry minced onion
½ cup coarse bread crumbs
¼ cup Parmesan cheese, grated
1 tablespoon butter, melted

Wash and dry squash, cut crosswise into ¼ inch slices. Thoroughly rinse shrimp under cold water and drain. Heat 2 tablespoons butter in saucepan. Blend in flour, salt, and pepper. Cook until it bubbles. Remove from heat and add chicken broth gradually, stirring constantly. Bring to boil for 1-2 minutes. Blend in cream and minced onion. Add raw shrimp. Put layer of squash in bottom of 1½-quart casserole. Spoon half shrimp sauce over squash. Repeat layers. Cover tightly and cook in 400° oven for 30 minutes. Meanwhile, toss crumbs and Parmesan cheese with melted butter. After 30 minutes baking time, remove casserole from oven. Reduce heat to 350°. Remove cover and top with bread crumbs. Bake uncovered another 15 minutes or until crumbs are golden brown.

NANCY REAGAN

Former First Lady Nancy Reagan sent us this favorite recipe which was featured in the first Hullabaloo in the Kitchen.

Baja California Chicken

8　chicken breasts, boned
Seasoning salt and pepper,
　to taste
2　cloves garlic, crushed

4　tablespoons olive oil
4　tablespoons tarragon vinegar
$^2/_3$　cup dry sherry

Sprinkle chicken with seasoning salt and pepper. Place crushed garlic into oil and vinegar in skillet. Sauté chicken pieces until golden brown, turning frequently. Remove. Place in 9×13-inch baking dish. Pour sherry over pieces and place in 350° oven for 10 minutes. Serves 8.

U. S. SENATOR PHIL GRAMM

Our "Aggie" Senator, Phil Gramm, says this chili recipe from he and his wife, Wendy, is a great favorite in the Gramm household. He also sends his best wishes.

Senator Gramm's Award Winning Chili

2　pounds meat, part ground
　and part cut into sugar-
　cube size
1　small onion, minced, OR
1　heaping tablespoon
　dehydrated onion
2　(8-ounce) cans tomato sauce
2　(8-ounce) cans water

1-2 teaspoons salt
2　teaspoons paprika (optional)
1　tablespoon ground cumin
　(optional)
½-1 teaspoon red pepper (optional)
2　cloves garlic, minced
4-6 tablespoons flour
4　tablespoons chili powder

Brown meat in onion and drain, if necessary. Add tomato sauce, water, chili powder, salt, paprika, cumin, red pepper, garlic, and 2-3 tablespoons flour. Cook 1-2 hours. Add 2-3 tablespoons flour to chili and cook 15 more minutes. Enjoy!

U. S. SENATOR
KAY BAILEY HUTCHISON

Senator Kay Bailey Hutchison won for Texas the coveted Congressional Club Chili Cook-off with this chili recipe. She says it is "controversial" in that it included beans, and for pro-beans-in-chili advocates and anti-beans-in-chili purists, this is akin to the longstanding Aggie-t.u. rivalry in the amount of fervor it produced.

Kay's Shadywood Showdown Chili

2½ pounds ground sirloin	4 tablespoons molé sauce
1 tablespoon olive oil	2 (8-ounce) cans tomato sauce
2 green peppers, diced	3 cups water
2 medium yellow onions, diced	4 tablespoons chili powder mix.
Salt, pepper, garlic powder to taste	1 (16-ounce) can kidney beans (or pinto beans), drained

Sauté half the onions and peppers in 1 tablespoon olive oil. Add salt, pepper, and garlic powder to taste. Brown meat separately, leaving in chunks. Drain fat. Add onion/pepper mixture to meat. Add 3 tablespoons molé to mixture. Transfer to large pot. Add tomato sauce, 2-3 cans water, 3 tablespoons chili powder. Bring to boil. Add remaining molé, if desired. Simmer 1 hour. Season and stir occasionally. Sauté remaining onions and peppers as above. Add to pot, along with drained beans. Add final chili powder to taste. Finish heating, about 15 minutes, and serve with favorite fixin's.

GOVERNOR GEORGE W. BUSH

 Governor and Mrs. Bush sent this recipe for Texas Pecan Pie. Governor Bush says desserts like this one keep him jogging every day!

Texas Pecan Pie

1½ cups Texas pecan halves	1 cup dark corn syrup
1 (9-inch) pie shell, unbaked	1 tablespoon vanilla
3 eggs	1 cup sugar
1 tablespoon butter, softened	1 tablespoon all-purpose flour

Arrange pecans in pie shell. Set aside. Beat eggs until light. Add butter, corn syrup, and vanilla. Stir until blended. Combine sugar and flour. Blend into egg mixture. Pour into pie shell. Let stand until pecans rise to the surface. Bake in 350° oven for 45 minutes.

JOE BARTON

 Congressman Joe Barton, '72, representative of the 6th District, Texas, sent us this recipe for Bean Soup along with the story of how it came to be on the menu of the U. S. House of Representatives Restaurant every day. Bean Soup had been a featured item on the menu of the House of Representatives Restaurant since long before that day in 1904 when the Speaker of the House, Joseph G. Cannon, of Illinois, came into the House Restaurant and ordered Bean Soup. Then, as now, Bean Soup was a hearty, zesty, and filling dish. But it was hot and humid in Washington that day, and, therefore, Bean Soup had been omitted from the menu. "Thunderation", roared Speaker Cannon, "I had my mouth set for Bean Soup." And, he continued, "from now on, hot or cold, rain, snow, or shine, I want it on the menu every day." And so it has been. Bean Soup has been on the menu every single day since.

Bean Soup

(Served in the U. S. House of Representatives Restaurant)

2 pounds white Michigan beans	Ham hock, smoked
Water	Salt and pepper to taste

Cover beans with cold water and soak overnight. Drain and re-cover with water. Add a smoked ham hock and simmer slowly for about 4 hours until beans are cooked and tender. Then add salt and pepper to suit taste. Just before serving, bruise beans with large spoon or ladle, enough to cloud. Serves 6.

JOHN SHARP

John Sharp, '72, Comptroller of Public Accounts for the State of Texas, sent us three recipes.

John Sharp's Chorizo Melt

1½ pounds Monterey Jack cheese
2 links chorizo sausage

¼ cup hot sauce/salsa
1 avocado

Sauté chorizo and drain well. Slice cheese and place on an ovenproof/microwaveable platter. Crumble chorizo over cheese. Melt cheese, heat thoroughly, either in oven or microwave. If cooked in a microwave, cover with plastic wrap. Remove from oven and spread hot sauce/salsa over melted cheese. Top with sliced avocado. Serve with tortilla chips.

John Sharp's Aggie Swirl Brownies

2 sticks butter
4 tablespoons cocoa
4 eggs
2 cups sugar
1 cup flour
2 teaspoons vanilla

1 (8-ounce) package cream cheese, softened
½ cup sugar
1 egg
1 teaspoon vanilla

Melt butter and mix with cocoa. Mix eggs, sugar, flour, and vanilla. Add butter and cocoa mixture. Pour ½ brownie mixture into greased 9×13-inch pan. Mix cream cheese and sugar until smooth. Add egg and vanilla. Add cream cheese mixture to brownie mixture in pan and top with remaining brownie mixture. Bake at 350° for 35-40 minutes.

John Sharp's Lemon Quail

8 quail
Salt, pepper and
Cavender's Greek Seasoning
1 stick butter

3 lemons
2 tablespoons
Worcestershire sauce

Clean quail well. Lightly brown quail in melted butter in a Dutch oven on top of stove. Lightly season all sides with salt, pepper, and Cavender's Greek Seasoning, while browning. After browning, arrange quail breast-side up in the Dutch oven. Mix lemon juice and Worcestershire sauce and pour over birds. Cover and cook over medium heat on top of stove for 30 minutes. Baste birds with sauce while cooking. Serve with wild rice and recipe's sauce.

GARRY MAURO

 Garry Mauro '70, Texas Land Commissioner, took time out from his busy schedule to send along his recipe for Taco Soup.

Taco Soup

2 pounds ground beef
1 onion, chopped
2 (10-ounce) cans Rotel
tomatoes and chilies, diced
1 (15-ounce) can whole
kernel corn, drained

3 (16-ounce) cans pinto beans
with jalapeños
1 package taco seasoning
1 package Hidden Valley
Ranch dip (dry)

Sauté ground beef and onion together. Drain and place in a large pot and add, tomatoes, corn, pinto beans, taco seasoning, and ranch dip. Cover and simmer about 1 hour. When serving, add a dollop of sour cream.

RICK PERRY

Rick Perry, Texas State Agriculture Commissioner, sends three recipes using Texas products, of course. The 1015 Onions were developed by the Aggies and are a contender for sweetest tasting onion with the Vidalia Onion. The 1015 Onion was so named because it was originally planted on October 15.

Lone Star-Style Whole Roasted Onions

4   (14-16-ounces each)   Olive oil
    Texas SpringSweet
    or Texas 1015 SuperSweet
    Onions

Place whole, unpeeled onions in as small a baking pan as possible. Drizzle lightly with olive oil. Roast uncovered at 375°. Onions are done when easily pierced with a fork (soft, but not mushy), about 1 hour and 15 minutes, depending on size. To serve, cut an X through the top of each onion and squeeze slightly at the bottom so it opens like a baked potato. Season with salt and pepper to taste and garnish with sour cream and chives, or try with your favorite baked potato toppings. Makes 4 servings.
An excellent substitute for baked potatoes.

Texas Barbecue Beef-Stuffed Onions

4   Lone Star-Style Whole   ¼   cup barbecue sauce
    Roasted onions without   3   ounces cheddar cheese,
    X cut, at room temperature   grated
6   ounces lean deli roast beef,
    cut into ½-inch squares.

Cut a thin slice off the top of the cooked onions. Gently squeeze each onion from the root end. Remove center to leave a shell of about ½-inch. Finely dice the onion centers. In a medium bowl, toss diced onion with roast beef, barbecue sauce, and cheese. Stuff each onion shell with ¼ of the mixture. Reheat at 375° until hot, about 15 minutes. Makes 4 servings. If Texas barbecued beef brisket is available, it can be substituted for the roast beef and barbecue sauce.

Texas Red Grapefruit Salad with Southwest Vinaigrette

6   cups mixed greens
1   Texas Red Grapefruit,
    peeled and sectioned
½   medium Texas SpringSweet
    or Texas 1015
    SuperSweet onion

¼   cup black olives, sliced
¼   cup Monterey Jack or
    cheddar cheese, shredded
Southwest Vinaigrette
(see recipe below)

Rinse greens. Pat dry. Place greens in a large salad bowl. Cut grapefruit sections crosswise into halves. Add grapefruit and onion. Pour Southwest Vinaigrette over salad. Toss well. Garnish with olives and cheese. Makes 4-6 servings.

Southwest Vinaigrette

3   tablespoons Texas Red
    grapefruit juice,
    freshly squeezed
2   tablespoons water
1   tablespoon white or
    red wine vinegar

¼   cup olive oil
1   garlic clove, minced
¼   teaspoon ground cumin
¼   teaspoon chili powder
¼   teaspoon dried oregano leaves
⅛   teaspoon salt

Mix all ingredients together. Shake well. Makes ½ cup.

MARGARET RUDDER

Margaret Rudder, widow of Earl Rudder '32, president of Texas A&M from 1959 until his death in 1970, is a gracious contributor to our cookbook, and good friend to Aggie Moms.

Easy Rum Cake

1 package yellow or white cake mix	1 cup pecans, chopped
1 (3.4-ounce) package vanilla pudding mix	½ cup cool water
4 large eggs	½ cup vegetable oil
	½ cup rum

GLAZE-

½ cup water	1 stick margarine
¼ cup rum	1 teaspoon vanilla
1 cup sugar	

Empty cake and pudding mix into bowl. Add rum, water, oil, and eggs. Beat for 2-3 minutes. Place pecans into well-greased and floured tube or bundt pan. Pour in batter and bake 1 hour at 350°. Remove from pan. Punch small holes in cake. Pour glaze over hot cake. For glaze, mix all glaze ingredients and bring to hard boil for 1 minute. Then pour over cake.

Kahlua Pecan Cake

1 (18-ounce) package butter cake mix	¾ cup vegetable oil
	1 teaspoon vanilla
4 eggs	1 cup brown sugar, packed
1 cup sour cream	⅓ cup Kahlua
1 (3.4-ounce) package instant French vanilla pudding	1¼ cups pecan, chopped

GLAZE-

1½ tablespoons margarine	1 tablespoon Kahlua
½ cup powdered sugar	¼ cup pecans, chopped

Place cake mix in medium mixing bowl. Add eggs, 1 at a time, beating well after each. Add sour cream, vanilla pudding, vegetable oil, and vanilla. Blend well. In a separate bowl, combine sugar, Kahlua, and pecans. Add half the cake batter to Kahlua mixture and blend well. Layer mixtures alternately in a bundt pan, ending with Kahlua mixture. Swirl with a knife to marbelize. Bake at 350° for 1 hour. Cool completely before glazing. To make glaze, cream margarine and sugar. Add Kahlua. Mixture should be watery. If too stiff, add a small amount of milk. Drizzle over cake and sprinkle with pecans.   Serves 10.

RAY M. BOWEN

Dr. Ray Bowen, '58, president of Texas A&M University, sent us this recipe for his favorite pound cake.

Buttermilk Pound Cake

3	cups sugar	3	cups flour
1	cup shortening	1	cup buttermilk
	(½ cup shortening	½	teaspoon salt
	plus ½ cup butter)	¼	teaspoon baking soda
6	eggs	2	tablespoons lemon extract

Cream shortening. Add sugar and blend. Add egg yolks one at a time. Add flavoring. Sift dry ingredients and add alternately with the buttermilk, beginning and ending with flour. Fold in beaten egg whites. Bake in 10-inch greased and floured loaf pan (or bundt pan) for 1 hour and 10 minutes at 350°. Let stand in pan for 10-15 minutes before removing.

DIONEL E. AVILÉS

Dr. Dionel E. Avilés, '53, is a member of the Board of Regents for the Texas A&M University System. He says that even though he is not the inventor of this recipe for Black Bean Salsa, he submits it because it is always a big hit at gatherings and especially at the tailgate parties after Aggie football games.

Black Bean Salsa

2	(16-ounce) cans black beans, drained and rinsed	6	teaspoons dried cilantro
		4	tablespoons vegetable oil
10-12 cherry tomatoes, finely chopped		2	tablespoons fresh lime juice
		1	teaspoon ground cumin
8	green onions, finely chopped with tops	½	teaspoon salt
		½	teaspoon pepper
2	cloves garlic, crushed		Tortilla chips
6	tablespoons fresh chopped cilantro OR		

In a medium bowl, combine all ingredients. Cover and refrigerate for 8 hours. Drain liquid before serving with tortilla chips. Enjoy!

FRED MCCLURE

Fred McClure, '76, another member of the Board of Regents, sent us these two recipes for Taco Soup and Chili Pork Chops. He says he acquired the recipe for Taco Soup from someone and he says it is very enjoyable!

Taco Soup

2 pounds ground beef
1 large onion, chopped
1 (15-ounce) can Ranch Style Pinto Beans with jalapeños
1 (15-ounce) can Ranch Style beans
1 (15-ounce) can hominy, drained
1 (15-ounce) can whole kernel corn, drained
1 (7-ounce) can chopped green chilies
1 (10-ounce) can Rotel diced tomatoes and green chilies
1 (15-ounce) can stewed tomatoes with onion, celery, and green peppers
2 tablespoons seasoned salt
1 (1.25-ounce) package taco seasoning
1 (1-ounce) package dry Ranch dressing
Monterey Jack cheese, shredded

Brown ground beef in large pot with chopped onion (may be prepared in microwave in covered dish on high for 10-13 minutes). Add remaining ingredients except cheese and cook on medium for 45 minutes, stirring occasionally. Spoon cheese on top. Makes 5 quarts.

Chili Pork Chops

4-6 lean pork chops
1 (20-ounce) can cream-style corn
1 (20-ounce) can whole kernel corn, drained
½ teaspoon salt
2½ teaspoons chili powder
⅛ teaspoon pepper
1 teaspoon minced onion
¼ cup sweet pepper flakes
½ cup bread crumbs
2 tablespoons melted butter

Preheat oven to 350°. Trim excess pork from chops. Rub each side with salt and pepper. Brown chops in vegetable oil. Place in casserole dish. Combine corn, salt, chili powder, pepper, onion, and pepper flakes. Spoon over chops. Cover casserole and bake 35 minutes. Blend bread crumbs with melted butter. Sprinkle over casserole and bake, uncovered, for 15 minutes longer. Serves 4-5.

ANNE ARMSTRONG

Anne Armstrong, a member of the Board of Regents, sent this recipe for Carmela's Enchiladas from the Armstrong Ranch. It is quick and easy.

Carmela's Enchiladas

FILLING -

²/₃ cup chile con carne (no beans)

½ cup Velveeta cheese, grated

2 tablespoons onion, chopped

SAUCE-

¹/₃ cup chile con carne

½ cup beef consomme

1 tablespoon chile powder

10 tortillas

½ to 1 cup Velveeta, grated

2 tablespoons onions, chopped

Mix chile con carne, 2 tablespoons onion, and ½ cup Velveeta without heating and let stand. Combine sauce ingredients. Heat each tortilla over burner to soften. Then place heaping tablespoon of filling in each tortilla and roll up. Place in 9×13-inch casserole dish, one layer deep, and pour sauce over it. Top with grated Velveeta and onions. Bake 10-15 minutes in 375° oven.

J. MALON SOUTHERLAND

Dr. J. Malon Southerland, '65, is director and vice president for Student Services at Texas A&M. He says this dip is a huge favorite after football games. Be sure you serve something cool to drink.

Malon's Dip

1 (8-ounce) jar Pace's Picante Sauce, medium hot

1 (8-ounce) package cream cheese

1 cup cooked small shrimp or crabmeat

Mix all ingredients. Serve with your favorite dipping veggie or tortilla chips and enjoy!

ERLE NYE

Erle Nye, '58, another member of the Board of Regents, sends his "world famous" recipe for Chocolate Chip Cookies. Aggie Moms who have tasted these cookies say they live up to their reputation!

Chocolate Chip Cookies

1 cup butter	1 teaspoon baking soda
1 cup sugar	2½ cups oatmeal
1 cup brown sugar	1 (12-ounce) bag chocolate chips
2 eggs	1 (4-ounce) Hershey's Chocolate
1 teaspoon vanilla	bar, grated
2 cups flour	1½ cups nuts, chopped

Cream together butter, sugar, and brown sugar. Add eggs and vanilla. Mix together flour, baking soda, and oatmeal (blended into a fine powder - measure before blending). Add chocolate chips, Hershey bar, and nuts. Place golf ball-sized cookies 2 inches apart on ungreased cookie sheet. Bake at 350° for 9 minutes.

JOHN H. LINDSEY

John H. Lindsey, '44, a member of the Board of Regents, sends his favorite recipe for Taco Stew, along with a hearty "Gig 'Em!"

Taco Stew

1 pound lean ground beef	1 (1 ¼-ounce) package
1 medium onion, chopped	taco seasoning
1 (15-ounce) can whole kernel corn, undrained	1 (10-ounce) can condensed tomato soup
1 (10-ounce) can diced tomatoes with chilies, undrained	1 cup water
	Baked tortilla chips
	Monterey Jack cheese, grated
1 (15-ounce) can pinto beans in chili sauce, undrained	

In Dutch oven, brown beef and onion. Add corn, tomatoes with chilies, beans, taco seasoning, undiluted soup, and water. Simmer on low until thoroughly heated. To serve, crumble tortilla chips into soup bowls and cover with generous helping of stew. Sprinkle with grated cheese. Serves 4-6.

SALLIE SHEPPARD

Dr. Sallie Sheppard, associate provost for Undergraduate Programs and Academic Services at A&M, says this Pineapple Surprise recipe is "yummy."

Sallie's Pineapple Surprise

2 (15 ¼-ounce) cans
   pineapple tidbits, drained
²/₃ cup sugar
5 tablespoons flour

Cheddar cheese, grated
1 roll Ritz crackers, crushed
½ stick butter

Place pineapple in an 8-9-inch square baking dish. Sprinkle sugar and flour on top of pineapple. Grate cheese on top. Mix crackers and butter and sprinkle on top. Heat in 350° oven for 30 minutes. Cover with foil loosely if crackers get brown. Do not cover to keep crackers fresh.

ROBERT WALKER

Director of Development Dr. Robert Walker, '58, serves this stew in the wintertime to lots of Aggies and they all want more! He said it is great for camping, cold weather, or anytime!

Easy and Delicious Stew

2 pounds ground beef or
   turkey
1 medium onion, chopped
Garlic salt, pepper to taste
3 (16-ounce) cans
   Ranch Style beans
1 (10-ounce) can Rotel
   tomatoes and chilies

2 (10½-ounce) cans
   minestrone soup
1 (16-ounce) can beef broth,
Tortilla chips
Cheddar cheese, grated
Cornbread

Sauté meat and onions. Drain excess fat. Add garlic salt and pepper. Add beans, tomatoes, minestrone soup, and beef broth (or may add 1 can more of liquid washed from cans of beans, tomatoes, and soup). Heat through and serve over or with tortilla chips, grated cheese on top, or with cornbread.

JERRY GASTON

Dr. Jerry Gaston, vice-president of Administration and Finance at A&M, offers this recipe for Vegetable Soup which he says is perfect when cornbread is served with it and will taste better after being frozen, thawed, and warmed up with leftover cornbread.

Vegetable Soup

2   cups onions, chopped
4-6 large garlic cloves, chopped
2   cups celery, chopped
    (use inner green leaves too)
1   cup any assorted green
    peppers/green onions
6   large carrots, cut anyway
    you like to see them
4   large white potatoes OR
    8 red potatoes, cut into
    ¾-inch chunks
1   (32-ounce) can of
    V-8 or tomato juice
1   (16-ounce) can whole
    kernel corn

1   (16-ounce) can of ANY of these -
    pinto beans, black beans,
    blackeyed peas, navy beans,
    or white beans
¼   cup olive oil
Salt and pepper to taste
Your choice of the following to
    taste-Tabasco Sauce, fresh or
    pickled jalapeños, or
    Worcestershire sauce
2   cups chicken, chopped OR
    any other meat you may
    have available (optional)
Cornbread

Heat olive oil in large stock pot. Sauté onions, celery, garlic, and other fresh ingredients. No need to overcook. Add V-8 or tomato juice, at least 1 quart of water, and bring to a boil. Add more water to make sure vegetables are always covered and you can add as much as you like for your personal desire relative to "soupiness". Add potatoes, carrots, corn, beans, and season to taste. Bring to boil, and cook for about 20 minutes. Add any cooked meat. Then reduce heat to lowest setting and make your cornbread. Soup will be perfect when cornbread is ready. Soup will freeze nicely and will taste better when thawed and warmed up with leftover cornbread.

JIM REYNOLDS

Jim Reynolds, director of the Memorial Student Center, claims this is the best venison recipe he has found. It is truly "to die for".

Venison To Die For

2-4 pounds venison back strap
  (back strap should be a
  minimum of 2½-inches
  in diameter)
Red wine
¼ cup red wine vinegar

Olive oil
Garlic powder
Onion Powder
Bay leaf
Tony Chachere's Cajun Seasoning

Marinate venison back strap for 48 hours in the following mixture - enough red wine to half cover the venison, ¼ cup red wine vinegar, sprinkles of garlic and onion powders, and bay leaves placed on exposed side. Turn 4 times to marinade. After 48 hours, dry the venison and rub with olive oil. Sprinkle liberally with Cajun seasoning. In a 400° oven, roast 5 minutes per side on top rack of oven (to crust surface of meat). Remove and place in a baking dish. Add 2 cups of red wine and cover dish. Simmer at 200° for 15 minutes (center should remain slightly pink). Don't overcook! Serve 1-inch medallions of venison over wild rice pilaf.

MICHAEL FRIEDLAND

Dr. Michael Friedland is dean of the College of Medicine at TAMU. He sends his best wishes and says this is one of his favorite recipes which he has prepared many times to his family's delight!

Sausage and Bean Chowder

1 pound medium hot sausage
2 (16-ounce) cans kidney beans
1 (28-ounce) can crushed
  tomatoes
1 (16-ounce) can whole
  kernel corn,
  or use frozen corn

1 medium onion, chopped
1 bay leaf
Salt and pepper to taste
8-12 ounces water

Brown the sausage and pour off fat. Add all the other ingredients and simmer for 1 hour. This recipe is best if served the next day. May be frozen. Great for cold Sundays and football games. Served best with buttered French bread.

DONALD DYAL

 Dr. Donald Dyal, Ph.D. '80, is director of the Cushing Library. He sends this recipe that E.B. Cushing himself was known to enjoy. "Although he did not live to a ripe old age, a caveat may be in order, but this is sure good!"

Old Style New Orleans Roast Pork Loin

Pork loin (don't get a lean cut - you need some fat)
Fresh parsley

Applesauce
Horseradish

Cut or score the loin with lines about ½-inch apart. Dredge the loin with salt and pepper and place in a roasting pan fat side up. Cook at 325° for about 25 minutes for each pound or to 185° on a meat thermometer. Make sure the pork is well done. The old recipe called for basting every 5 minutes for the first 30 minutes and every 10 minutes thereafter. This is a little harder to do now because our pork today is much leaner than it was 75-100 years ago. When done, remove the loin from the baking pan and place on a hot serving dish. Garnish with fresh parsley and serve with applesauce and horseradish.

WILLIAM B. KRUMM

 Vice-President of Finance and Controller William Krumm sent this recipe for Cranberry Pudding, guaranteed to be yummy!

Cranberry Pudding

1½ tablespoons butter
½ cup sugar
¼ cup water
¼ cup evaporated milk

1 cup cranberries, cut in half
1 cup flour
½ teaspoon salt
1 teaspoon baking soda

FOAMY SAUCE-
1 stick butter
1 cup sugar

½ cup evaporated milk
1 teaspoon vanilla

Blend butter and sugar. Add dry ingredients alternately with milk and water. Fold in cranberries. Bake in greased muffin tins at 350° for 22 minutes. Do not overcook. For foamy sauce, mix butter, sugar, evaporated milk, and vanilla in top of double boiler or a heavy saucepan. Cook until slightly thickened. Serves 12.

44

ED HILER

Dr. Ed Hiler, dean of the College of Agriculture, and his wife, Patricia, '77, sent this recipe for Fig Preserve Cake. Pat said this comes from a friend whose husband was Class of '44. Dr. Hiler says "Promote Texas products!"

Fig Preserve Cake

CAKE-

2	cups flour	3	eggs
1	teaspoon baking soda	1	cup buttermilk
1	teaspoon salt	1	cup fig preserves, mashed
1½	cups sugar	1	teaspoon vanilla
1	cup butter or vegetable oil	3	cups nuts, chopped

ICING-

1	cup sugar	1	tablespoon white corn syrup
1	stick margarine	½	cup buttermilk
1	teaspoon vanilla	½	teaspoon baking soda

Mix all ingredients for cake and pour into a 9×13-inch greased and floured loaf pan. Bake 35-40 minutes in 350° oven. While still warm, prick holes in cake and pour icing. For icing, mix all icing ingredients, but do not cook. Pour over cake.

JOE T. HANEY

Colonel Joe T. Haney, '48, retired director of the Fightin' Texas Aggie Band, says this recipe is a winner with Aggies of all ages.

Bevo Burger Filets

2	pounds lean ground beef	1	(8-ounce) can mushrooms, chopped
1	onion, chopped		
1	(6-ounce) can ripe olives, chopped	1	cup fresh Parmesan cheese, grated
1	green pepper, chopped	8	slices bacon

Flatten ground beef in rectangle shape on foil and top with remaining ingredients, except bacon. Roll up long side as a jelly roll, and cut into 1½-inch "filets". Wrap each slice with bacon and skewer with a toothpick. Grill over coals 8 minutes on each side.

C. ROLAND HADEN

Roland Haden, dean of the College of Engineering, and his wife, Joyce, enjoy this cheesecake and say it has been a hit at several gatherings.

Chocolate Turtle Cheesecake

2   cups vanilla wafer crumbs
6   tablespoons butter
1   (14-ounce) bag caramel candies
1   (5.3-ounce) can evaporated milk
1   cup pecans, toasted and chopped
2   (8-ounce) packages cream cheese, softened

½   cup sugar
1   teaspoon vanilla
2   eggs
½   cup semisweet chocolate chips, melted
Whipped cream, chopped nuts, and maraschino cherries for garnish

Combine crumbs and butter. Press into bottom of a 9-inch springform pan. Bake 10 minutes at 350°. Melt caramels in milk in heavy 1½-quart saucepan over low heat, stirring frequently until smooth. Pour over crust. Top with pecans. Combine cream cheese, sugar, and vanilla in large bowl of electric mixer. Mix at medium speed until well-blended. Add eggs, one at a time, mixing well after each. Blend in chocolate. Pour cream cheese batter over pecans. Bake at 350° for 40 minutes or until done. Loosen cake from rim of pan. Chill. Garnish with whipped cream, chopped nuts, and maraschino cherries. Makes 10-12 servings.

RICHARD E. EWING

Dean Richard E. Ewing (College of Science) contributed a wonderful recipe for French Toast Casserole. He recommends Otto's Bread from the "Farm Patch" in Bryan.

Sunday Morning French Toast Casserole

4	large slices sourdough bread, cut into 1-inch cubes	6	eggs
1	(8-ounce) package cream cheese, cut into cubes	1	cup milk
		1¾	teaspoons cinnamon
1	large Granny Smith apple, peeled and chopped	3	tablespoons powdered sugar, sifted
			Maple syrup

Put half of the bread cubes into an ungreased 7×11-inch casserole dish. Spread cream cheese cubes evenly over the bread. Spread apple over both evenly. Cover with remaining bread cubes. Beat together eggs, milk, and cinnamon until well-blended. Pour over bread/cheese/apple mixture. Cover and refrigerate overnight. Bake at 375° for 35 minutes. Sprinkle with powdered sugar. Serve with maple syrup. Makes 4-5 servings.

M. T. (TED) HOPGOOD

Major General Ted Hopgood, '65, is the commandant of the Corps of Cadets. He is retired from the Marine Corps. This cake recipe is quick and easy.

Chocolate Chip Cake

1	butter recipe fudge cake mix	½	cup salad oil
1	(4½-ounce) package instant chocolate pudding	½	cup water
1	cup sour cream	1	(12-ounce) package semisweet chocolate chips
4	eggs		

Grease bundt pan. Preheat oven to 350°. Mix all ingredients, except chocolate chips, in mixer until smooth. Fold in chips by hand. Pour into bundt pan. Bake approximately 50 minutes until toothpick comes out clean. Cool 10 minutes. Invert cake onto wire rack. Once completely cool, sprinkle with powdered sugar.

THOMAS G. DARLING

Major General Tom Darling. '54, (USAF retired) who is commander emeritus of the Corps and executive director for Corps Development, enjoys this enchilada casserole. General Darling was commandant when the Dallas County Aggie Moms designed and made the Corps Quilt which hangs in the Sanders Corps Center.

General Darling's Enchilada Casserole

1½ pounds lean ground beef
½   cup onion, chopped
1   cup cooked rice
1   (15-ounce) can Ranch
    Style beans
1   (14-ounce) can
    enchilada sauce

1   (10½-ounce) can cream of
    mushroom soup
1   (4.5-ounce) can green chilies,
    chopped
12 corn tortillas
½   pound cheddar cheese, grated

Spray 2-quart casserole with vegetable spray. Line bottom of casserole with half of tortillas that have been torn into pieces. Brown beef with onion. Drain. Add rice, beans, sauce, soup, and chilies. Simmer briefly. Pour half of the meat mixture over tortillas. Sprinkle with half of the cheese. Add remainder of tortillas, meat mixture, and top with cheese. Bake in 350° oven for 30 minutes or until bubbly and heated through. May be prepared early in the day and refrigerated. Allow extra time for heating. Serves 6-8.

FRANK COX

Frank Cox, '65, author of "I Bleed Maroon," and his wife, Cheryl (also an Aggie Mom), gave us this recipe for Dallas Burgers. Frank and Cheryl are parents of Aggies, John Blair Cox, '95, and Cristy Cay Cox, '98.

Dallas Burgers

1   pound ground beef
Chopped onion to taste
1   (10 ½-ounce) can chicken
    gumbo soup

3   tablespoons ketchup
2   tablespoons mustard
2   tablespoons brown sugar

Sauté ground beef and onion. Drain grease. Add other ingredients and simmer 10 minutes. Serve open-faced on hamburger buns. A great quick meal!

BOB FRYMIRE

Bob Frymire, '45, of Frymire Engineering Company, agreed that this met his engineering standards for good eating when he submitted it for the first edition of Hullabaloo in the Kitchen.

Spinach Casserole

3   (10-ounce) packages frozen
    chopped spinach
4   ounces cream cheese,
    softened
1   medium onion, chopped

¼   cup margarine
½   pint sour cream
1   (7-ounce) can artichoke
    hearts
Paprika to garnish

Cook spinach as directed. Drain well and add cream cheese to hot spinach, blending well. Sauté onion in margarine. DON'T BROWN. Add sour cream and stir into spinach mixture. Pour into medium casserole dish. Drain artichokes and put on top of casserole, pushing artichokes down until only the tops show. Sprinkle with paprika and bake in 325° oven for 25-30 minutes.

JERRY COOPER

Jerry Cooper, '63, editor of The Texas Aggie, says he is proud to have been editor for the past 26 ½ years. These sand tarts, originally made by his "Aggie Mom", almost melt in your mouth!

Mom's Sand Tarts

½   pound butter
5   heaping tablespoons
    powdered sugar

2   cups flour
1½ teaspoons vanilla
1   cup nuts

Cream butter. Add sugar and flour alternately. Add vanilla and nuts. Make into small balls about the size of a quarter and drop on ungreased cookie sheet. (Leave peaks on dough if desired.) Cook about 15-20 minutes until barely golden brown. (No temperature was included in his mother's recipe. He guesses the temperature to be about 350°.) While still hot, roll in powdered sugar and then place on cooling rack.

Maroon Velvet Cake

Jerry Cooper tells us that he once won a blue ribbon for this recipe. It was originally called Red Velvet Cake, but careful attention when mixing the food coloring and the cocoa can result in a beautiful Aggie Maroon. Aggies call this the "Maroon and White Cake." Many a cake has been cut with a senior's saber!

CAKE-

2 ounces red food coloring	2¼ cups cake flour
3 tablespoons cocoa	1 teaspoon salt
½ cup shortening	1 teaspoon vanilla
1½ cups sugar	1 tablespoon vinegar
2 eggs, beaten	1 teaspoon baking soda
1 cup buttermilk	

ICING-

½ cup soft butter	3 tablespoons flour
½ cup shortening	⅔ cup milk, room temperature
1 cup powdered sugar	1 teaspoon vanilla

FOR CAKE-

Mix red food coloring with cocoa and set aside. Cream shortening and sugar. Add beaten eggs, then coloring paste. Beat well. Sift cake flour and salt 3 times. Add to creamed mixture along with buttermilk. Add vanilla and beat well again. Remove from mixer and add mixture of vinegar and baking soda. Mix by hand until blended. Pour into 2 8-inch round cake pans which have been greased and floured. Bake for 350° for 30-35 minutes.

FOR ICING-

Cream butter and shortening with sugar. Add flour 1 spoonful at a time. Add milk and vanilla. Beat a long time with mixer until icing is light and fluffy.

RANDY MATSON

Randy Matson, '67, is director of the Association of Former Students. He also holds gold and silver medals from the 1968 Olympics. His cookies are both beautiful and tasty.

Whole Wheat Chocolate Chip Cookies

1 cup shortening	1 teaspoon baking soda
1½ cups brown sugar, packed	½ teaspoon salt
2 eggs	2 cups pecans, chopped
1 teaspoon vanilla	1 cup (6-ounces)
2¼ cups whole wheat flour (sift 3 times, then measure)	semisweet chocolate chips

Cream shortening, brown sugar, eggs, and vanilla. Sift flour three times then measure 2 ¼ cups, then sift together with baking soda and salt. Add to creamed mixture. Stir in pecans and chocolate chips. Drop by large rounded teaspoonsful onto ungreased cookie sheet. Bake at 375° approximately 8-10 minutes until light brown.

C. E. "PAT" OLSEN

C. E. "Pat" Olsen, '23, for whom the TAMU baseball stadium, Olsen Field, is named, contributed this "home run" cookie recipe for our first Hullabaloo in the Kitchen.

Oatmeal Cookies

1 cup sugar	1 teaspoon baking soda
½ cup shortening	1 teaspoon cinnamon
½ cup butter	⅛ teaspoon salt
2 eggs, beaten	2 cups dry oatmeal
2 cups flour	1 cup pecans, chopped
1 cup raisins or currants	

Cream sugar, shortening, and butter in large bowl. Add eggs, flour, baking soda, cinnamon, and salt. Beat until mixed well. Fold in oatmeal, pecans, and raisins by hand. Chill 2-4 hours. Drop by teaspoonsful on slightly greased cookie sheet. Bake at 375° for 12-15 minutes. As soon as cookies cool on cake racks, put in jar or tins that can be tightly closed. Yield - 9 dozen.

DR. JOHN KOLDUS

Dr. John Koldus, retired vice president for Student Services, and much-loved by students who came in contact with him, shared a tasty recipe from his Hungarian heritage.

Hungarian Stuffed Cabbage

1- 1½ pounds ground beef or
mixture of half ground beef,
half ground pork
¼ cup onion, chopped
Salt and pepper to taste

¾ cup white rice
1 head cabbage
1 (28-ounce) can
whole tomatoes
½ can water

Brown meat and onions. Salt and pepper to taste. Precook rice. Mix with meat and onions. Core cabbage and steam in covered saucepan about 15 minutes until leaves are pliable. Drain. Separate each leaf of cabbage and slice bulk off back veins so leaf can be manipulated. Place 2 tablespoons of meat stuffing mixture on 12-14 cabbage leaves. Roll up each and tuck in ends. Place any remaining cabbage leaves in bottom of saucepan. Arrange all cabbage rolls on top of bed of cabbage leaves. Pour tomatoes on top. Add water and, if desired, more salt and pepper. Cover saucepan and cook on low heat on top of stove until cabbage is tender, about 45 minutes.

JANE GANTER

Jane Ganter, mother of 12 children, including Don Ganter, owner of the Dixie Chicken, has been a Dallas resident for over 50 years. She contributed this recipe for Tuna and Rice Casserole.

Tuna and Rice Casserole

1 (10½-ounce) can cream of
mushroom soup
1 (12-ounce) can tuna, grated
1 teaspoon curry powder
2 cups cooked white rice

½ cup onion, chopped
(sautéed in 1 tablespoon butter)
½ cup celery, chopped
(sautéed in 1 tablespoon butter)

In large 3-4-quart casserole dish, combine the above ingredients. Mix thoroughly. Cook at 350° for 30 minutes or until thoroughly heated.

CINDY BOETTCHER

Cindy Boettcher, '76, author of "Anna Meagan: An Aggie Cinderella Story;" "Whoop!: An Aggie Football Weekend", and "A Is For Aggie," sends us these two recipes for baked chicken and sugar cookies. She said she always seems to double or triple the cookie recipe because one batch is never enough.

My Family's Favorite Sugar Cookies

½ cup butter	½ teaspoon vanilla
1 cup sugar	½ teaspoon salt
1 egg	2 teaspoons baking powder
1 tablespoon milk	1¾ cups plus 2 tablespoons flour

COOKIE GLAZE-

3 cups powdered sugar, sifted	1 tablespoon white corn syrup
¼ cup warm water	¼ teaspoon vanilla

Cream together butter and sugar, then add egg. Beat well. Add milk and vanilla. Sift together salt, baking powder, and flour. Add these ingredients ¼ cup at a time to the butter/sugar/egg mixture. Form into balls and chill AT LEAST 8 hours. Roll out and cut into desired shapes. Bake at 375° for 8-9 minutes. For cookie glaze, mix all ingredients together and heat slightly. This sets very fast. Add hot water if necessary to make spreading easier. Tint with food coloring as desired. This makes a smooth semi-gloss coating for cookies. The glaze is very sweet!

Cindy says this chicken is very tender when you add buttermilk to the batter and bake. This is great served over rice pilaf.

Buttermilk Baked Chicken

6 boneless chicken breasts	¼ teaspoon pepper
1½ cups buttermilk	¾ stick margarine
¾ cup flour	1 (10¾-ounce) can
1½ teaspoons salt	cream of chicken soup

Dip chicken in ½ cup buttermilk. Roll in flour seasoned with salt and pepper. Melt margarine in 9×13-inch pan. Put chicken in pan and bake uncovered at 425° for 30 minutes. Turn chicken and bake another 15 minutes. Blend remaining soup and 1 cup of buttermilk and pour AROUND chicken pieces and bake another 15 minutes. Serves 6.

CHRISTIE CARTER

Christie Carter, '88, past president of the Dallas A&M Club, shares this outstanding recipe for Tortilla Soup. It is thicker than most tortilla soups and DELICIOUS!

Homemade Tortilla Soup

1   onion, chopped
2   cloves garlic, minced
1   tablespoon vegetable oil
1   (10-ounce) can
     Rotel tomatoes
1   (16-ounce) can
     pureed tomatoes
3   (16-ounce) cans
     chicken broth

1   teaspoon chili powder
1   teaspoon cumin
Salt to taste
4   corn tortillas, cut into
     thin strips
1   cup smoked chicken, diced
Diced avocado, grated
Monterey Jack , cheddar cheese,
or sour cream to garnish

In large saucepan, sauté onions and garlic in 1 tablespoon vegetable oil, about 5 minutes. Add Rotel tomatoes, pureed tomatoes, chicken broth, chili powder, cumin, and salt. Heat to boiling, reduce heat and simmer 20-30 minutes. Meanwhile, cut tortillas into thin strips and fry until crisp in oil. Drain on paper towels. Add chicken and tortilla strips to soup and heat through, about 5 minutes. Garnish each serving with sprinkling of diced avocado, cheese, and a scoop of sour cream. Makes 8 servings.

KRISTINE KAHANEK

Meteorologist Kristine Kahanek, '89, of Dallas' WFAA-TV, Channel 8, sends one of her favorite recipes from college days. "There was a big group of us that must have had a party at least once a week. One of my friends made this dish that lasted only as long as it took to cut it!"

Breakfast Pizza

2-3 cans of refrigerator
   crescent rolls
1   pound of breakfast sausage
5   eggs
1   cup cheddar cheese or
   preference

1   cup frozen hash browns,
   crumbled
½   cup milk
Salt and pepper to taste

Brown sausage. Drain off grease. Let cool, then crumble. Roll crescent rolls on pizza pan or cookie sheet. Mix eggs, milk, salt, and pepper. Beat well, then add cheese. Set aside. Spread sausage over rolls, then pour egg mixture over sausage. Add hash browns. Bake at 350° for 30-45 minutes. I always add more cheese, bacon, or mushrooms. It is one of those suit to taste recipes that is always good.

DAVID FINFROCK

David Finfrock, '76, meteorolgist for KXAS-TV, NBC-5, and good friend to Aggie Moms, contributed recipes for Turkey Spinach Enchiladas and Spanish Rice along with a "Gig 'Em!"

Turkey Spinach Enchiladas

1	pound ground turkey	1	(8-ounce) package low-fat cream cheese, cubed
2	cups picante sauce		
1	(10-ounce) package frozen chopped spinach, thawed	12	7-inch flour tortillas
		1	(16-ounce) can stewed tomatoes
2	teaspoons cumin	1	cup cheddar cheese, shredded
½	teaspoon salt		

Squeeze thawed spinach until dry. Cook turkey in nonstick skillet until no longer pink. Add 1 cup picante, spinach, 1½ teaspoons cumin, and salt. Cook and stir 5 minutes or until most of the liquid has evaporated. Add cream cheese, stirring until melted. Remove from heat. Grease a 9×13-inch baking dish. Fill tortillas with turkey mixture. Place in pan seam side down. Mix tomatoes, 1 cup picante, and ½ teaspoon cumin. Pour over enchiladas. Bake at 350° for 20 minutes. Sprinkle with cheese and bake 2 more minutes.

Spanish Rice

½	cup green bell pepper, chopped	½	teaspoon dried basil, crushed
		2	tablespoons oil
¼	cup onion, chopped	1	cup rice
1	clove garlic, minced	1	(16-ounce) can stewed tomatoes
½	teaspoon dried rosemary, crushed	1	teaspoon salt
		¼	teaspoon pepper

In skillet, cook green pepper, onion, garlic, basil, and rosemary in hot oil until vegetables are tender. Stir in rice, chopped tomatoes, salt, pepper, and 2 cups water. Cook, covered, over low heat for about 20 minutes or until rice is done. Makes 6 servings.

"RED" CASHION

"Red" Cashion, '53, retired NFL referee and chairman of the board of ANCO Insurance in Bryan, calls this one a touchdown every time.

Texas Jambalaya

8	tablespoons bacon drippings	2	tablespoons Worcestershire sauce
2	large onions, chopped		
2	large garlic cloves, minced	1	(20-ounce) can tomato juice
8	ribs celery, chopped	1	(20-ounce) can tomatoes
2	green peppers, chopped	4	tablespoons flour
1	teaspoon thyme	4	tablespoons cold water
½	teaspoon pepper	4	pounds raw shrimp, cleaned
1	teaspoon paprika	2	(1-pound) packages frozen lump crab meat
2	whole bay leaves		
4	tablespoons fresh parsley, chopped	2	(10-ounce) cans clams
4	teaspoons salt		

Melt drippings in skillet. Add vegetables and seasonings. Cook about 10 minutes, until tender. Blend flour and water and add to gravy to hasten thickening. Add shrimp, crab meat, and clams. Simmer 20 minutes and serve over hot rice with hot French bread.

ROBERT L. BOONE

Robert L. Boone, retired director of the Singing Cadets, says he is a transplanted Chesapeake Bay boy, and therefore, seafoods are his favorite. He submits the following gumbo, which he says is great served with a tossed salad and warmed, crusty French bread.

Shrimp and Crab Gumbo

1 pound fresh okra	1 quart boiling water
4 tablespoons cooking oil	Salt and pepper to taste
(bacon drippings add flavor)	1 pound cleaned and
1 medium white onion, diced	deveined shrimp
1 medium bell pepper, diced	½-1 pound crab claw meat
4 garlic cloves, diced	
or crushed	

ROUX-

2 tablespoons margarine   4 tablespoons flour

½- 1 pound cooked rice
(keep warm)

Wash, dry, and slice okra into ¼-½-inch pieces. Fry in 4 tablespoons of cooking oil. Cook 20 minutes over medium heat, stirring frequently. Add diced onion, pepper, and garlic. Continue cooking until all vegetables are browned. Add boiling water. Salt and pepper to taste. Cook 30-45 minutes over medium heat. During this time, clean and devein shrimp. Add to vegetables, cooking about 20 minutes more. Clean crab meat, removing bits of claw and membrane. Add about 10 minutes before serving. For roux, use separate skillet. Melt margarine and sprinkle in flour, stirring constantly until dark brown. Be careful not to burn. Stir into gumbo. Add more water, depending on how soupy you like your gumbo. If water is added, allow enough time for all the wonderful flavors to spread. Serve in a bowl over cooked, warm rice.

R. C. SLOCUM

Head Football Coach R. C. Slocum tells us that this has become a favorite at Cain Dining Hall where the athletes eat.

Crunchy Squash Casserole

2 (10-ounce) packages frozen sliced yellow squash
1 cup onion, chopped
1 tablespoon margarine
1 (8-ounce) carton sour cream
1 (10¾-ounce) can cream of chicken soup, undiluted
1 (8-ounce) can water chestnuts, drained

1 (6-ounce) package chicken flavored stuffing mix
¼ cup plus 2 tablespoons margarine, melted
Squash slices (optional)
Celery leaves (optional)

Cook the squash according to package directions. Drain well. Sauté onion in 1 tablespoon margarine. Combine the squash, onion, sour cream, soup, and water chestnuts. Combine stuffing mix and ¼ cup plus 2 tablespoons melted butter. Stir well. Add ¾ of stuffing mixture to squash mixture. Spoon into a lightly greased 2-quart casserole. Sprinkle remaining stuffing mixture over casserole. Bake at 350° for 20 minutes or until bubbly. Garnish casserole with thawed squash slices and celery leaves, if desired.

TOM LANDRY

Former Dallas Cowboys Coach Tom Landry says these popover-type corn bread muffins are his favorite, and should "score" at your home, too!

Tom Landry's Corn Bread Muffins

1¼ cups cornmeal
1 teaspoon salt
2 tablespoons baking powder
¾ cup flour

½ tablespoon sugar
2 cups milk
2 small eggs
2 tablespoons shortening

Sift dry ingredients. Beat eggs well. Add a little more than half of the milk to the eggs and beat well. Add egg mixture to flour mixture and beat well. Stir in rest of milk and melted shortening. Fill hot, well-greased muffin tins about half full. Bake at 500° for about 15 minutes. Makes 12 muffins. And YES, 500° is the correct temperature!!

JOHN DAVID CROW

Heismann Trophy Winner John David Crow, '58, and his wife, Carolyn, survived on this recipe during their A&M days. John Crow is also an All-American Halfback, NFL player, and former Athletic Director at TAMU.

Carolyn's Vegetable Soup

1   tablespoon oil
1½ pounds lean
     stew meat, cubed
2   tablespoons flour
1   quart water
1   tablespoon salt
1   teaspoon pepper
1   large onion, chopped
3   ribs celery, chopped
3   carrots, chopped
1   (8½-ounce) can
     small lima beans

1   (16-ounce) can cream corn
1   (16-ounce) can
     tomatoes, quartered
1   (8-ounce) can tomato sauce
1   potato, chopped, or
¼   cup rice, uncooked
1   bay leaf
1   tablespoon sugar
1   (10-ounce) box
frozen okra (optional)

In large Dutch oven, brown meat in oil and remove. Brown flour in drippings. Stir until dark brown. Add water, tomatoes, tomato sauce, and seasonings. Let simmer 5 minutes. Add meat and vegetables, except okra. Let simmer until vegetables are done, several hours for full flavor. Add okra the last 30 minutes.

ROGER STAUBACH

Former outstanding Dallas Cowboy quarterback Roger Staubach (also an Aggie Dad), shares with us his favorite salad, a guaranteed winner.

Roger Staubach's Spinach Salad

1 bag fresh spinach	¼ teaspoon paprika
4 ounces blue cheese	1 (10½-ounce) can
1 (2.8-ounce) can	tomato soup
French-fried onion rings	¾ cup oil
¾ cup sugar	¾ cup vinegar
½ teaspoon salt	1 onion, quartered
1 teaspoon dry mustard	

Wash and remove stems from spinach. Tear in bite-sized pieces. Crumble blue cheese and onion rings over spinach. In a tall bottle, mix dry seasoning ingredients first. Add liquid ingredients (soup, oil, vinegar) and shake well. Put onion in for flavor, but remove before serving. The dressing will be enough for 2 bags of spinach.

GENE STALLINGS

Former A&M, and recently retired Alabama, Head Coach Gene Stallings, '57, added this recipe to his family's collection while he was a coach with the Dallas Cowboys. This is a man pleaser!

Gene's Baked Potatoes

10 large new potatoes	1½ cups Colby cheese, grated
¾ cup butter	Bacon bits
5 green onions, chopped	1 pint sour cream
Salt and pepper to taste	

Boil potatoes until fork tender. Pour off water and peel while hot. Mash by hand, leaving in medium-sized chunks while mixing in butter, salt, pepper, onions, bacon bits, and half the cheese. Stir in sour cream and pour into a 9×13-inch baking dish. Top with remaining cheese and bake 20-30 minutes until bubbly at 325°.

BUCK WEIRUS

 Buck Weirus, '42, the late executive director of the Association of Former Students, included this favorite of his in our first Hullabaloo in the Kitchen. The Buck Weirus "Student Spirit Awards" are given each year to several students in his memory.

Waffles

4 eggs, separated	2 tablespoons cooking oil
1 cup All-Bran cereal	1 teaspoon baking soda
1 cup flour	½ teaspoon salt
2 cups buttermilk	

After separating eggs, stir the yolks and add cereal, flour, buttermilk, oil, baking soda, and salt. Beat egg whites until fluffy. Fold into batter. Bake in hot waffle iron.

HOWARD KRUSE

 CEO of Blue Bell Creameries Howard Kruse, '52, and his wife, Verlin, enjoy this salad whenever they can.

Broccoli Salad

1 head broccoli, cut in bite-sized pieces	1 cup raisins
1 small red onion, chopped	6 slices bacon, fried crisp and crumbled
1 cup sunflower seeds (kernels)	

DRESSING -

1 cup mayonnaise	2 tablespoons red wine vinegar
¼ cup sugar	

Combine salad ingredients. Prepare dressing a few hours before serving. Pour over salad. Enjoy!

MELVIN ZIEGENBEIN

Blue Bell Ice Cream's Vice President and Dallas Division Manager Melvin Ziegenbein, '66, and his wife, Karla, sent us these three delicious recipes.

Mexican Corn Casserole

2   (8-ounce) packages
    cream cheese
Small bunch green onions,
    chopped
1   (4-ounce) can
    green chilies, chopped

Small fresh jalapeño pepper,
    chopped, no seeds
1   can Mexicorn
1   pound package frozen corn
½   stick butter, sliced

Soften cream cheese on low heat until smooth. Add green onions, green chilies, and jalapeño. Mix well. Place corn in casserole dish. Add cream cheese mixture, mixing all together. Top with butter. Bake at 350° until hot, about 30 minutes.

Oriental Cabbage Slaw

DRESSING-
1   flavor packet from
    Oriental Ramen-style
    noodles
2   tablespoons sugar

3   tablespoons vinegar
⅓- ½ cup vegetable oil
½   teaspoon pepper

SALAD-
2   tablespoons sesame seeds
½   cup slivered almonds
½   large head cabbage (5 cups),
    shredded

4   green onions, chopped
1   (3-ounce) package
Oriental Ramen-style noodles

Make dressing early in the day. Mix well and refrigerate. Toast sesame seeds and almonds in 350° oven for 15 minutes. Combine shredded cabbage, onions, and uncooked noodles (which have been broken into pieces by hand). Mix lightly. Before serving, add dressing, seeds, and nuts. Toss lightly. Serve immediately. Makes 10 servings.

Heavenly Pineapple

1	(3-ounce) package lemon gelatin	1	cup sharp cheddar cheese, shredded
¾	cup pineapple juice	2	cups frozen whipped topping
1	tablespoon lemon juice	2	small cans crushed pineapple

Dissolve lemon gelatin in 1 cup boiling water. Add pineapple juice and lemon juice. Chill until slightly thick. Fold in crushed pineapple (drained), shredded cheese, and whipped topping. Pour into bowl. Chill until firm.

EDDIE DOMINGUEZ

 Eddie Dominguez, '66, a former member of the Fightin' Texas Aggie Basketball Team, as well as owner of Tupinamba Restaurant, recommends this recipe as a traditional favorite.

Spanish Rice

½	cup cooking oil	2	chicken flavor bouillon cubes
1	cup long grain rice	2	teaspoons salt
2	cups water	½	teaspoon garlic salt
1	medium white onion, chopped	1	teaspoon pepper
2	medium tomatoes, chopped		

Heat oil and brown rice, stirring to prevent burning. Drain oil off. Add water, onion, tomatoes, bouillon cubes, salt, pepper, and garlic salt. Cook until water has boiled down to top of rice. Turn heat to low and cover. Keep covered until water has completely evaporated. Stir and serve.

Appetizers
and
Beverages

Crab Aspic

1½ cups V-8 juice
1 (3-ounce) package
    lemon gelatin
1 tablespoon lemon juice
¼ teaspoon salt
¼ teaspoon paprika
1 (6-ounce) can crab meat

¼ cup celery, diced
2 eggs, hard-boiled
    and diced
8 olives, sliced
½ teaspoon minced onion
3 tablespoons green
    bell pepper

SAUCE-
1 cup mayonnaise
2 tablespoons chili sauce

2 tablespoons Roquefort cheese

Boil the V-8 juice, add the gelatin, lemon juice, salt, and paprika. Let cool. Arrange the rest of the ingredients on a 9-inch ring mold. Pour the gelatin mixture over the ring mold and refrigerate until set. Mix the sauce ingredients together and serve in center of crab mold. Can be served as a salad course.

Mary Aasterud, President ('94-'95)
Valerie Aasterud McLaughlin '94

Mom's Tomato Aspic Spread

1 (10.5-ounce) can
    tomato soup, undiluted
1 (3-ounce) box lemon gelatin
8 ounces cream cheese,
    softened
¹/₃ cup mayonnaise

5 green onions, chopped
1 (6-ounce) bottle
    stuffed olives, chopped
1 small green bell pepper,
    chopped

Heat tomato soup in saucepan. Stir in gelatin and remove from heat. Beat in cream cheese. Add remaining ingredients, mixing well. Pour into ring mold and refrigerate until set. Serve cold with crackers.

Susan Saiter
Rob Saiter '90
David Saiter '98

Chili Relleno

2 (7-ounce) cans green
   chilies, chopped
¾ pound Monterey Jack
   cheese, grated

¾ pound sharp cheddar
   cheese, grated
8 ounces sour cream
10 eggs, beaten

Grease 9×12-inch baking dish. Cover bottom with green chilies. Layer with cheeses. Pour sour cream and beaten eggs over mixture. Bake at 350° for 45 minutes. Cut into squares. Serves 12.

Jo Rowlett

Stuffed Mushrooms

12-16 large mushrooms
1 teaspoon margarine
1 tablespoon minced onion
4 ounces pastrami or other
   luncheon meat, finely chopped

3 ounces smoked cheese, grated
2 tablespoons ketchup

Scoop out inside of mushrooms and place in a skillet with the margarine. Add the onion and meat and cook until tender. Add the cheese and ketchup and stir until the cheese is melted. Fill the mushroom caps with the mixture and bake at 375° for 10-15 minutes until fluffy. Makes 12-16 mushrooms.

Mary Aasterud, President ('94-'95)
Valerie Aasterud McLaughlin '94

Sausage Pinwheels

2	pounds sausage	4	teaspoons baking powder
½	cup shortening	2	teaspoons sugar
⅔	cup milk	½	teaspoon salt
2	cups flour		

Cook the sausage until brown and drain well. Mix the other ingredients together to make a soft dough. Divide the dough into 2 balls. Place the dough on a floured surface and roll into a rectangle. Spread the sausage on the dough. Roll the dough as for a jelly-roll and freeze. Cut into thin slices and bake at 425° for 10 minutes. Yield - 2 rolls or about 100 pieces.

Janis Haydel
Sally Haydel '97
Chris Haydel '02

Tortilla Pinwheels

1	cup sour cream	1	(2.25-ounce) can ripe olives, chopped
8	ounces cream cheese, softened		Red pepper to taste
1½	cup cheddar cheese, grated	1	(10-count) package large tortillas
1	tablespoon onion, chopped		
1	teaspoon garlic powder	1	cup mild picante sauce
1	(4-ounce) can green chilies, chopped		

Mix all ingredients, except tortillas and picante sauce. Spread the mixture on tortillas, and roll up tight. Refrigerate. Slice ½-inch thick and serve with picante sauce. Yield - about 100-120 pieces.

Mary Aasterud, President ('94-'95)
Valerie Aasterud McLaughlin '94

Best Cheese Ball

1   (8-ounce) package
    low-fat cream cheese
1   ounce blue cheese
1   stick butter
    (do not substitute)

1/3   cup ripe olives, chopped
1/8   teaspoon garlic salt
1   cup pecans, chopped

Mix cream cheese, blue cheese, and butter. Add ripe olives and garlic salt. Mix well. Shape into 1 large ball or 2 small balls. Roll in nuts. Chill. Yield - 1 large or 2 small balls.

Lillian Gips
Bruce Holmes '78 (son)
Jeff Broaddus '98 (grandson)

Cheese Ball

2   (8-ounce) packages
    cream cheese
4   green onions, chopped
1   (4-ounce) can ripe olives,
    chopped

3   ounces shaved
    sandwich meat, chopped

Soften cream cheese. Mix in remaining ingredients. Form into ball. Chill. Serve with crackers of your choice. Yield - 1 ball.

Lynne Charbonneau
Scott Charbonneau '98
Mark Charbonneau '01

Cheese Pats

2   sticks margarine, softened
1/2 pound sharp cheddar
    cheese, grated
2   cups flour

2   cups Rice Crispies
Dash of Tabasco Sauce
Dash of salt
Dash of cayenne pepper

Mix softened margarine and cheese. Stir in flour, cereal, Tabasco Sauce, salt, and cayenne pepper. Roll into large marble-sized balls. Flatten with a fork. Bake at 325° for 15 minutes. Yield - About 100 pats.

Nina Cox, President ('96-'97)
Chris Cox '92

Terry's Cheese Ball

12 ounces cream cheese, softened
1 (5-ounce) jar Roka Blue cheese, softened
1 (5-ounce) jar Old English cheese, softened
$\frac{1}{8}$ teaspoon garlic powder
$\frac{1}{2}$ teaspoon Accent
1 onion-flavored bouillon cube
1-2 cups pecans, finely chopped

Blend cheeses. Add garlic powder and Accent. Dissolve bouillon cube in 1 teaspoon hot water. Mix all ingredients, except pecans. Roll into 1 or 2 balls. Roll each ball in chopped pecans. Keep refrigerated. Yield - 1 large or 2 small balls.

Terry Moomaw
Adam Moomaw '01

Anna's Chicken Cheese Ball

1 (8-ounce) package cream cheese, softened
$\frac{1}{2}$ cup stuffed olives, diced
1 (4.2-ounce) can chicken sandwich spread
1 cup Italian-flavored bread crumbs

Combine all ingredients. Mix well. Form mixture into a ball. Roll in bread crumbs. Chill. Serve with crackers. Yield - 1 ball.

Can be made a day ahead.

Anna Sheffield
Ann Sheffield Kuebler '97
Kevin Kuebler '97

Pineapple Cheese Ball

2 (8-ounce) packages
   cream cheese
1 (8-ounce) can crushed
   pineapple
½ cup pecans, chopped

½ cup onion, grated and drained
1-2 tablespoons green
   bell pepper, diced
1 teaspoon seasoned salt
½ teaspoon Accent

Drain pineapple well. Mix all ingredients together except pecans. Shape into ball, then sprinkle with pecans. Refrigerate. Yield - 1 ball.

Marion Crawford (Don '64)
Kristin Crawford '91
Julie Crawford '95

Holiday Cheese Log

1 pound sharp cheddar
   cheese, grated
1 (3-ounce) package
   cream cheese, softened
1 teaspoon garlic powder
2 tablespoons mayonnaise

3 dashes Tabasco Sauce
½ cup pecans, chopped
   Chili powder
60 Ritz crackers
20 stuffed olives, sliced

Mix softened cheeses well. Add garlic powder, mayonnaise, Tabasco Sauce, and pecans. Form into 2 logs and roll in chili powder to cover. Wrap logs in plastic wrap or foil and chill about 2 hours or until firm. When ready to use, slice and place on Ritz crackers. Top each with an olive slice. Yield - 60 servings.

The logs can be made the day before a party.

Mary Lou Laden, President ('80-'81) (Sam '56)
Gary Laden '81

71

Cheese Roll

1 pound sharp cheddar
cheese, grated
8 ounces cream cheese
½ cup pecans, finely chopped

2-3 cloves of garlic, finely chopped
Cayenne pepper to taste
Paprika to cover

Soften cheeses at room temperature. Blend well. Add pecans, garlic, and pepper. Divide mixture into 2 parts. Form into logs. Coat well with paprika and wrap in heavy freezer paper. Chill for 3 days. Slice and serve on crackers. Yield - 2 logs.

Ruby Lee Sandars, Federation Officer

Cheese Straws

½ cup butter, softened
2 cups sharp cheddar
cheese, grated

Cayenne pepper to taste
Salt to taste
1½ cups flour

Cream butter and cheese thoroughly. Add salt and cayenne pepper. Gradually work in flour. Place on lightly floured board. Roll to ⅛ to ¼-inch thickness and cut into strips. (May be put through cookie press.) Make each straw about 2 inches long and place on an ungreased cookie sheet. Bake at 350° for 10-12 minutes. Yield - 2-2½ dozen.

Anna Sheffield
Ann Sheffield Kuebler '97
Kevin Kuebler '97

Cheese Wafers

1   stick margarine, softened
1   (5-ounce) jar Old English
    cheese spread
1½ cups flour

Cayenne pepper to taste
1½ cups pecans,
    finely chopped

Blend margarine and cheese. Add flour and cayenne pepper. Stir in pecans. Roll mixture on floured board into several nickel-sized rolls. Refrigerate 2 hours. Slice and bake at 350° for 10-12 minutes.

Anna Sheffield
Ann Sheffield Kuebler '97
Kevin Kuebler '97

Miniature Cheeseburgers

1   pound ground beef
1   package Pepperidge
    Farm party rolls (or any
    small rolls, 20 to a package)

1   (6-ounce) jar Cheez Whiz
    (may use jalapeño-style)

Make 20 tiny beef patties and cook until done. Leaving the rolls connected, slice the rolls in half. Spread the cheese spread on both sides of the rolls. Place the patties between rolls. Heat at 350° for 15 minutes or until warm. Separate the rolls into individual pieces. Makes 20 pieces.

Janis Haydel
Sally Haydel '97
Chris Haydel '02

Crab Meat Casserole

1	pound crab meat or imitation crab meat	1	(10½-ounce) can cream of mushroom soup
1	(2.8-ounce) can French fried onion rings	¾	cup cracker crumbs

Mix all ingredients. Place in buttered casserole dish. Bake at 350° for 30 minutes. Serves 4-6.

Christina Trevino (David '72)
Maria '00

Meatball Appetizers

1	pound ground beef	2	tablespoons butter
1	teaspoon Accent	3	tablespoons molasses
¾	teaspoon salt	3	tablespoons prepared mustard
1	tablespoon onions, chopped	3	tablespoons vinegar
½	cup soft bread crumbs	¼	cup ketchup
¼	cup milk	¼	teaspoon thyme
1	tablespoon flour		

Break up meat with a fork. Sprinkle with Accent, salt, and onion. Mash together crumbs and milk. Add to meat mixture and toss lightly until all ingredients are combined. Form into fifty ¾-inch balls and roll in flour. Brown in butter in skillet. Combine remaining ingredients and blend until smooth. Add to meatballs. Simmer 8 to 10 minutes. Stir occasionally until sauce thickens and meatballs are glazed. Bake at 300° for 1 hour. Serve in chafing dish. Yield - 50 meatballs.

Meatballs may be made several days in advance and frozen.

Judy Greenwood

Party Meatballs

2 pounds lean ground beef
1 egg, beaten

1 small onion, grated
Salt and pepper to taste

SAUCE-
1 (15-ounce) bottle
   chili sauce

1 cup grape jelly
1 teaspoon lemon juice

Mix together ground beef, egg, onion, salt, and pepper. Shape into small balls. Drop into simmering sauce. Cook until tender. Serve hot. Yield - About 60 meatballs.

Anna Sheffield
Ann Sheffield Kuebler '97
Kevin Kuebler '97

Sausage Balls

2 cups dry biscuit mix
1 pound sausage,
   uncooked

1 cup cheddar cheese,
   finely grated
Tabasco Sauce to taste

Combine all ingredients in a mixing bowl. Knead until mixture is thoroughly mixed. Place small balls of dough on a lightly greased baking sheet. Bake at 350° for 20 minutes or until golden brown. Yield - About 2 dozen.

Low-fat baking mix and low-fat cheese can be substituted without altering the taste. Great as a breakfast food or appetizer.

Patricia Perez
Jose Perez '99

Sausage Biscuits

8 ounces cream cheese
1 pound pork sausage, browned

3½ cups dry biscuit mix

Melt cream cheese in a double-boiler or microwave. Add sausage and mix well. Stir baking mix into mixture. Roll into small balls. Bake at 350° until brown. Yield - 2 dozen.

These freeze well.

Debbie Cauthen
Christopher Cauthen '00

Aggie Pizzas

1 pound hot breakfast-type sausage

1 pound Velveeta cheese
1 loaf party rye bread

Fry and crumble sausage until brown. Drain well. Cube Velveeta and melt in microwave. Combine cheese and sausage. Spread mixture on individual slices of party rye bread. Place on cookie sheets and freeze. When frozen, place in plastic bags and keep frozen until ready to serve. Preheat oven to 425°. Place frozen slices on ungreased cookie sheet and bake for 10 minutes. Yield - 40 slices.

Great served with soup for a meal or as an appetizer at parties. Men especially love them.

Carla Bergstrom (Paul '63)

VARIATION-

Add 1 pound ground beef, cumin to taste, and garlic salt to taste. Do not freeze. Bake at 350° for 10-15 minutes. Serve hot.

Anna Sheffield
Ann Sheffield Kuebler '97
Kevin Kuebler '97

Vegetable Bars

2	(8-count) cans crescent roll dough	¾	cup green onion, chopped
¾	cup mayonnaise	1½	cups fresh broccoli, chopped
½	cup sour cream	1½	cups fresh carrots, chopped
2	(8-ounce) packages cream cheese, softened	1½	cups fresh cauliflower, chopped
1	(1-ounce) package ranch dressing mix	¾	cup cheddar cheese, shredded
¾	cup green bell pepper, chopped		

Spread crescent roll dough out to cover an ungreased 11×17-inch pan. Bake at 350° for 8 minutes or until brown. Let cool. Combine all other ingredients, except cheddar cheese. Spread mixture over cooled crust. Chill thoroughly. Sprinkle with cheese. Cut into bars to serve. Yield - 2 dozen.

Lisa Bell, Aggie Aunt
Jose Perez '99

VARIATION-

Omit sour cream. Reduce mayonnaise to ¼ cup and fresh broccoli to ½ cup. Add ¾ cup red bell pepper, chopped, and ½ cup fresh mushrooms, chopped. Cut into 1¼-inch squares.

Phyllis Condit
Matthew Condit '01

Baked Cheese Dip

1	cup sharp cheddar cheese, grated	1	cup mayonnaise
		1	onion, minced fine

Bake 20 minutes, uncovered at 350°. Serve with tortilla chips and/or wheat crackers.

Peggy Erickson, President ('85-'86),
Federation President ('95-'96)
Kelle Erickson '85
Traci Erickson Thomas '89
Ashlee Erickson '95

Zucchini Appeteasers

3	cups zucchini, grated	2	tablespoons parsley,
1	cup dry biscuit mix		chopped
½	cup onion,	¼	teaspoon salt
	finely sliced	¼	teaspoon garlic salt
½	cup Parmesan cheese	½	teaspoon seasoned salt
½	cup oil	½	teaspoon oregano
4	eggs		Dash of black pepper

Mix all ingredients and spread in greased 9×13-inch pan. Bake at 350° for 30 minutes or until golden brown. Cut into small squares. Yield - 3-4 dozen.

Betty Donahue, Aggie Grandmother
Megan Donahue '99
Ryan Donahue '02

Black-Eyed Pea Dip

4	cups cooked black-eyed peas, drained	¼	cup onion, chopped
3	small jalapeño peppers, chopped	½	teaspoon garlic powder
		½	pound sharp cheddar cheese, grated
1	tablespoon juice from jalapeño peppers	1	cup margarine, softened
1	(4-ounce) can green chilies, chopped		

Mash peas, add remaining ingredients and mix thoroughly. Serve with corn chips or tortilla chips.

Sylvia Clark

Dip for Fruit

1	(8-ounce) jar marshmallow cream	1	teaspoon orange rind, grated
8	ounces cream cheese		Orange juice to make right consistency for dipping

Combine all ingredients.

Aggie Mom

78

Zesty Texas Caviar (Hot Black-Eyed Peas)

2   (15-ounce) cans black-eyed
    peas with jalapeños,
    drained
½   cup green bell pepper,
    diced
½   cup onion, diced

1   (4-ounce) jar chopped
    pimentos, drained
¼   teaspoon garlic, minced
1   (8-ounce) bottle Italian
    salad dressing
1   cup picante sauce

Carefully stir all ingredients together. Refrigerate overnight. Drain mixture and serve with chips.

Cindy Etier
Emily Etier '01

Chili Tamale Dip

8   ounces sharp
    cheddar cheese
1   (4-ounce) stick
    garlic cheese
1   (15-ounce) can chili

1   (15-ounce) can
    hot tamales, mashed
Tabasco Sauce to taste
Worcestershire sauce to taste

Heat cheeses slowly in a skillet. In a separate pan, heat chili and mashed tamales. Pour chili and tamale mixture into cheeses and mix thoroughly. Season with Tabasco Sauce and Worcestershire sauce. Serve hot with tortilla chips.

Anna Sheffield
Anna Sheffield Kuebler '97
Kevin Kuebler '97

Joann's Hot Artichoke Dip

1   (14-ounce) can artichoke
    hearts, drained

1   cup mayonnaise
1   cup Parmesan cheese, grated

Put artichoke hearts in blender. Mash well. Add mayonnaise and Parmesan cheese. Put into a greased 9×9-inch casserole dish. Heat at 325° until warm. Serve with plain crackers.

Susan Saiter
Rob Saiter '90
David Saiter '98

Dill Dip

1   cup sour cream
1   cup mayonnaise
2   teaspoon Beau
     Monde seasoning
2   heaping teaspoons
     dill weed

2   tablespoons green onion,
     chopped
2   tablespoons
     parsley flakes

Mix all ingredients together. Let stand in refrigerator overnight. Serve with pumpernickel bread.

JaNahn Rodriguez, President ('97-'98)
David Rodriguez '94
Cindy Rodriguez '95
Dan Rodriguez '99

Layered Nacho Dip

1   (16-ounce) can refried beans
½   of a (1.25-ounce) package
     taco seasoning mix
1   (6-ounce) carton avocado dip
8   ounces sour cream
1   (4.5-ounce) can ripe olives,
     chopped

2   large tomatoes, diced
1   small onion, finely chopped
1   (4-ounce) can green chilies,
     chopped
1½ cups Monterey Jack cheese,
     shredded

Combine beans and seasoning mix. Spread bean mixture in a 12×8×2-inch dish. Layer remaining ingredients in the order they are listed. Serve with tortilla chips.

Martha Tucker
Jennifer Tucker '97

Shrimp Dip

1   (4.5-ounce) can tiny shrimp
2   teaspoons lemon juice
8   ounces sour cream

8   ounces cream cheese
1   (0.75-ounce) package dry
     Italian salad dressing mix

Wash and drain shrimp. Mix remaining ingredients until smooth. Add shrimp. Refrigerate at least 3 hours before serving. Serve with chips or crackers. Serves 15.

Martha Tucker
Jennifer Tucker '97

THE DIXIE CHICKEN

Is the Dixie Chicken an Aggie Tradition? Yes! Texas A&M is more than the University campus. It encompasses the entire Bryan-College Station area. Students build as many college memories within the community as they do on campus.

Just as students, faculty, and parents support area businesses, the community enthusiastically supports the goals of Texas A&M. The community is there whenever needed. In 1994, the bonfire stack fell just two weeks prior to the t.u. game. Disappointment soon became determination as the B-CS community helped the student body rebuild in time for Bonfire. The Spirit of Aggieland permeates Bryan-College Station, and the Aggies are proud of their community!

This page provided by the generous support of

The Dixie Chicken
307 University Drive
College Station, TX 77840

(Thank you for your continuous support for over twenty five years.)

Dixie Chicken Photo
By
Richard Korczynski

Yummy Layered Dip

4   ounces cream cheese,
    softened
2   (15-ounce) cans black beans,
    rinsed, drained, and mashed
1   cup picante sauce, (divided)
1   teaspoon cumin

1   teaspoon chili powder
½   teaspoon garlic salt
1   cup Monterey Jack cheese,
    shredded, (divided)
½   cup green bell pepper,
    chopped

GARNISH-
Tomato, chopped
Ripe olives, chopped

Fresh cilantro, minced
Avocado, chopped

Soften cream cheese in microwave for 30-45 seconds. Add mashed beans, ½ cup picante sauce, cumin, chili powder, and garlic salt. Mix well. Spread into a microwave-safe (9-inch) pie plate. Top evenly with remaining picante sauce. Sprinkle with ½ cup cheese and green bell pepper. Cover loosely with wax paper and microwave 4 to 5 minutes, rotating after 2 minutes. Sprinkle with remaining cheese. Garnish, as desired, with tomatoes, olives, cilantro, or avocado and serve warm with chips or vegetables. Serves 6-8.

Sue Duncan
Nikki Duncan '97
Stephen Duncan '99

Polynesian Ginger Dip

1   cup mayonnaise
1   cup sour cream
¼   cup onion, finely
    chopped
¼   cup water chestnuts,
    finely chopped

¼   cup parsley, minced
1   tablespoon candied ginger,
    finely chopped
1   tablespoon soy sauce
Dash of salt
2   cloves garlic, minced

Mix mayonnaise and sour cream. Add other ingredients. Makes 2 cups. Serve with sesame seed crackers or toast or cauliflower and carrot sticks.

Mary Aasterud, President ('94-'95)
Valerie Aasterud McLaughlin '94

Pizza Dip

8 ounces cream cheese, softened	½ cup meat (browned hamburger, sausage, or diced pepperoni)
½ cup sour cream	¼ cup green onion, chopped
1 teaspoon oregano	¼ cup green bell pepper, chopped
⅛ teaspoon garlic powder	
⅛ teaspoon crushed red pepper	½ cup mozzarella cheese, shredded
½ cup pizza sauce	¼ cup Parmesan cheese

Beat together cream cheese, sour cream, oregano, garlic powder, and red pepper. Spread in pie plate or quiche dish. Cover with pizza sauce and top with meat and vegetables. Bake at 350° for 10 minutes. Sprinkle with cheeses and bake 5 minutes more. Serve with pita bread chips, crackers or chips. Serves 8.

Susie Donahue
Megan Donahue '99
Ryan Donahue '02

Spinach Dip

1 (10-ounce) package frozen chopped spinach	1 cup mayonnaise
	1 cup sour cream
1 (0.9-ounce) package Knorr vegetable soup mix	¼ cup onion, chopped
1 (8-ounce) can water chestnuts, chopped	

Thaw spinach and squeeze out excess water. Mix all ingredients together. Cover and refrigerate.

Marion Crawford (Don '64)
Kristin Crawford '91
Julie Crawford '95

Spinach Con Queso Dip

1	(10-ounce) package frozen chopped spinach	½	cup milk
1	pound Mexican Velveeta, cubed	1	small onion, chopped
		1	medium tomato, diced

Thaw spinach and squeeze out excess water. Combine cheese, milk, and onion in top of double boiler and heat until melted. Add spinach and tomato. Serve with tortilla chips. Serves 10-12.

Susie Donahue
Megan Donahue '99
Ryan Donahue '02

Vegetable Dip

8	ounces cream cheese	½	cup green bell pepper, chopped
½	cup mayonnaise	½	cup onion, chopped
1	tablespoon green goddess salad dressing	1	(8-ounce) jar dried beef

Combine and serve with vegetables or crackers.

JaNahn Rodriguez, President ('97-'98)
David Rodriguez '94
Cindy Rodriguez '95
Dan Rodriguez '99

Yogurt Dip

1½	cups no-fat yogurt	2	teaspoon dried dill
1	cup mayonnaise (may use no-fat style)	1	teaspoon celery seed
		1½	teaspoons lemon juice

Combine all ingredients. Serve with raw vegetables. Makes 2½ cups.

Make a Christmas tray by using cherry tomatoes, radishes and red bell pepper for the red and broccoli florets, cucumber slices, asparagus, Brussels sprouts, celery sticks and green bell pepper for the green.

Mary Aasterud, President ('94-'95)
Valerie Aasterud McLaughlin '94

Marlene's Hot Sauce

3 (16-ounce) cans
   whole tomatoes
1½ tablespoons garlic powder
2 tablespoons crushed
   red pepper
1½ tablespoons vinegar

1 tablespoon oil
½ jalapeño pepper
Salt and pepper to taste
Dash dried onion flakes
Dash dried bell pepper flakes

Drain juice from tomatoes, and pour juice into blender. Add all ingredients, except tomatoes, to blender and blend. Add tomatoes last and pulse blender until sauce is chunky. Keeps in refrigerator for several weeks.

"Betcha can't eat just one bite."

Paula Lively
Carrie Lively Patterson '96
Jim Lively '96
Troy Patterson '93

Charlie's Party Mix

9 tablespoons margarine
4 tablespoons Worcestershire
   sauce
1 teaspoon hot sauce
1 teaspoon garlic powder

2 cups Cheerios
2 cups Bran Chex
2 cups Rice Chex
2 cups pretzels
2 cups mixed nuts

Combine margarine, Worcestershire sauce, hot sauce, and garlic powder. Heat until margarine is melted. Stir well. Combine cereals, pretzels, and nuts. Spread cereal mixture on a large jelly roll pan. Pour margarine mixture evenly over the cereal mixture. Bake at 250° for 45 minutes, stirring every 15 minutes. Spread on paper towels until cool. Store in airtight container.

Pat Hardi, President ('93-'94)
Steven Hardi '91, '94

Party Snack Mix

3   cups small pretzels
2   cups canned shoestring
    potatoes
2   cups Spanish peanuts
1½ cups seasoned croutons

1   (3-ounce) can French-fried
    onion rings
1   stick margarine, melted
½   cup Parmesan cheese, grated

In a large bowl, mix pretzels, potatoes, peanuts, croutons, and onion rings. Pour melted margarine over mixture. Sprinkle with Parmesan cheese. Mix well. Spread on a 15×10-inch jelly-roll pan or shallow roasting pan. Bake at 250° for 1 hour, stirring twice during cooking. Keeps well. Serves 12.

Susan Saiter
Rob Saiter '90
David Saiter '98

Minted Pecans

2   cups sugar
Dash of salt
¾   cup evaporated milk

1   tablespoon butter
    or margarine
1   teaspoon peppermint extract
4   cups pecan halves

Place 2 large sheets of aluminum foil on counter top in readiness for spreading out pecans. In a heavy 2-quart saucepan, combine sugar, salt, evaporated milk, and butter. Heat over low heat, stirring constantly, until sugar is dissolved (about 5 minutes). Cook over medium heat, stirring constantly, to soft-ball stage (234-240°), about 7 minutes. Remove from heat and stir in extract. Stir in pecans and coat well. Pour onto one sheet of foil. Break the clusters into individual nuts and place onto the second sheet of foil. Cool thoroughly. Store in airtight container.

Martha Tucker
Jennifer Tucker '97

Mexican Pick-up Sticks

2 (3-ounce) cans
   French fried onion rings
1 (7-ounce) can shoestring
   potatoes

2 cups Spanish peanuts
⅓ cup margarine, melted
1 (1-ounce) package taco
   seasoning mix

Combine onion rings, potatoes, and peanuts. Place in 9×13-inch pan. Pour margarine over the mixture and stir well. Sprinkle with taco seasoning and mix well. Bake at 250° for 45 minutes, stirring every 15 minutes.

Cindy Etier
Emily Etier '01

Oyster Crackers Parmesan

1 (1-ounce) package dry
   ranch salad dressing mix
¼ cup Parmesan cheese

¾ cup salad oil
1 (10-ounce) package
   oyster crackers

Stir ranch dressing mix and cheese into oil. Using a brown paper bag, toss together the crackers and oil mixture. Set aside for 1 hour, stirring occasionally. Store in an airtight container.

Anna Sheffield
Ann Sheffield Kuebler '97
Kevin Kuebler '97

Sugar and Spice Nuts

¼ cup butter
3 cups pecan halves
½ cup sugar
3 tablespoons sugar

1 tablespoon cinnamon
½ teaspoon ginger
½ teaspoon nutmeg

In 10-inch skillet, melt butter and stir in nuts and ½ cup of sugar. Cook over medium heat, stirring occasionally, until sugar melts and nuts brown (8-12 minutes). Meanwhile, in large bowl, combine remaining ingredients. Stir in caramelized nuts. Spread on waxed paper and cool completely. Break clusters into individual nuts. Store in airtight container. Yield - 3 cups.

This is great for gift-giving at Christmas.

Janie Wallace
Rachel Wallace '01

Almond Tea

3 tablespoons lemon-flavored instant tea, unsweetened	2 (6-ounce) cans frozen lemonade
1 cup sugar	3 teaspoons vanilla extract
2 cups boiling water	3 teaspoons almond extract

Mix tea and sugar. Pour boiling water into mixture. Add thawed lemonade and extracts. Add enough water to above mixture to make 1 gallon of tea. It can be stored in the refrigerator for several days. Yield - 1 gallon.

Camille Dillard '68 (Don '64)
Danylle Dillard Leeds '91
Jason Leeds '92

Hot Almond Tea

2 cups boiling water	10 tablespoons lemon juice
3 small tea bags	1 teaspoon almond extract
4 cups water	½ teaspoon vanilla extract
¾ cup sugar	

Pour boiling water over tea bags and steep 10 minutes. Combine 4 cups water and sugar in a saucepan and boil for 5 minutes. Stir in lemon juice, almond extract, and vanilla extract. Mix together with the brewed tea. Serve hot. (Can be kept in the refrigerator.) Makes about 7 cups.

Cindy Etier
Emily Etier '01

Hot Cranberry Tea

2 cups sugar	2 cups orange juice
4 cinnamon sticks	3 tablespoons lemon juice
2 cups water	4 cups water
2 quarts cranberry juice cocktail	4 cinnamon sticks
	Additional cinnamon sticks

In stock pot, bring sugar, 4 cinnamon sticks, and 2 cups water to a boil. Add juice and stir in remaining 4 cups of water and 4 cinnamon sticks. Simmer until steaming but not boiling. Garnish with additional cinnamon sticks. May be prepared ahead and reheated. Yield - 16 (8-ounce) servings.

Julee White '80

Friendship Tea

1 (3-ounce) jar instant tea
2 cups sugar
2 (5-ounce) packages instant lemonade mix

1 (16-ounce) jar instant orange drink
½ teaspoon ground cloves
½ teaspoon ground cinnamon

Mix ingredients thoroughly. Use 2 rounded teaspoons in 1 cup of boiling water. Keep in air-tight container. A great gift for friends, teachers, or anyone.

Anna Sheffield
Ann Sheffield Kuebler '97
Kevin Kuebler '97

Hot Chocolate Mix (For a Crowd)

1 (20-quart) box nonfat dry milk mix
32 ounces instant chocolate drink mix

16 ounces non-dairy coffee creamer
7½ cups powdered sugar
1 (13-ounce) jar chocolate malt

Mix all ingredients in a large airtight container. Use ⅓ cup of the mix and ⅔ cup of hot water per cup. Serves a family of four for an entire winter.

Robin Luffy
Jennifer Luffy '00
Brian Luffy '02

Spiced Hot Chocolate

1 quart milk
4 ounces German sweet baking chocolate, finely chopped

½ teaspoon ground cinnamon
Whipped topping, thawed

In a medium saucepan, beat milk, chocolate, and cinnamon over medium heat, stirring constantly. Cook until chocolate is melted and mixture just comes to a boil. Pour into serving cups. Serve with a spoonful of whipped topping. Serves 4.

Sharon Reid
Ethan Reid '96

Instant Cocoa Mix

8½ cups nonfat dry milk	1½ cups powdered sugar
3 cups instant chocolate drink mix	1½ cups non-dairy coffee creamer

Combine all ingredients. Store in air-tight container. To serve - mix ½ cup mixture with 9 ounces boiling water. Yield - 14 cups mixture or 30 servings.

Anna Sheffield
Ann Sheffield Kuebler '97
Kevin Kuebler '97

Almond Tea Punch

1 cup lemon juice from concentrate	2 tablespoons pure vanilla extract
4 cups sugar	4 tablespoons pure almond extract
2 cups strong brewed tea	
2 quarts water	4 liters ginger ale

Mix first 6 ingredients. Freeze in a 1-gallon plastic bag. Remove from freezer 2 hours before serving. Immediately before serving, mash with a fork and add ginger ale. Yield - 40 (5-ounce) servings.

Anna Sheffield
Ann Sheffield Kuebler '97
Kevin Kuebler '97

Cherry Bounce (Cherry Liqueur)

1 pound dark, sweet cherries, stemmed	2 cups sugar
	1 fifth of bourbon

Combine all ingredients in a 64-ounce glass jar. Close tightly. Turn and shake container every day for a week until sugar is dissolved. Do not open for four to six months. When "bounce" is ready, strain liqueur into containers of your choice. Cherries may be used on ice cream after seeds are discarded. Fresh Bing cherries are only available in late July. Cherry Bounce will be ready for Christmas gift giving. This is an old Louisiana recipe. The cheapest bourbon works fine.

Grace Durand, Aggie Aunt
Dr. Malon Southerland '65

The Texas Governor's Mansion Summer Peach Tea

2	cups sugar	1	(6-ounce) can frozen lemonade
1	cup water		
3	family-sized tea bags	1	(32-ounce) can peach nectar
6	cups water		
2	cups fresh mint, loosely packed	1	liter ginger ale, chilled
		1	liter club soda, chilled

Bring 2 cups of sugar and 1 cup of water to boil. Boil slowly until syrup is clear (about 4 minutes). Bring 6 cups of water to a boil, remove from heat, and add tea bags and mint. Let steep for 10 minutes and remove tea bags. When the tea has cooled to room temperature, strain tea into a 2-gallon container. Add lemonade, peach nectar, and syrup. Chill. Just before serving, add ginger ale and club soda. Yield - 1½ gallons.

Judy Boldt (Bob '68)
Laura Boldt '94
David Boldt '97

Frozen Pineapple Punch

1	(46-ounce) can pineapple juice	2	cups sugar
1	(16-ounce) can frozen orange juice	5	bananas, blended
½	cup lemon juice	2	(2-liter) bottles lemon-lime soda

Mix all ingredients together, except for lemon-lime soda. Freeze. When ready to serve, add soda. Yield - 40 (5-ounce) servings.

JaNahn Rodriguez, President ('97-'98)
David Rodriguez '94
Cindy Rodriguez '95
Dan Rodriguez '99

Peppermint Ice Cream Punch

½ gallon peppermint
  ice cream

1 quart eggnog
1 liter ginger ale

Mix all ingredients together in a punch bowl. Hang candy canes on the side of the punch bowl. Serve immediately. Yield - 1 gallon. Pretty and festive for holidays.

Nancy Bagwell
Lauren Bagwell '99
John Bagwell '03

Red Holiday Punch

1 (2-quart) package
  unsweetened cherry Kool-Aid
1 (2-quart) package
  unsweetened strawberry
  Kool-Aid

1 (6-ounce) can frozen orange
  juice
1 (6-ounce) can frozen
  lemonade
1 quart ginger ale

Mix Kool-Aid as directed on package. Mix orange juice and lemonade as directed on packages. Add Kool-Aids, orange juice, lemonade, and ginger ale together. Freeze for several hours until slushy. (Ginger ale may be added just before serving, instead of before mixture is frozen.) Yield - 1 gallon.

Sharon Cornwell

Teaberry Punch

¾ cup lemon-flavored
  ice tea mix with sugar
3 cups cranberry juice cocktail
1 (6-ounce) can frozen
  orange juice, thawed

1 (6-ounce) can frozen
  lemonade, thawed
1 quart water, chilled
1 liter ginger ale, chilled

In a 1½-gallon container, combine all ingredients, except ginger ale. Just before serving, add chilled ginger ale. Serve over ice. Yield - 20 (5-ounce) servings.

Cindy Etier
Emily Etier '01

Fruit Smoothies

1½ cups frozen strawberries,   1   banana, sliced and frozen
    sliced and sweetened   1½ cups skim milk

Put frozen berries, frozen bananas, and milk in a blender. Blend together. Can use other fruit combinations, such as peaches, blackberries, or raspberries. Yield - 2 servings.

A low fat, refreshing drink, especially when it is hot.

Nina Cox, President ('96-'97)
Chris Cox '92

Lime Mint Frost

1   (6-ounce) can frozen limeade   2   cups lime sherbet
1   large banana, cut into chunks   ⅛   teaspoon mint extract

Combine limeade (diluted according to directions on can) and banana in blender and blend until smooth. Add sherbet and mint extract. Blend on medium speed until smooth (about 10 seconds). Pour into glasses and freeze for 1 hour. Serves 3-4.

Wilma Green

Orange Soda Supreme

6   ounces sugar-free   ½   teaspoon vanilla extract
    orange soda   ¼   teaspoon coconut extract
1½ teaspoon nonfat dry milk   Ice cubes
½   cup unsweetened frozen
    strawberries

In a blender, whip all ingredients together, except ice cubes. Add ice cubes one at a time until mixture is thick and foamy. Add more orange soda, if necessary. Yield - 1 serving.

Cindy Etier
Emily Etier '01

Soups,
Sandwiches,
and Sauces

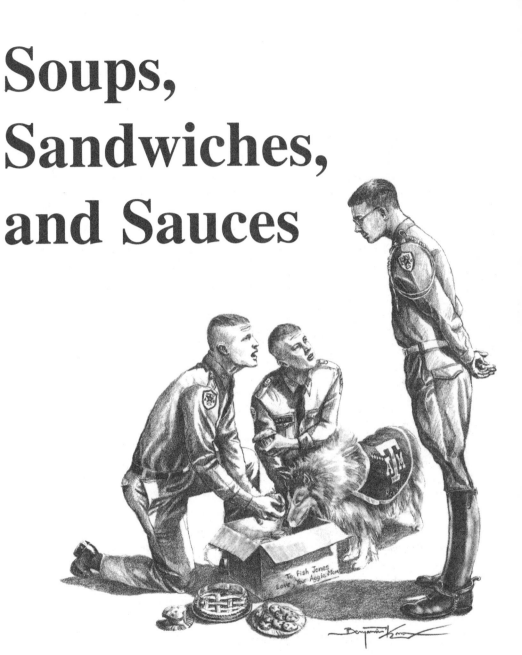

Black Bean Soup

1 tablespoon olive oil
1 cup onion, chopped
2 small cloves garlic, minced
2 (15-ounce) cans black beans, drained
1 (14½-ounce) can "no-salt added" stewed tomatoes, chopped and undrained

1 (10½-ounce) can low-sodium chicken broth
½ cup picante sauce (mild or medium)
¼ cup water
1 teaspoon ground cumin
2 tablespoons fresh lime juice
Chopped fresh cilantro (optional)

Heat oil in large nonstick saucepan over medium heat until hot. Add onion and garlic and sauté until tender. Add beans and next five ingredients. Stir well. Bring to a boil. Reduce heat and simmer, uncovered, for 15 minutes. Remove from heat. Stir in lime juice. Ladle soup into bowls and garnish with cilantro, if desired. Yield - 6 cups. Serves 4-6. Serve with cornbread muffins.

Sharon Corry
Trey Corry '01

Broccoli-Cheese Soup

1 tablespoon butter
¾ cup onion, chopped
6 cups water
6 bouillon cubes (chicken or beef)
1 (8-ounce) package fine egg noodles
1 teaspoon salt

2 (10-ounce) packages frozen chopped broccoli
⅛ teaspoon garlic powder
6 cups milk
1 pound American cheese or cheese spread
Pepper to taste (optional)

Heat butter and sauté onion. Add water and bouillon cubes. Boil and gradually add noodles and salt. Cook in water 3 minutes. Stir in broccoli and garlic powder. Cook for 3 minutes. Add milk, cheese, and pepper. Stir constantly until cheese melts. Makes 4 quarts.

This soup will freeze and keep for one month.

Trudy Lewis, President (El Paso Mothers' Club '87-'88)
Stan Lewis '88

Cheese Soup

1	(10-ounce) package carrots, shredded	2	(10½-ounce) cans potato soup
3	ribs of celery, chopped	1	(8-ounce) carton sour cream
1	large onion, chopped	8	ounces American cheese slices
2	tablespoons butter		Tabasco Sauce to taste
2	(14-ounce) cans chicken broth		

Sauté first 4 ingredients in large pan. Add broth and simmer 20 minutes. Add potato soup, sour cream, and cheese slices. Stir until smooth. Add Tabasco Sauce. Serves 6-8. Very good winter soup—easy to make.

Vara Buchanan
Adie Buchanan '01

Cold Black Cherry Soup

3	cups cold water	1	tablespoon arrowroot
1	cup sugar	2	tablespoons water
1	cinnamon stick	¼	cup heavy cream
4	cups canned black cherries	¾	cup dry red wine, chilled

In two-quart pan combine water, sugar, and cinnamon stick. Boil. Add cherries and cover. Simmer over low heat for ten minutes. Remove cinnamon stick. Mix arrowroot and 2 tablespoons water into paste, then beat into soup. Stir, bringing soup to boil. Reduce heat and simmer for two minutes or until clear and slightly thickened. Pour into shallow or stainless bowl and refrigerate until completely chilled. Just before serving, stir in cream and wine. Makes 8 servings.

Use leftovers over ice cream.

Eileen Buis
Josh Buis '97
Jordan Buis '99

Chicken Gumbo

1 large onion, chopped	½ (10-ounce) package frozen corn
2 tablespoons salad oil	
4 cups chicken broth	½ (10-ounce) package frozen lima beans
2 cups canned tomatoes with liquid	
	1 tablespoon seasoned salt
4 cups frozen cut okra	12 drops Tabasco Sauce
1 fryer, cooked, skinned and diced	2 teaspoons filé powder

Sauté onion in oil until tender but not brown. Combine onion, broth, tomatoes, okra, chicken, corn, and lima beans in a large pot and simmer about 30 minutes. Stir in seasoned salt, Tabasco, and filé. Serve over mounds of hot rice. Serves 4-6.

This is a good way to use leftover turkey.

Paula Lively
Jim Lively '96
Carrie Lively Patterson '96
Troy Patterson '93

Chicken Lime Soup

1 onion, chopped	1 teaspoon cumin
2 cloves of garlic, minced	1 tablespoon Molly McButter (butter substitute)
1 tablespoon olive oil	
4 (12-ounce) cans fat-free chicken broth	Pepper to taste
	Freshly squeezed juice from 2 limes
2 (12-ounce) cans chopped tomatoes	3 tablespoons fresh chopped cilantro
2 pounds boneless, skinless chicken, cooked and cubed	8 ounces fat-free Monterey Jack or mozzarella cheese, grated
2 teaspoons garlic powder	8 ounces tortilla chips, crushed

Brown onion and garlic in one tablespoon olive oil in soup pot. Add chicken broth, tomatoes, and chicken. Add garlic powder, cumin, butter substitute, and pepper. Add lime juice and cilantro. Simmer for 15 minutes. To serve-Add cheese to bottom of soup bowl. Add crushed tortilla chips. Serve soup over cheese and chips. Serves 8.

Cindy Rodriguez '95

Black Bean Chili Marsala

1	large onion, chopped	2-3	(4-ounce) cans sliced mushrooms, drained
2	cloves garlic, minced	3-4	tablespoons chili powder
3	tablespoons vegetable oil	2	teaspoons seasoned salt
1	(15-ounce) can kidney beans, drained	1	teaspoon freshly ground pepper
1	(15-ounce) can pinto beans, drained	2	(15-ounce) cans black beans, undrained

1   (15-ounce) can red beans, drained
1   (29-ounce) can tomato sauce
2   (6-ounce) cans tomato paste
1   cup Marsala wine (1 cup Chablis or other dry white wine plus 1½ tablespoons brandy may be substituted)

Hot cooked rice
Garnish - strips of lime rind or cilantro sprigs

Cook onion and garlic in oil in a Dutch oven over medium high heat, stirring constantly, until tender. Add next 8 ingredients. Bring to a boil. Cover, reduce heat, and simmer 1 hour, stirring occasionally. Add black beans and cook until thoroughly heated. Serve over rice. Garnish, if desired. Yield - 3 quarts.

Helen Moese
Linda Moese '97

Clam Chowder

2	slices bacon	1	cup water
1	cup onion, chopped	2	(6-ounce) cans clams
2	cups potatoes, cubed	2	cups half-and-half
1	teaspoon salt	2	tablespoons butter or margarine

Dash of pepper

Chop bacon. Sauté in large kettle until almost crisp. Add onion and cook about 5 minutes. Add potatoes, salt, pepper, and water. Cook, uncovered, until potatoes are tender. Add clams, half-and-half, and butter. Heat through. Serves 4.

Martha Tucker
Jennifer Tucker '97

Chili Blanco with Chicken

3   pounds chicken thighs or
    breasts, skinned and boned
1½ teaspoons white pepper
1   teaspoon garlic powder
3   tablespoons vegetable oil
1   small onion, diced
2   (15-ounce) cans great
    Northern beans
2   (14-ounce) cans chicken broth

2   (4-ounce) cans chopped
    green chilies
1   (10½-ounce) can cream of
    chicken soup
3   tablespoons jalapeño pepper
    juice
2   tablespoons fresh cilantro,
    minced
1   teaspoon salt

GARNISH-
6-8 flour tortillas
1   cup sour cream

1½ cups grated Monterey Jack
    cheese

Cut chicken into small pieces and season with white pepper and garlic. Sauté chicken in oil in a stockpot for 3 minutes. Add remaining soup ingredients and bring to a boil. Reduce heat and simmer for 30 minutes.

Cindy Rodriguez '95

Chili Cookoff Winner I

3   pounds lean beef, coarsely
    ground
1   large onion, chopped
1   teaspoon garlic powder
1   tablespoon cumin
4   tablespoons chili powder
Crushed red pepper (optional)

4   tablespoons Worcestershire
    sauce
2   teaspoons salt, or to taste
2   (8-ounce) cans tomato sauce
4   cups hot water
10 saltine crackers, crushed

In a heavy Dutch oven, cook meat over medium heat until gray. Add onions, cook until translucent. Stir in next 6 items. Add tomato sauce and water. Lower heat and simmer for 3 hours or more (lid slightly ajar). Stir occasionally. May be thickened with a paste of crackers mixed with water. Pour the paste into the chili, stirring constantly to avoid lumping. Simmer for an additional 30 minutes. Serves 8-10.

Buddy Blankenship
Clay Blankenship '82
Ruth Ellen Blankenship Heaton '90

Chili Cookoff Winner II

2	pounds ground round	½	teaspoon cayenne pepper
1	pound Cajun sausage, out of casing	1	teaspoon cumin seeds, whole
3	tablespoons olive oil	1	teaspoon salt
2	cups shallots, coarsely chopped	2	tablespoons chili powder
2	tablespoons garlic, finely chopped		Black pepper
1	(10-ounce) can green chilies, chopped	4	cups beef broth
		1	(6-ounce) can tomato paste
		1	teaspoon oregano

In a large heavy skillet, brown meat and sausage. Transfer to a 4-quart pot. In the same skillet, add beef stock and bring to a boil. Remove stock from heat. Set this aside in a separate bowl. Add olive oil to the skillet and cook the shallots and garlic for 5 minutes, stirring frequently. Remove from heat. Add canned chilies, oregano, cumin seeds, cayenne pepper, chili powder, salt, and a few grindings of black pepper. Stir together, then add tomato paste and beef stock. Mix together thoroughly. Add this to meat and bring to a boil. Stir. Reduce heat and simmer in half-covered pot for 1½ hours or more. Serves 8-10.

Carol Smith, President ('92-'93) (Wilburn '60)
Stephanie Smith McVay '85
Martin McVay '83
Darryl Smith '90

Quick Corn Chowder

1	(15-ounce) can cream-style corn	1	(10½-ounce) can potato soup
1	(10½-ounce) can jalapeño soup	1	soup can of milk
		1	soup can of water

Mix all ingredients, heat, and serve.

Lillian Gips
Bruce Holmes '78
Jeff Broaddus '98

South of the Border White Chili

2   tablespoons olive oil
1   medium onion, chopped
3   cloves garlic, minced
2   (10-ounce) cans tomatoes
    with green chilies, chopped
1   medium jalapeño, seeded
    and chopped
2   cups chicken stock
    OR 2 (12½-ounce) cans
    chicken broth
1   (17-ounce) can chopped
    green chilies
2   cups baked chicken, chopped

½   teaspoon oregano
½   teaspoon cumin
¼   cup (heaping) chopped
    cilantro
2   (19-ounce) cans cannellini
    beans
1   tablespoon lime juice
Salt and pepper to taste
8   ounces sour cream
8   ounces shredded Monterey
    Jack cheese
8   ounces fried tortilla strips

Heat the oil in a large stockpot over medium high heat. Add onion. Sauté for 3-5 minutes until softened. Add garlic. Cook for 1-2 minutes longer; do not brown. Add tomatoes and jalapeño. Cook, stirring occasionally. Add chicken stock, green chilies, chicken, oregano, cumin, cilantro, beans, and lime juice. Cook until heated through, stirring frequently. Season with salt and pepper. Serves 8-10. To serve- Ladle chili into serving bowls. Garnish with a dollop of sour cream, cheese, and tortilla strips.

This chili won the 1997 Chili Cook-off Aggie Bonfire Award.
Serving Suggestion - Serve with a salad and chips on a cold winter night.

Nina Cox, President ('96-'97)
Chris Cox '92

Suzanne's Chili

1½	pounds ground sirloin	1	teaspoon cumin
1	large onion, chopped	1	teaspoon paprika
½	cup green bell peppers, chopped		Pepper to taste
1	(15-ounce) can Ranch Style beans	1	tablespoon freshly squeezed lemon juice
2	(15-ounce) cans tomato sauce	¾	cup mild picante sauce
1	(15-ounce) can diced tomatoes	1½	cups water
3	tablespoons chili powder	8	ounces cheddar cheese, grated

Brown sirloin and drain. Combine sirloin and next 11 ingredients in large Dutch oven. Add water. Bring to a boil, turn heat to medium low and cook 5 hours. Serve with grated cheese on top.

Suzanne Blaney
Erin Blaney '01

Vegetarian Chili

2	tablespoons vegetable oil	⅔	cup bulghur wheat
1	large onion, chopped	1	(8-ounce) can tomato sauce
1	large green bell pepper, chopped	1	(6-ounce) can tomato paste
2	cloves garlic, minced	1	(4-ounce) can diced green chilies
1	(28-ounce) can stewed tomatoes, undrained	1	teaspoon ground cumin
1	cup ripe olives, sliced	1½	tablespoons chili powder
2	(15-ounce) cans pinto beans, drained	¾	teaspoon salt
1½	cups water	1	teaspoon sugar
		¼	teaspoon crushed red pepper flakes

Heat oil in a large pan. Sauté onion, bell pepper, and garlic in oil until vegetables are tender, about 5 minutes. Pour in tomatoes with juice. Stir in remaining ingredients. Cover and simmer until bulghur is tender and flavor develops, about 45-60 minutes. Stir occasionally. If chili seems dry, add more water as needed. Yields 2 quarts or 6 servings.

Cindy Etier
Emily Etier '01

The Great Vogeli Chili

1   ounce olive oil
2   pounds coarsely ground beef
2   medium onions, ¼-inch diced
4   cloves garlic, finely chopped
2   jalapeño peppers,
    ¼-inch diced
6   ancho chilies, soaked in
    1-quart of hot water,
    blended in the
    blender, and strained (hold)

2   teaspoons paprika
½   teaspoon oregano
½   teaspoon ground cumin
3   bay leaves
2   (12-ounce) cans, V-8 juice
2   tablespoons flour
1   quart or more cooked
    pinto beans
Cayenne pepper (optional)

In a large pot, sauté onions and garlic in olive oil. Add beef and brown. Add paprika, oregano, bay leaves, and cumin. Add jalapeño. Roast briefly, and add flour. Remove from fire and stir in flour. Add V-8 juice and blended ancho chilies. Simmer until beef is tender, or about 45 minutes. Season to taste with pepper and salt. For extra heat, add cayenne pepper. If chili is too thick, add beans with the juice. If not, drain beans to add to chili. Serves 8-10.

Tilly Vogeli (Champion Chili Cook)
Michael Vogeli '94

White Turkey Chili

1   pound turkey meat, cut in
    bite-sized pieces
½   cup carrots, sliced
½   cup celery, sliced
3   (14½-ounce) cans chicken
    or turkey broth
2   (16-ounce) cans navy beans,
    undrained

1   (4-ounce) can green chilies,
    chopped and drained
½   tablespoon oregano
½   tablespoon cumin
½   tablespoon black pepper
½   cup sour cream
1½ cups shredded Monterey
    Jack cheese

Simmer turkey, carrots, and celery in broth about 10 minutes until turkey is no longer pink. Add beans, chilies, and spices. Simmer for 10 minutes. Top each serving with shredded cheese and a dollop of sour cream. Serves 8.

Serving Suggestion - Serve with crackers or corn chips.

Susan Saiter
Rob Saiter '90
David Saiter '98

Mexican Soup

2	pounds hamburger meat	2	(15-ounce) cans Ranch Style
1	onion, chopped		beans
3	(10½-ounce) cans minestrone soup	2	(10-ounce) cans Rotel tomatoes

Brown hamburger meat and onion and drain. Mix all ingredients in large pan. Cook one hour. Serves about 6.

VARIATIONS:
Substitute cooked chicken for hamburger (you may need to add liquid). Serve over tortilla chips and top with shredded cheese.

Linda Murphy
Kristina Murphy '91
Karin Murphy Harbour '93
Sean Harbour '92

New Year's Day Soup

1½	cups dried black-eyed peas	4	garlic cloves, minced
4	tablespoons butter	1½	teaspoons thyme (divided)
1	cup onion, chopped	8	cups chicken stock
3	leeks, sliced	1	ham hock
4	ribs celery, coarsely chopped		Salt and pepper to taste
3	carrots, peeled and chopped		

Soak peas overnight. Drain off water. In large pot, sauté onions, leeks, celery, carrots, and garlic in butter until tender. Stir in one teaspoon thyme and stock. Add ham hock and peas. Bring to boil. Add salt and pepper. Reduce heat and simmer until peas are tender, about 40 minutes, skimming occasionally. Remove ham hock and let cool slightly. Remove meat from bones and return meat to soup. Correct seasoning. Before reheating, add another ½ teaspoon thyme. Makes 8-10 servings.

Sue Duncan
Nikki Duncan '97
Stephen Duncan '99

Creole Onion Soup

1½ cups unsalted butter or margarine

5 large onions, chopped

2 teaspoons sugar

½ cup flour

6 cups canned beef broth or veal and pork stock

6 cups poultry stock or canned chicken broth

Salt to taste

½ teaspoon freshly ground pepper

Garlic bread (see below)

10 slices of Gruyere cheese, ¼-inch thick

GARLIC BREAD-

10 French bread slices, ½-inch thick

¼ cup olive oil

6 large garlic cloves

Salt to taste

To prepare soup, melt butter or margarine in a heavy 5-6 quart soup pot over medium heat. Add onions, stirring often, until very limp and completely transparent, about 20 minutes. Sprinkle sugar over onions and stir to blend. Increase heat to medium high. Cook, stirring, until onions are lightly brown and slightly crisp on edges (about 5-6 minutes). Reduce heat to medium. Add flour all at once and stir until combined. Cook 3-4 minutes, stirring. Slowly stir in stock or broths. Bring to a boil to thicken slightly. Reduce heat. Season with salt and pepper. Simmer one hour, stirring occasionally. Taste for seasoning and adjust if necessary.

GARLIC BREAD- Position oven rack 6 inches below broiler. Pre-heat broiler. Using a pastry brush, brush both sides of bread lightly with olive oil. Place on an ungreased cookie sheet. Broil until crisp, turning once. Cool slightly. When toast is cool enough to handle, rub garlic cloves on one side of each piece. Salt lightly and set aside.

TO SERVE - Ladle soup into flameproof bowls. Place a garlic bread slice on each bowl of soup. Top each bread slice with a cheese slice. Broil under broiler until cheese melts (1-2 minutes). Serve hot. Makes 6-8 servings.

Artie J. Jenkins
Altie Jenkins '00

Cheese Potato Soup

6-8 medium potatoes, cooked
2 carrots, sliced and cooked
2 celery stalks, sliced and cooked
1 small onion, diced and cooked
3 cups water
5 chicken bouillon cubes

¾ teaspoon Spike (all-purpose seasoning)
½ teaspoon thyme
½ teaspoon rosemary
Dash of garlic powder
Dash of pepper
2 cups skim milk
1 (16-ounce) package Velveeta, cubed

Simmer first 11 ingredients for 20-30 minutes in medium pot. Mash ingredients with a potato masher. Add skim milk and cheese. Heat until cheese melts. Serves 10. Wonderful potato soup served with cornbread.

Helen Beasley, President ('91-'92)
Nancy Beasley '90

Dill Potato Soup

2 (10½-ounce) cans cream of potato soup
1½ cups water
1¾ cups milk

½ teaspoon dill weed
White pepper to taste
½ teaspoon salt
1 cup sour cream

Heat soup and water. Add milk, but do not boil. Add remaining ingredients and heat through.

Sooo good!

Paula Lively
Jim Lively '96
Carrie Lively Patterson '96
Troy Patterson '93

Potato Soup

3 cups diced potatoes
2 stalks celery, sliced
1 small onion, chopped
1 cup water
1 teaspoon salt
1 teaspoon parsley

$^1/_8$ teaspoon pepper
1 teaspoon instant chicken
   bouillon granules
2 cups milk (divided)
3 tablespoons flour
3 tablespoons butter or margarine

GARNISHES-
8 ounces cheddar cheese, grated
4 slices bacon, fried crisp and
   crumbled

8 ounces sour cream
2 tablespoons chives

Combine potatoes, celery, onion, water, spices, and bouillon. Cook over medium heat until tender, then mash. Using a jar with a tight-fitting lid, shake together $^1/_8$ cup of milk with flour until well blended. Combine with remaining milk and butter and add to potato mixture. Cook over medium heat until boiling, stirring constantly. Garnish with any combination of cheese, bacon, sour cream, and/or chives. Serves 8-10.

Anna Sheffield
Ann Sheffield Kuebler '97
Kevin Kuebler '97

Also submitted by Lynne Charbonneau
Scott Charbonneau '98
Mark Charbonneau '01

Santa Fe Soup

1 pound ground meat
1 (15-ounce) can diced tomatoes
1 (10-ounce) can Rotel tomatoes
1 (15-ounce) can kidney beans
1 (3-ounce) package taco or chili seasoning mix
1 (15-ounce) can corn
1 (15-ounce) can carrots
1 (0.4-ounce) package ranch dressing mix (dry)
1 beef bouillon cube

Brown meat and drain. In a large pot, mix meat and all ingredients. (It is not necessary to drain the liquids from the cans.) Add water, if necessary. Simmer and serve.

Since all of the ingredients are canned, this can be made up and served in a hurry!

Cindie Deasey
Beth Williamson '02

Cindy's Taco Soup

1 pound ground beef
½ onion, chopped
1 (28-ounce) can diced tomatoes
1 (3-ounce) package taco seasoning mix
1 (0.4-ounce) package ranch dressing mix
4 ounces picante sauce
1 (8-ounce) can tomato sauce
2 (14½-ounce) cans niblet corn
½ (14½-ounce) can pinto beans
2 cups water

Brown ground beef with onion. Add remaining ingredients. Simmer for 45-60 minutes. Serves 8.

Serving Suggestion - Serve over chips, grated cheese, and sour cream.

Cindy Rodriguez '95

Ranch-Style Taco Soup

2   pounds ground beef, browned
1   medium onion, chopped
2   (15-ounce) cans Ranch Style beans
1   (3-ounce) package dry taco seasoning mix
1   (0.4-ounce) package dry ranch dressing mix
1   (15-ounce) can diced tomatoes
1   (15-ounce) can Rotel tomatoes
1   (15-ounce) can white hominy
1   (15-ounce) can yellow hominy
1-2 cups water

Do not drain liquid from any of the vegetables. Mix all ingredients. Simmer 1-2 hours. Serves 6.

Nancy Tong
Paul Tong '99

Tortellini Soup

1   tablespoon butter
½   cup sliced mushrooms
3   cups water
1   package Knorr's vegetable soup mix (dry)
1   cup tortellini, fresh or frozen
3   tablespoons grated Parmesan cheese

Sauté mushrooms in butter. Add water and bring to a boil. Add remaining ingredients and heat 20-30 minutes. Serve with Parmesan cheese sprinkled over the top.

Paula Lively
Jim Lively '96
Carrie Lively Patterson '96
Troy Patterson '93

La Madeleine's Tomato Basil Soup

4 cups (8-10) tomatoes, peeled, seeded, and chopped OR 4 cups canned whole tomatoes, crushed
4 cups tomato juice OR part juice and part vegetable or chicken stock
12-14 fresh basil leaves
1 cup heavy cream
¼ pound sweet, unsalted butter
¼ teaspoon crushed black pepper
Salt to taste

Combine tomatoes, juice and/or stock in saucepan. Simmer 30 minutes. Puree, along with the basil leaves, in small batches, in blender or food processor. Return to saucepan and add cream and butter while stirring over low heat. Add salt and pepper. Garnish with basil leaves and serve with French bread.

Cindy Thompson, Aggie Aunt
Megan Donahue '99
Ryan Donahue '02

Tortellini Stew

1½ pounds Italian sausage
1 cup onions, coarsely chopped
2 cloves garlic, sliced
5 cups beef broth
½ cup water
½ cup red wine
4 medium tomatoes, chopped
1 cup carrots, thinly sliced
1½ cups zucchini, sliced
1 medium green bell pepper, chopped
½ teaspoon basil
½ teaspoon oregano
1 (8-ounce) can tomato sauce
2 cups dried cheese-filled tortellini
3 teaspoons parsley, chopped
Parmesan cheese, freshly grated

Brown sausage. Remove from pan. Sauté onions and garlic in pan drippings. Add everything else and simmer until vegetables are tender. Garnish with grated Parmesan. If you like more broth than stew, add more beef broth. Serves 6 - 8.

Eileen Buis
Josh Buis '97
Jordan Buis '99

Taco Soup with Jalapeños

1	pound ground beef	1	onion, chopped
1	(15-ounce) can jalapeño beans	1	(10-ounce) can Rotel
1	(17-ounce) can corn	1	(8-ounce) can tomato sauce
1	package taco seasoning mix	1	package ranch dressing mix

Cook all together. Serve over rice or with cornbread muffins. Serves 4.

Cora Nell Sneary, Grandmother
Shannon Sneary '00

Neiman-Marcus Tortilla Soup

½	large onion, finely chopped	2	(3-ounce) packages cream cheese
3	tablespoons unsalted butter	1	(14½-ounce) can chicken broth
1½	(4-ounce) cans mild green chilies, drained, seeded, and finely chopped	1½	cups half-and-half
		4	teaspoons fresh lemon juice
			Garlic powder to taste
2	(14½-ounce) cans plum tomatoes, drained, seeded, and finely chopped		Cayenne pepper to taste
			Cumin to taste
			Salt to taste

GARNISH-
Julienne tortilla strips,   Green onions, chopped
fried crisp   Monterey Jack cheese, grated

Cook onion in butter over moderately low heat in a saucepan, stirring occasionally, until onion is softened. Add chilies and tomatoes. Cook mixture 8-10 minutes over moderate heat, stirring occasionally, until liquid evaporates. Stir in cream cheese. Maintain moderate to low heat until cheese melts. Stir in chicken broth, half-and-half, lemon juice, garlic powder, cayenne pepper, cumin, and salt. Heat soup over moderate heat until hot, but do not boil. Sprinkle tortilla strips, green onions, and Monterey Jack cheese over individual servings. Serves 4-6.

Cindy Thompson, Aggie Aunt
Megan Donahue '99
Ryan Donahue '02

Zesty Vegetable Rice Soup

2	cups onion, chopped	1	cup carrots, sliced
1	cup celery, chopped	½	cup rice, uncooked
2	cloves garlic, minced	½	cup picante sauce
Olive oil		2	teaspoons basil
2	(14-ounce) cans beef broth	1	large white leek, sliced into rings
1	(14-ounce) can Mexican-style		(including green parts)
	stewed tomatoes	¼	cup parsley, chopped

Sauté onion, celery, and garlic in olive oil. Add beef broth, tomatoes, carrots, rice, picante sauce, and basil. Bring to a boil. Reduce heat, cover, and simmer for 15 minutes. Stir in leek, cover, and simmer 10 minutes. Stir in parsley and simmer 10 minutes. Serves 4-6.

Sue Anderson, Federation Officer

Veggie Spread

½	pound cheddar cheese, grated	½	bunch green onions, chopped
½	pound Swiss or Monterey		(include tops)
	Jack cheese, grated	1	(4-ounce) jar chopped pimientos
3	large carrots, grated	Mayonnaise to moisten	
		1	(8-ounce) carton plain yogurt

Mix ingredients together and moisten with mayonnaise and yogurt.

Great sandwich spread and is especially good on whole grain or homemade bread. Makes a LOT!

Lillian Gips
Bruce Holmes '78
Jeff Broaddus '98

Cucumber Sandwiches

1 (0.75-ounce) package Good
   Seasons garlic salad dressing
   mix (dry)
6 tablespoons sour cream
2 (3-ounce) packages cream
   cheese, softened

2 loaves party rye bread
2 medium cucumbers, peeled,
   scored with fork and sliced
Stuffed green olives, sliced

Blend together garlic salad dressing mix, sour cream, and cream cheese. Spread on rye bread. Add sliced cucumbers and olives for garnish.

Anna Sheffield
Ann Sheffield Kuebler '97
Kevin Kuebler '97

Cucumber and Cheese Sandwiches

1 large cucumber
1 (8-ounce) package cream
   cheese, softened
1 tablespoon minced onions

½ teaspoon salt, or more to taste
¼ teaspoon pepper
1 large loaf (1½ pounds) white
   bread, buttered if desired

Peel, seed, and mince cucumber. Mix cream cheese and cucumber with onion, salt, and pepper. Spread on bread. May be cut into halves or quarters. Will keep a number of days in refrigerator. Yields enough filling for 1½ pound loaf of bread.

Marilyn Jones

Pimiento Cheese

1 (8-ounce) package cream
   cheese
1 (12-ounce) package extra
   sharp cheddar cheese, shredded

Mayonnaise to moisten
1 (4-ounce) jar pimientos, chopped

Mix thoroughly and serve on bread or as a dip.

Phyllis Condit
Matthew Clifton '01

BONFIRE

What began as a casual custom of gathering scrap wood in the 1920's has become a tradition of building the world's largest bonfire. The event is always held before the Aggie-Longhorn game. The spiraling flames are symbolic of the undying Aggie Spirit.

But there's more to Bonfire than tradition and symbolism. It is a highly organized effort, implemented by student leadership. Thousands of students don hard hats and spend countless hours cutting, hauling, and unloading the logs. They build and guard the stack. It is a unique effort of students working together—a synthesis of camaraderie, enthusiasm, hard work, pride in their school, and pride in their accomplishment.

Bonfire Photo
By
Richard Korcyznski

Creamy Nutty Tuna

1   (8-ounce) package cream cheese, softened
2   tablespoons lemon juice
½   cup mayonnaise
½   cup chopped ripe olives
1   (7-ounce) can tuna, drained
¼   teaspoon salt
1   cup nuts, chopped (pecans or walnuts)

Mix cream cheese with lemon juice. Stir in remaining ingredients and mix well. Refrigerate. May be served with crackers or used as a sandwich spread.

Nina Cox, President ('96-'97)
Chris Cox '92

Chicken Salad Stuffed Croissants

1   cup mayonnaise
½   cup heavy cream, whipped
2½ cups cooked chicken, cubed
1   cup celery, chopped
1   cup green grapes, sliced in half
½   cup slivered almonds
2   teaspoons parsley, minced
1   teaspoon salt
12 medium croissants

Combine above ingredients. Fill croissants with chicken salad. Makes 12.

Eileen Buis
Josh Buis '97
Jordan Buis '99

113

Mock Philadelphia Cheese Steak Sandwiches

1 pound ground sirloin	1 tablespoon water
½ cup onions, sliced	Salt and pepper to taste
½ cup green bell pepper, sliced	6 hoagie buns
½ cup mushrooms, sliced	6 slices Provolone cheese
1 teaspoon flour	

Brown ground sirloin and drain. Add sliced onion, green bell pepper, and mushrooms. Cook until tender. Add flour and water. Season with salt and pepper. Stir well. Cover and cook 5-10 minutes. Put hot mixture in sliced hoagie buns. Top with Provolone cheese. Serve hot. Yield - 6 sandwiches.

Suzanne Blaney
Erin Blaney '01

Stuffed Pita Bread

½ cup celery, thinly sliced	½ cup raisins
2 cloves garlic, peeled and minced	3 very ripe tomatoes, peeled and chopped or 1 (16-ounce) can tomatoes, drained and chopped
½ cup green onions, chopped	
½ cup green bell pepper, chopped	½ teaspoon oregano
½ cup oil	Salt and pepper to taste
2 tablespoons butter	4 pita pockets
½ pound ground lean meat	4 slices mild cheddar cheese

Sauté celery, garlic, onion, and green pepper in the oil and butter. Add meat. Cook and stir. Add raisins, tomatoes, and oregano. Cook until thick. Season with salt and pepper. Stuff the pita bread with the meat mixture. Put slice of cheese on top of each pita pocket. Put under broiler, just until cheese is melted. Serves 4.

GOOD!

Helen Beasley, President ('91-'92)
Nancy Beasley '90

Barbecue Sauce for Grilling Chicken

½	cup margarine	2	tablespoons ketchup
¼	cup lemon juice	2	teaspoons salt
3	tablespoons horseradish	½	teaspoon Worcestershire sauce
2	tablespoons vinegar	¾	teaspoon Tabasco Sauce

Heat while blending sauce. Sauce will baste 8 pieces of chicken. Grill meat low and slow for about 45 minutes. Continue basting chicken while grilling.

I prefer to use boneless, skinless chicken breasts.

Sandra Bruns
Frances Bruns Yoder '94
John Yoder '93
Charlotte Bruns Franta '96

Eileen's Caesar Salad Dressing

3	tablespoons wine vinegar	1	teaspoon crushed garlic
1	teaspoon salt	1	egg
½	teaspoon dry mustard	1	cup olive oil (extra virgin)
3	teaspoons lemon juice		

In blender put all ingredients except olive oil. Blend at highest speed for 10 seconds. While still blending, carefully remove center of lid and drizzle olive oil into whirring mixture. This will be very thick. Immediately refrigerate dressing. Must be used within 3-4 days.

Eileen Buis
Josh Buis '97
Jordan Buis '99

Blender Hollandaise Sauce

3   egg yolks
2   tablespoons lemon juice
Pinch of cayenne pepper

¼   teaspoon salt
1½ sticks butter

Place first four ingredients in blender. Heat butter to bubbling stage, but do not brown. Cover blender container and turn on high. After three seconds, remove lid and pour in the bubbling butter in a steady, slow stream. By the time the butter is poured in, about 30 seconds, the sauce should be finished. Serve at once or keep sauce warm by immersing blender container in warm water.

This is a quick and easy way to make a classic sauce to serve over broccoli, asparagus, or other vegetables. This sauce may be frozen and reconstituted over hot water in a double boiler.

Judy Boldt (Bob '68)
Laura Boldt '94
David Boldt '97

Honey Glaze for Ham

½   cup Heinz 57 Sauce

¼   cup honey

Blend sauce and honey well. Brush on ham.

Phyllis Condit
Matthew Clifton '01

Honey Lime Salad Dressing

¼   cup olive oil
¼   teaspoon grated lime peel
3   tablespoons fresh lime juice
3   tablespoons honey

½   teaspoon dry mustard
¼   teaspoon seasoned salt
¼   teaspoon paprika
Dash of white pepper

Mix all ingredients in blender and pour over fresh greens.

Eileen Buis
Josh Buis '97
Jordan Buis '99

Raisin Sauce

1½ cups brown sugar
2 tablespoons cornstarch
Dash ground cloves
Dash salt

½ cup raisins
1½ cups cranberry juice
½ cup orange juice

Bring all ingredients to slow boil for 10 minutes. Serve immediately.

Delicious with ham.

Paula Lively
Jim Lively '96
Carrie Lively Patterson '96
Troy Patterson '93

Steak Marinade I

¼ cup onion, chopped
¼ cup soy sauce
5-6 dashes Worcestershire sauce
2 cloves garlic, crushed

$^1/_8$ teaspoon ginger
2 tablespoons sugar
Meat tenderizer

Sprinkle meat with meat tenderizer. Combine other ingredients and marinate steaks at least 1 hour, turning occasionally. Broil steaks 15 minutes until well done or as desired. Marinates 4 steaks.

Lynne Charbonneau
Scott Charbonneau '98
Mark Charbonneau '01

Steak Marinade II

$^1/_3$ cup soy sauce
½ clove garlic, minced
2 teaspoons sugar

2 tablespoons dry sherry
¼ teaspoon rosemary

Combine all ingredients. Baste steak 6-8 hours before broiling.

JaNahn Rodriguez, President ('97-'98)
David Rodriguez '94
Cindy Rodriguez '95
Dan Rodriguez '99

Sweet Southern Dressing

1½ cups sugar
3 tablespoons purple onion, chopped
2 teaspoons Dijon mustard
2 teaspoons salt
²/₃ cup apple cider vinegar
2 cups vegetable oil
3 tablespoons pecans, chopped

Blend sugar, onion, mustard, salt, and vinegar in food processor or blender. Add oil in steady stream until blended and thick. Stir in pecans. Store covered in refrigerator.

Keeps for up to 6 months. Serve over red lettuce, spinach and egg, or apples.

Pat Hardi, President ('93-'94)
Steven Hardi '91, '94

Tomatillo Sauce

12 ripe tomatillos (more if desired)
1 bunch cilantro
Several garlic cloves (to taste), chopped
1-2 serrano peppers, chopped (fresh if available)
Salt and pepper to taste

Slowly boil tomatillos until "mushy" after removing any loose outer skin. Chop 2 tablespoons of cilantro, more if desired. Chop serrano peppers. Blend together cooked tomatillos, chopped garlic (to taste), chopped serrano peppers (to taste), and cilantro. Add salt and pepper to taste. Makes enough to top 4 servings of sour cream chicken enchiladas or 4 servings of poached chicken pieces.

Will keep well in the refrigerator for several days.

Patricia Bradfield
Quisha Albert '00

Salads

Ambrosia Salad

1   (3-ounce) package orange gelatin
1   cup boiling water
¾   cup reserved juice from Mandarin oranges (add cold water to make ¾ cup)

1   cup heavy cream, whipped, or use whipped topping
1   (11-ounce) can Mandarin orange slices, drained (reserve juice)
1   banana, sliced and quartered
²/₃ cup flaked coconut

Dissolve gelatin in boiling water. Add Mandarin orange juice. Chill until thickened, about 1½ hours. Fold in whipped cream. Fold in remaining ingredients. Spoon into a 1½-quart mold or 8 individual molds. Chill until firm. Unmold and garnish with additional whipped cream, coconut, and fruit. Serves 8.

Judy Boldt (Bob '68)
Laura Boldt '94
David Boldt '97

Apricot Salad

2   (3-ounce) packages apricot gelatin
²/₃ cup water
2   (4-ounce) jars apricot baby food

1   (20-ounce) can crushed pineapple, undrained
1   (14-ounce) can condensed milk
1   (8-ounce) package cream cheese
1½ cups pecans, chopped

Mix the gelatin and water in small saucepan and bring to a boil. Remove from heat and stir in apricots and pineapple. Cool. Mix condensed milk and cream cheese together until smooth. Stir into gelatin mixture. Add pecans. Pour into a 9×13-inch pan and refrigerate until firm. Serves 16.

Janice Myers, President ('95-'96) (Tony '65)
Greg Myers '92
Cindy Myers Crook '96

Carolyn's Blueberry Salad

2   (3-ounce) packages black
    cherry gelatin
2   cups boiling water
1   (15-ounce) can blueberries,
    undrained
1   (8-ounce) can crushed
    pineapple, undrained

1   (8-ounce) package cream
    cheese, softened
¼   cup sugar
½   pint sour cream
½   teaspoon vanilla

Dissolve gelatin in water. Add blueberries and pineapple. Pour into 10×12-inch dish. Refrigerate until congealed. Beat cream cheese and sugar until fluffy. Add sour cream and vanilla. Mix well. Spread over gelatin. Refrigerate until ready to serve. Serves 10-12.

Eva Gay Brown

Cherry Freeze Salad

1   (14-ounce) can sweetened
    condensed milk
1   (20-ounce) can cherry pie
    filling
¼   cup lemon juice

1   (15-ounce) can crushed
    pineapple, drained
¼   teaspoon almond extract
1   pint whipping cream, whipped

Mix all ingredients together, except whipping cream. Fold in whipped cream. Pour into paper-lined muffin cups. Freeze. Let thaw 5 minutes before serving. Yield - 12 servings.

Cindy Etier
Emily Etier '01

Cranberry-Grape Salad

1   (16-ounce) package fresh
    cranberries
2   cups sugar
2   cups seedless grapes

2   cups miniature marshmallows
1   pint whipping cream
1   cup pecans, chopped

Mix cranberries and sugar and refrigerate overnight. Drain well. Add remaining ingredients. Let stand several hours in refrigerator until firm. Serves 12.

Anne Turano '84

Coke Salad (It is maroon and white!)

1 (16-ounce) can sour pie cherries in water (reserve juice)
1 (8-ounce) can crushed pineapple (reserve juice)
1 (3-ounce) package cherry gelatin
1 (3-ounce) package raspberry gelatin
2 (12-ounce) bottles of Coca-Cola
1 (8-ounce) package cream cheese, cut into small cubes
1 cup pecans, chopped

Drain cherries and pineapple. Heat the juice and dissolve gelatins in it. Cool. Add Coke, cherries, and pineapple. While this mixture is chilling, put cream cheese in freezer so it will be hardened and easier to cube. When gelatin is almost congealed, fold in cheese and pecans. Pour into mold and refrigerate until ready to serve.

Paula Lively
Jim Lively '96
Carrie Lively Patterson '96
Troy Patterson '93

Cottage Cheese/Lime/Pineapple Salad

1 (3-ounce) package lime gelatin
1 cup boiling water
1 (8-ounce) can crushed pineapple
½ cup nuts, chopped
1 cup cottage cheese
1 cup miniature marshmallows
1 (8-ounce) container of Cool Whip

Pour hot water over lime gelatin and stir until gelatin is dissolved. Add pineapple and mix well. Refrigerate until it thickens. Fold in nuts, cottage cheese, and marshmallows. Mix well. Refrigerate until it thickens again. Add Cool Whip. Stir until well mixed. Pour into 9×9-inch pan or mold. Refrigerate until ready to serve. Serves 6-8.

Trudy Lewis, President (El Paso Mothers' Club '88-'89)
Stan Lewis '88

Cranberry Fruit Salad

1 (3-ounce) package cherry gelatin	2 oranges, peeled and diced
1 cup boiling water	Peel of 1 orange, grated
12 large marshmallows	1 apple, chopped
1 pound cranberries, ground	1½ cups sugar
	½ cup nuts, chopped

Combine gelatin and water and stir until dissolved. Add marshmallows and allow to melt. Stir in cranberries, oranges, orange peel, apple, sugar, and nuts. Pour into mold. Chill. Serves 12.

JaNahn Rodriguez, President ('97-'98)
David Rodriguez '94
Cindy Rodriguez '95
Dan Rodriguez '99

Cranberry/Pineapple Salad

1 cup raw cranberries	1 cup pineapple syrup
1 cup sugar	1 cup crushed pineapple, drained
1 (3-ounce) package lemon gelatin	½ cup walnuts, chopped
1 cup hot water	1 cup celery, chopped

Combine cranberries and sugar. Dissolve gelatin in hot water. Add syrup to gelatin. Chill until partially set. Add cranberry mixture, pineapple, walnuts, and celery. Pour into greased 9×9-inch pan. Chill until firm. Serves 12.

Betty Pennington
Shelley Lenamond '98
Mitchell Lenamond '99

Judy's Cranberry Orange Relish

1	(1-pound) package fresh cranberries		Peel from ½ orange
2	oranges, peeled	2	Winesap or Braeburn apples
		1	cup honey

Grate all fruit using food processor. Pour into bowl and stir in honey. Chill.

This nutritious condiment is a great accompaniment to any meat. It has been a holiday tradition at our house for many years. This relish freezes well.

Judy Boldt (Bob '68)
Laura Boldt '94
David Boldt '97

Fruit Basket Salad

1	(16-ounce) can sliced peaches, drained and cut into bite-sized pieces	1	(16-ounce) can pears, drained and cut into bite-sized pieces
1	(16-ounce) can pineapple tidbits, drained	1	(3.4-ounce) box instant vanilla pudding mix
		1	(10-ounce) package frozen strawberries

Put canned fruit in a glass bowl. Sprinkle with dry pudding mix. DO NOT STIR. Place frozen strawberries on top of fruit and pudding mix. Cover tightly and refrigerate overnight. Stir well before serving. Serves 8-10.

Helen Beasley, President ('91-'92)
Nancy Beasley '90

Glazed Fruit Salad

1	(20-ounce) can peach pie filling	1	(10-ounce) package frozen strawberries, drained
3	bananas, sliced	1	(11-ounce) can Mandarin oranges, drained
1	(20-ounce) can pineapple chunks, drained		

Mix all ingredients together and refrigerate. Serves 6-8.

Quick and easy!

Anna Sheffield
Ann Sheffield Kuebler '97
Kevin Kuebler '97

Luscious Red Leaf Lettuce and Fruit Salad

1	large head red leaf lettuce (green leaf or mixed greens work, too)	½-1	cup fresh raspberries or fresh strawberries, sliced
1	(11-ounce) can Mandarin oranges, drained	¼	cup pecan pieces, toasted
½	cup green grapes	8	ounces low-fat raspberry salad dressing

Wash lettuce, pat dry, and tear into bite-sized pieces. Combine with fruit and pecans in a large salad bowl. Add dressing and toss just before serving. Serves 8.

Marilyn McBride
Shannon McBride '98

Golden Glow Salad

1	(6-ounce) box orange gelatin	1	(16-ounce) can crushed pineapple (reserve juice)
		1	cup carrots, grated

Prepare gelatin according to package directions, reducing the amount of water and substituting juice from pineapple to make up the difference. Add pineapple and carrots. Refrigerate, stirring occasionally as salad congeals. Serves 6.

Lynne Charbonneau
Scott Charbonneau '98
Mark Charbonneau '01

Green Grape Delight

1 (3-ounce) package cream cheese	Dash garlic powder (or rub bowl with garlic)
1 tablespoon mayonnaise	4 cups (2 pounds) seedless green grapes, halved
1 tablespoon sugar	1 cup pecans, chopped
Dash of cayenne pepper	

Combine first 5 ingredients and mix until smooth. Gently fold in grapes and nuts. Chill thoroughly, about 2 hours. Serve on lettuce leaves. Serves 4-6. It is a simple, easy recipe. The combination of grapes and garlic sounds a bit unusual, but try it. This is absolutely delicious!

Ann Grubbs
Mitch Cogbill '93
Heath Hayes '93
Donna Chafin Cogbill '94

Lime/Cream Cheese/Pineapple Salad

2 (3-ounce) packages lime gelatin	½ pint whipping cream
2 cups boiling water	1 (3-ounce) package cream cheese, at room temperature and cut into small pieces
½ cup mayonnaise	
½ cup pecans, chopped	
1 (8-ounce) can crushed pineapple, drained	

Dissolve gelatin in 2 cups boiling water. Let stand until syrupy. To gelatin mixture add mayonnaise, pecans, and pineapple. Whip the whipping cream. Add cream cheese and mix. Add this mixture to gelatin mixture. Stir gently. Pour into mold. Refrigerate until firm. Serves 6-8.

Marion Crawford (Don '64)
Kristin Crawford '91
Julie Crawford '95

Mandarin Orange Toss

½ cup salad oil
½ teaspoon Tabasco Sauce
1 tablespoon salt
¼ cup sugar
¼ cup tarragon vinegar
8 ounces canned
  Mandarin oranges, drained

½ head salad greens,
  torn into pieces
2 celery ribs, chopped
1 tablespoon parsley flakes
2 tablespoons chives or
  scallions, chopped
¼ cup almonds, slivered and
  toasted

Mix first 5 ingredients together and refrigerate for several hours before serving. In a salad bowl, mix the oranges and vegetables together and toss. Just before serving, add the salad dressing and almonds and toss again. Serves 6.

Mary Aasterud, President ('94-'95)
Valerie Aasterud McLaughlin '94

Orange Salad Supreme

1 (6-ounce) package orange
  gelatin
1 (20-ounce) can crushed
  pineapple, drained (reserve
  juice)
1 cup nuts, chopped (divided)
8 ounces Dream Whip
  (2 envelopes)

1 (8-ounce) package cream cheese,
  softened
2 eggs, beaten
¾ cup sugar
1 tablespoon fresh lemon juice
2 tablespoons flour

Prepare gelatin according to package directions. Refrigerate. After gelatin has begun to congeal, add drained pineapple. Sprinkle with ½ cup nuts. Prepare Dream Whip according to package directions. Fold in softened cream cheese and blend well. Spread over gelatin. Add enough water to reserved pineapple juice to make 1 cup. Add eggs, sugar, lemon juice, and flour. Cook until thick. Refrigerate until cool. Spread over the Dream Whip. Top with remaining nuts. Can be prepared a day ahead. Serve on lettuce leaves. Serves 12.

Anna Sheffield
Ann Sheffield Kuebler '97
Kevin Kuebler '97

Patriotic Salad (Raspberry-Blueberry)

FIRST LAYER-

1 (3-ounce) package raspberry gelatin

2 cups hot water

SECOND LAYER-

1 envelope plain gelatin
½ cup cold water
1 cup cream
1 cup sugar

1 teaspoon vanilla
1 (8-ounce) package cream cheese, softened
½ cup nuts, chopped

THIRD LAYER-

1 (3-ounce) package raspberry gelatin

1 cup hot water
1 (16-ounce) can blueberries

To make first layer, dissolve raspberry gelatin in 2 cups hot water. Pour into 9×13-inch pan and chill. To make second layer, soften plain gelatin in ½ cup cold water. Heat cream and sugar until hot. Add softened gelatin and stir until dissolved. Add vanilla and cream cheese. Blend until smooth. Stir in nuts. When cool, pour over first layer. Put in refrigerator and chill. To make third layer, dissolve raspberry gelatin in 1 cup hot water. Add blueberries. When cool, pour over second layer and chill. Serves 12-15.

JaNahn Rodriguez, President ('97-'98)
David Rodriguez '94
Cindy Rodriguez '95
Dan Rodriguez '99

Easy Spiced Peaches

2 (29-ounce) cans peach halves
2 tablespoons cider vinegar
1 teaspoon whole allspice

1 teaspoon whole cloves
4 cinnamon sticks

Drain peaches well, reserving 1½ cups juice. Mix all ingredients together, including reserved juice. Refrigerate for several days. Serves 6-8.

Easy, do-ahead addition to a special meal. Great with ham!

Judy Boldt (Bob '68)
Laura Boldt '94
David Boldt '97

Spiced Pineapple Chunks

1 (20-ounce) can pineapple chunks or spears (reserve juice)	½ cup sugar
	5 whole cloves
	2 cinnamon sticks
¼ cup apple cider vinegar	

Drain pineapple well. Save juice. Combine pineapple juice, vinegar, sugar, cloves, and cinnamon sticks. Bring to a boil and continue cooking for 5 minutes. Add pineapple and simmer for 3 minutes. Remove cloves and cinnamon sticks. Refrigerate, tightly covered, for 24-48 hours. Serves 10-12.

The longer they are refrigerated, the better. Can be made several days ahead. Excellent with Mexican food.

Helen Beasley, President ('91-'92)
Nancy Beasley '90

Pretzel Salad

CRUST-

2 cups pretzels, crushed	3 tablespoons sugar
¾ cup butter, softened	

MIDDLE LAYER-

1 (8-ounce) package cream cheese, softened	1 (9-ounce) container Cool Whip
	¾ cup sugar

TOP LAYER-

1 (6-ounce) package strawberry or raspberry gelatin	1 (20-ounce) package frozen strawberries or raspberries, thawed

Mix pretzels, butter, and sugar together and pat gently into a 9×13×2-inch baking dish. Bake at 400° for 10 minutes. Cool. To make middle layer, mix cream cheese, Cool Whip, and sugar together. Pour over cooled crust. For top layer, make gelatin according to package directions. Refrigerate and let set slightly. Gently fold in fruit and pour over middle layer. Refrigerate until salad congeals. Serves 10-12. I call this a dessert, but my mom insists it's a salad!

Matthew Clifton '01

129

Raspberry/Cranberry Molded Salad

1 (10-ounce) package frozen raspberries
1 cup water
1 (16-ounce) can whole berry cranberry sauce

1 (6-ounce) package raspberry gelatin
1 (8-ounce) can crushed pineapple, undrained

Thaw berries. In 2-quart saucepan, put 1 cup water and cranberry sauce and bring to a boil (until sauce is melted). Remove from heat and stir in raspberry gelatin until dissolved. Add pineapple and raspberries. Pour into 8×8-inch pan and thoroughly chill. Cut into 2×4-inch portions and serve on bed of red-tipped green lettuce. Makes 8 servings.

This is beautiful for 4th of July, Thanksgiving, and Christmas!

Eileen Buis
Josh Buis '97
Jordan Buis '99

VARIATIONS-
Add ½ (¼-ounce size) package of plain gelatin and increase water to 2 cups. Increase pineapple to 1 20-ounce can undrained. Add ½-1 cup chopped nuts. A 7-9 cup oiled mold may be used.

Martha Tucker
Jennifer Tucker '97

Strawberry/Pineapple Molded Salad

1 (3-ounce) package lime gelatin
2 cups hot water (divided)
1 (8-ounce) package cream cheese
1 (8-ounce) can crushed pineapple, undrained

1 (3-ounce) package strawberry gelatin
1 cup (or more) commercial strawberry glaze
1 pint sliced strawberries

Dissolve lime gelatin in 1 cup hot water. Beat cream cheese with rotary beater. Mix lime gelatin, cream cheese, and pineapple. Pour into mold. Let set about 2 hours. Mix strawberry gelatin with 1 cup hot water. Mix strawberry gelatin, glaze, and strawberries and spread over lime layer. Chill. Serves 6-8.

Betty Pennington
Shelley Lenamond '98
Mitchell Lenamond '99

Couscous

1 cup water	⅛ teaspoon garlic powder
⅔ cup couscous, uncooked	1½ cups green bell pepper, chopped
¼ cup red wine vinegar	1¼ cups cucumber, chopped
2 tablespoons olive oil	1 cup onion, chopped
2 tablespoons Dijon mustard	¼ cup raisins
1 tablespoon parsley flakes	1 (15.25-ounce) can corn, drained
¼ teaspoon salt	1 chicken breast, cooked and
¼ teaspoon pepper	cubed (may substitute tuna)

Bring 1 cup water to boil. Add couscous and remove from heat. Cover and let stand for 10 minutes. Combine the next 7 ingredients and whisk together. Add the vegetables and the chicken to the vinegar mixture and mix well. Fluff the couscous with a fork and add to the vegetable mixture, mixing well. Chill and serve cold. Serves 2-3.

Valerie Aasterud McLaughlin '94 (Tim '90, '94)

Taj Mahal Chicken Salad

1 cup uncooked rice	2 tablespoons lemon juice
2 cups cooked chicken	1½ teaspoons curry powder
¼ cup green onion, thinly sliced	1 teaspoon salt
1½ cups mayonnaise	¼ teaspoon pepper

Prepare rice according to package directions. Add chicken and onion. Mix mayonnaise, lemon juice, curry powder, salt, and pepper. Stir into rice mixture. Chill 3-4 hours. Serves 8.

Sue Duncan
Nikki Duncan '97
Stephen Duncan '99

Mexican Taco Salad

2-3 medium tomatoes, chopped
1 medium onion, chopped
2 avocados, chopped
1 (8-ounce) bottle Italian salad dressing
1 pound ground beef
Garlic to taste

1 (2.5-ounce) envelope taco seasoning
1 (15-ounce) can kidney or pinto beans, drained and rinsed
1 small head lettuce, torn in pieces
10 ounces corn chips, slightly crushed
1 pound cheddar cheese, cubed

Marinate tomatoes, onion, and avocado in dressing while preparing salad. Brown ground beef with garlic. Add taco seasoning and beans. Simmer a few more minutes. Combine all ingredients and toss. Serves 6-8 generously.

Use as a main course with hot French bread.

Julie Thedford (Marvin '65)
Mary Helen Thedford Ramsey '93
Clay Ramsey '93
Katherine Thedford '98

Spam Summer Salad

1 (7-ounce) package macaroni
2 tablespoons salad oil
2 tablespoons vinegar
1 tablespoon onion, minced
½ teaspoon seasoned salt
¼ teaspoon seasoned pepper
1 cup cheddar cheese, diced
1 (12-ounce) can Spam luncheon meat, diced

⅓ cup mayonnaise or salad dressing
1 (10-ounce) package frozen peas, thawed
1 cup cucumber, diced
2 eggs, diced
½ cup bread and butter pickles, diced

Cook macaroni according to package directions. Drain. Do not chill. While still hot, drizzle with oil and vinegar. Add onion, seasonings, and cheese, and toss well. Gently mix in Spam and remaining ingredients. Chill thoroughly. Serves 8-10.

Mary Husa
Ben Husa '00

Macaroni Salad

1 (8-ounce) package elbow or shell macaroni
½ cup celery, chopped
½ cup green bell pepper, chopped
¼ cup green onion, chopped
1 tomato, diced
1 tablespoon prepared mustard
1½ teaspoons salt
½ teaspoon paprika
½ cup mayonnaise

Cook macaroni according to package directions. Rinse well and drain. Combine with other ingredients. Refrigerate until serving time. Serves 8-10.

If prepared a day ahead, add tomato 1-2 hours before serving.

Mary Rosen

Shrimp-Macaroni Salad

1 pound shelled shrimp, cooked
1½ cups macaroni shells, cooked and drained
4 ounces American cheese, cubed
½ cup celery, chopped
¼ cup green bell pepper, chopped
2 tablespoons onion, chopped
½ cup mayonnaise or salad dressing
½ cup sour cream
3 tablespoons vinegar
¾ teaspoon salt
Dash of hot pepper sauce

Cut up shrimp. Toss with macaroni, cheese, celery, green pepper, and onion. Blend remaining ingredients and toss with shrimp mixture. Cover. Chill. Before serving, stir salad. Serve on lettuce and top with green pepper rings. Serves 4-6.

June Bradfield, Grandmother
Quisha Albert '00

Linda's Summer Spaghetti

8	tomatoes, chopped	1	teaspoon paprika
2	medium onions, chopped	½	teaspoon oregano
12	green olives, quartered	3	tablespoons red wine vinegar
4	medium cloves of garlic, chopped	1	cup olive oil
⅔	cup parsley, chopped		Salt and pepper to taste
4	tablespoons dried basil	1	(16-ounce) package bow-tie macaroni
4	teaspoons capers		

Combine first 9 ingredients. Mix vinegar, olive oil, salt, and pepper. Pour over ingredients and marinate overnight. Boil one pound bow ties according to package directions. Drain and toss immediately with tomato mixture. Serves 12.

I also add cubes of salami, mozzarella cheese, chopped green bell peppers, and artichokes. This is great for salad luncheons.

Eileen Buis
Josh Buis '97
Jordan Buis '99

Vegetable Rice Salad

¾	cup low-fat mayonnaise	¼	teaspoon pepper
2	tablespoons cider vinegar	2	cups cooked rice
1	tablespoon minced onion	1	carrot, thinly sliced
	Small clove garlic, minced	¼	cup green bell pepper, diced
1	teaspoon salt		

In medium bowl, mix first 6 ingredients. Add remaining ingredients. Toss to coat well. Cover. Chill 2 hours. Makes 3 cups. Serves 6.

Anna Sheffield
Ann Sheffield Kuebler '97
Kevin Kuebler '97

Yummy Rice Salad

1	tablespoon vinegar
2	tablespoons corn oil
¼	cup mayonnaise
1	teaspoon salt
½	teaspoon curry powder

1⅓ to 1½	cups uncooked rice
2	tablespoons onion, chopped
1	cup celery, chopped
1	(10-ounce) package frozen English peas, undercooked

Mix vinegar, oil, mayonnaise, salt, and curry powder. Cook rice according to package directions until just done. Add rice to curry mixture. Add onion while rice is hot. When cooled, add celery and peas. Refrigerate. Serves 6-8.

Better the second day.

Berniece Smith

Asparagus Salad

2	pounds fresh asparagus
¼	cup water
1	(7.25-ounce) jar roasted red bell peppers, drained and cut into strips

½	cup almonds, sliced
½	cup feta cheese, crumbled
1	lemon, cut into wedges (for garnish)

DRESSING-

2	tablespoons olive oil
2	tablespoons cider vinegar

2	tablespoons lemon juice
1	tablespoon honey

Wash asparagus and place in 9×13-inch glass dish. Add ¼ cup water. Cover with plastic wrap and steam in microwave on High for 5-6 minutes, until fork-tender. Pour off water and chill. Place asparagus on serving platter. Top with pepper strips, almonds, and cheese. Whisk salad dressing ingredients together. Drizzle over salad. Garnish with lemon wedges. Serves 10-12.

Judy Boldt (Bob '68)
Laura Boldt '94
David Boldt '97

Bean Salad

½   cup oil
¾   cup vinegar
1   tablespoon water
1   cup sugar
¼   teaspoon black pepper
1   teaspoon salt
1   (15.25-ounce) can LeSeur
    peas, drained

1   (14.5-ounce) can cut green
    beans, drained
1   (11-ounce) can shoe peg corn,
    drained
1   green bell pepper, finely chopped
1   bunch green onions, chopped
1   cup celery, chopped
1   (2-ounce) jar pimiento, drained
    and chopped

Mix oil, vinegar, water, sugar, pepper, and salt and bring to a boil. Pour over
the mixed and drained vegetables. Let set overnight. Serves 8.

Martha Tucker
Jennifer Tucker '97

Five-Bean Salad

4   cups canned green beans,
    drained
1   cup black beans, cooked,
    rinsed, and drained
1   cup pinto beans, cooked,
    rinsed, and drained
1   cup small white beans,
    cooked, rinsed, and drained

1   cup kidney beans, cooked,
    rinsed, and drained
½   cup onion, chopped
1   rib celery, chopped
½   teaspoon seasoned salt
½   cup rice vinegar
½   teaspoon Italian seasoning

Combine beans. Add onion and celery. Combine salt, vinegar, and seasoning.
Stir gently into bean mixture. Chill. Serves 12-15.

Sue Duncan
Nikki Duncan '97
Stephen Duncan '99

Broccoli Salad

1	head broccoli, cut into small pieces	1	small red onion, finely chopped
½	cup raisins	6	slices of bacon, fried crisp and crumbled
		½	cup cheddar cheese, grated

DRESSING-
1	cup mayonnaise	2	tablespoons white vinegar
¼	cup sugar		

Mix first 5 ingredients together. Make dressing by combining mayonnaise, sugar, and vinegar. Mix salad with dressing and refrigerate several hours or overnight. Serves 6.

Betty Donahue, Grandmother
Megan Donahue '99
and Ryan Donahue '02

Broccoli Cauliflower Salad

1	bunch broccoli	1	(8-ounce) bottle Italian salad dressing
1	head cauliflower		
1	purple onion (optional)		8-10 fresh mushrooms, sliced (optional)

Wash and drain broccoli and cauliflower. Cut into bite-sized pieces. Slice onion and separate into rings. Pour salad dressing over vegetables and marinate in refrigerator overnight. Add sliced mushrooms just before serving.

Janice Myers, President ('95-'96) (Tony '65)
Greg Myers '92
Cindy Myers Crook '96

137

Greek Salad

1	bunch broccoli	1	(0.75-ounce) package Good
1	head cauliflower		Seasons Italian dressing
1	cup fresh mushrooms, sliced		mix (dry)
1	large red onion, thinly sliced	3	tablespoons Italian seasoning
1	(8-ounce) can water		
	chestnuts, drained and sliced		

Cut broccoli and cauliflower into bite-sized pieces. Mix with mushrooms, onion, and water chestnuts. Prepare dressing mix according to package directions. Add seasoning. Pour dressing over vegetables and marinate 24-36 hours. Toss occasionally. Store in refrigerator in covered container. Serves 10-12.

Terry Moomaw
Adam Moomaw '01

Cabbage Salad

1	(3-ounce) package chicken-flavored Ramen noodles, crushed	½	cup almonds, sliced
		½	cup vegetable oil
		3	tablespoons vinegar
6	cups cabbage, shredded	2	tablespoons sugar
4	green onions, chopped	½	teaspoon salt
½	cup toasted sunflower kernels	½	teaspoon pepper

Remove seasoning packet from noodle package; set aside. Mix cabbage, onions, sunflower kernels, and almonds. Combine seasoning packet and remaining ingredients. Mix with a wire whisk. Pour dressing over the cabbage mixture. Toss gently to coat. Cover and chill. Add noodles just before serving. Makes 6 servings.

Loretta Nouri
Julie Pickard '94
Bejan Nouri '99

Crunchy Coleslaw

1 head cabbage	1 cup vegetable oil
1 bunch green onions	1 cup vinegar
2 packages Ramen noodles	½ cup sugar
½ cup sunflower seeds	Salt and pepper to taste
⅔ cup almonds, slivered	

Chop cabbage and onions finely. Break up noodles (do not use enclosed seasoning packet). Mix all ingredients except noodles together. Chill. Add noodles just before serving. Serves 8-10.

Cindy Etier
Emily Etier '01

Kraut Salad

½ cup vinegar	1 green bell pepper, diced
½ cup salad oil	1 (2-ounce) jar pimiento, diced
1 cup sugar	1 onion, diced
½ teaspoon salt	1 stalk celery, diced
1 (16-ounce) can sauerkraut, drained (reserve juice)	

Boil vinegar, oil, sugar, salt, and sauerkraut juice for 2 minutes. Pour hot dressing over kraut and remaining ingredients. Refrigerate in airtight container overnight. Serves 6-8.

Helen Beasley, President ('91-'92)
Nancy Beasley '90

Clay's Potato Salad

5 medium potatoes	1 cup celery, diced
6-7 slices bacon, fried and crumbled (save bacon drippings)	5 eggs, hard-boiled and chopped
	1 teaspoon salt
	Pepper to taste
½ cup onion, diced	Mayonnaise to moisten

Boil and dice potatoes. Pour bacon drippings over potatoes. When cool, add remaining ingredients with enough mayonnaise to bind together. Stir in bacon. Refrigerate until well chilled. Serves 8-10.

Anne Turano '84

139

Corn Salad

2	stalks celery, chopped	¼	cup raspberry vinaigrette salad
½	red bell pepper, chopped		dressing
1	carrot, peeled and shredded	¼	cup red wine vinegar
1	jalapeño pepper, seeded and	½	cup oil
	chopped	1	teaspoon salt
2	tablespoons fresh parsley,	½	teaspoon pepper
	chopped	¼	teaspoon garlic powder
2	(11-ounce) cans corn, drained	¼	teaspoon onion powder

Mix all ingredients. Chill at least 1 hour. Stir before serving.

Best if allowed to marinate longer.

Gloria Gilpin, President ('98-'99) (Bobby '62)
Wes Gilpin '93
Katherine Gilpin '97

Marinated White Corn Vegetable Salad

1	(14½-ounce) can French cut	1	cup onion, chopped
	green beans, drained	1	cup celery, chopped
1	(14½-ounce) can baby peas,	1	cup green bell pepper, chopped
	drained	1	cup sugar
1	(14½-ounce) can white corn,	¾	cup white vinegar
	drained	½	cup salad oil

Layer the beans, peas, corn, onion, celery, and bell pepper in an 8-cup glass bowl. Combine sugar, vinegar, and oil and bring to a boil. Cool. Pour over vegetables. Refrigerate several hours before serving. Serves 12.

Keeps up to one week in refrigerator.

Lynne Charbonneau
Scott Charbonneau '98
Mark Charbonneau '01

Marinated Cucumber Salad

3 cucumbers, sliced

1 onion, sliced in rings (or 1 bunch green onion, chopped)

DRESSING-
3 tablespoons vinegar
3 tablespoons oil
1 tablespoon water

Salt and pepper to taste
½ teaspoon sugar

Slice vegetables and place in medium-sized bowl. Combine dressing ingredients and pour over vegetables. Refrigerate at least 1 hour. Serves 4.

Lynne Charbonneau
Scott Charbonneau '98
Mark Charbonneau '01

Potato Salad

3 tablespoons salad oil
1 teaspoon wine vinegar
1½ teaspoons salt
¹/₈ teaspoon pepper
2 cups warm cooked potatoes, diced
½ cup ripe olives, sliced

2 eggs, hard-boiled and sliced
½ cup dill pickles, diced
1 (2-ounce) jar diced pimiento
1 teaspoon onion, grated
1 tablespoon prepared mustard
¹/₃ cup mayonnaise

Blend together oil, vinegar, salt, and pepper. Pour over potatoes and toss lightly. Refrigerate. At serving time add olives, eggs, dill pickles, pimiento, onion, mustard, and mayonnaise. Serves 6.

Martha Tucker
Jennifer Tucker '97

Sweet Potato Salad

5	pounds sweet potatoes	½	cup dried, pitted cherries, dried
¼	cup fresh lemon juice		cranberries, or white raisins
2	cups celery, sliced	1	cup toasted pecans, coarsely
½	cup scallions, sliced		chopped (divided)

DRESSING-

1¼ cups salad dressing or
    mayonnaise
1   teaspoon grated orange or
    lemon rind
¼   cup fresh orange juice

2   tablespoons honey
2   teaspoons gingerroot, peeled
    and grated
Salt and pepper to taste

Peel sweet potatoes, quarter lengthwise, and cut in 1-inch chunks. Add water and cook 6-8 minutes. Do not overcook (they will not be as mushy as sweet potatoes that have been baked, boiled whole, or canned, though any of these could be used). Drain. Sprinkle with lemon juice and cool completely. Add celery, scallions, and fruit. Mix dressing ingredients together and pour over potato mixture, tossing gently. This could be prepared up to a day ahead. Just before serving, mix in ½ cup toasted pecans, and sprinkle the remaining ½ cup on top. Serves 12-15.

Lillian Gips
Bruce Holmes '78
Jeffrey Broaddus '98

Spinach Salad

1   pound fresh spinach
1   head lettuce
1   (10-ounce) package frozen
    peas, thawed and drained
6   hard-boiled eggs, sliced
1   bunch fresh green onions,
    chopped

6   slices bacon, fried crisp and
    crumbled (or bacon bits)
1   package ranch dressing mix
    (dry)
1   (16-ounce) carton sour cream

Tear up spinach and lettuce into bite-sized pieces in 9×13-inch dish. Add peas, eggs, onion, and bacon. Mix dry ranch dressing mix and sour cream. Spread over top. Cover with plastic wrap. Refrigerate 24 hours. Serves 8-10.

Sally Rasmussen
Matt Rasmussen '01

24-Hour Spinach Salad

3   cups torn fresh spinach
Salt, pepper and sugar to taste
1½ cups Swiss cheese, shredded
½ cup green onion, chopped
6   eggs, hard-boiled and chopped

½ pound bacon, fried crisp and crumbled
1   (10-ounce) package frozen green peas, thawed and drained (optional)
¾ cup buttermilk dressing

Place half of spinach in bottom of deep bowl. Sprinkle with salt, pepper, and sugar. Top with half of everything, except dressing, layering ingredients. Repeat layers. Spread dressing on top, sealing to edge of bowl. Garnish with additional bacon and green onion. Cover and refrigerate overnight. Serves 6-8.

Donna Bentley, Federation President ('98-'99)

Green Salad

Juice from 2 lemons
½ cup salad oil
1   tablespoon seasoned salt
8   green onions, chopped
2   ripe avocados, sliced

½ cup Parmesan cheese
½ head iceberg lettuce
½ head romaine lettuce
½ head leaf lettuce

In a large glass bowl, mix lemon juice, oil, salt, onions, and avocados. Place torn lettuce leaves on top of this mixture. DO NOT TOSS. Cover and refrigerate. Just before serving, add Parmesan cheese and toss. Serves 8-10.

Helen Moese
Linda Moese '97

Make-Ahead Tossed Salad

1 large head of lettuce, shredded	1 (10-ounce) package frozen peas, separated, but not cooked
1-2 green bell peppers, chopped	2 cups mayonnaise
1 bunch of green onions, cut up (include tops)	1-2 tablespoons sugar
	1 cup Parmesan cheese, grated
1 (8-ounce) can water chestnuts, sliced thin	1 (3.25-ounce) jar bacon bits

In a large glass bowl, layer first five ingredients. Combine sugar and mayonnaise. Spread on top, using a spatula. Sprinkle with Parmesan cheese. Cover with foil, and refrigerate 24 hours. Just before serving, add bacon bits and toss. Serves 8-10.

Phyllis Condit
Matthew Clifton '01

Taylor's Layered Salad

1 head lettuce, torn	2 cups frozen green peas, thawed and drained
¾ cup celery, chopped	
¾ cup green onions, chopped	2 cups mayonnaise
¾ cup green bell pepper, chopped	2 teaspoons sugar
	1 cup sharp cheddar cheese, shredded

Layer vegetables in 9×13-inch dish in the order given. Mix mayonnaise and sugar and spread over the layered vegetables. Spread shredded cheese over mayonnaise. Cover with plastic wrap and refrigerate overnight. Bacon may be sprinkled over the cheese layer. Serves 8-10.

Suzanne Blaney
Erin Blaney '01

Breads

Bacon Bread

1	(¼-ounce) package active dry yeast	¼	teaspoon baking soda
¼	cup water, very hot	1	teaspoon salt
2⅓	cups flour (divided)	1	cup sour cream
2	tablespoons sugar	1	egg
		8	slices bacon, fried and crumbled

Grease 9×5-inch loaf pan. In a large bowl, dissolve yeast in hot water. Add 1⅓ cups flour and next 5 ingredients. Blend, using electric mixer, for 30 seconds on low speed, scraping bowl constantly. Beat 2 minutes on high speed, scraping occasionally. Stir in remaining flour and bacon. Pour into pan and cover with a damp cloth. Let rise 50 minutes in warm place. Bake at 350° for 40-45 minutes. Yield - 1 loaf.

Martha Tucker
Jennifer Tucker '97

Banana Bread

½	cup butter	3	large or 4 small ripe bananas, mashed
1	cup sugar		
2	eggs	2	cups flour
1	teaspoon vanilla	1	teaspoon baking soda
		¼	teaspoon salt.

Cream butter and sugar together. Add eggs and vanilla. Stir until thoroughly mixed. Add mashed bananas. Fold in dry ingredients. Place in well greased 9×5×3-inch loaf pan. Bake at 325° for 55 minutes or until done. Yield - 1 loaf

Suzanne Blaney
Erin Blaney '01

Hawaiian Banana Nut Bread

3 cups flour	1½ cups oil
2 cups sugar	2 cups mashed bananas
1 teaspoon baking soda	1 (8-ounce) can crushed
1 teaspoon salt	pineapple, drained
1 teaspoon cinnamon	2 teaspoons vanilla
3 eggs, beaten	1 cup nuts, chopped

Combine flour, sugar, soda, salt, and cinnamon. Combine eggs, oil, bananas, pineapple, and vanilla. Add liquid mixture to the dry ingredients and mix together. Add nuts. Pour into 2 greased 9×5×3-inch loaf pans. Bake at 350° for 65 minutes. Yield - 2 loaves.

JaNahn Rodriguez, President ('97-'98)
David Rodriguez '94
Cindy Rodriguez '95
Dan Rodriguez '99

Juanita's Banana Bread

½ cup oil	1¾ cups flour
1½ cups sugar	1 teaspoon baking soda
1 cup mashed bananas	1 teaspoon baking powder
4 tablespoons sour cream	1 cup nuts, chopped
2 eggs, well beaten	

Preheat oven to 325°. Grease and flour 2 (9×5×3-inch) loaf pans. Cream oil and sugar together. Add bananas, sour cream and eggs. Mix well. Sift flour, baking soda, and baking powder together. Add to banana mixture and stir together. Add nuts. Bake at 350° for 50 minutes or until done. Do not over-bake. If using smaller pans, check periodically and adjust the time as needed. Yield - 2 loaves or more with smaller pans.

Gloria Gilpin, President ('98-'99) (Bobby '62)
Wes Gilpin '93
Katherine Gilpin '97

Low-Fat Banana Bread

3	ripe bananas, mashed	1	teaspoon baking powder
1	cup sugar	½	teaspoon baking soda
1	egg	1	teaspoon vanilla
2	cups flour	½	cup nuts, chopped (optional)

Mix all ingredients. Pour into a greased 9×5×3-inch loaf pan. Grate nutmeg on top, if desired. Bake at 350° for 45-50 minutes or until done. Absolutely no fat if you omit the nuts and use egg-substitute instead of the real egg. This recipe was given to my newly married mother by her landlord.

Nancy Pfrommer
Natasha Pfrommer '95
Nicole Pfrommer '97
Nerissa Pfrommer '99

Whole Wheat Banana Bread

9	ripe bananas, mashed	3	teaspoons baking soda
2	sticks margarine, melted	2	teaspoons salt
3	cups sugar	3	teaspoons vanilla
3	eggs	3	cups walnuts, chopped
4½	cups whole wheat flour		

Place all ingredients in mixing bowl and mix well. Pour into 3 (9×5×3-inch) greased loaf pans or 4 (8×4×3-inch) pans, filling ½ full. Bake at 300° for 75-90 minutes. Yield - 3-4 loaves.

Sue Duncan
Nikki Duncan '97
Stephen Duncan '99

Blueberry Applesauce Bread

3	cups flour	2	eggs, beaten
1	cup sugar	1	cup applesauce
1	tablespoon baking powder	¼	cup shortening, melted,
1	teaspoon salt		OR ¼ cup oil
½	teaspoon baking soda	2	cups fresh blueberries
½	teaspoon cinnamon		

Mix together the dry ingredients. Mix the eggs, applesauce, and shortening. Combine the two mixtures and fold in the blueberries. Pour into a greased 9×5×3-inch loaf pan and bake at 350° for 50-60 minutes. Yield - 1 loaf.

Anna Sheffield
Ann Sheffield Kuebler '97
Kevin Kuebler '97

Gingerbread

1½	sticks butter, softened	1	teaspoon nutmeg
1	box light brown sugar	2	teaspoons ginger
2	cups flour	2	eggs
1	teaspoon baking soda	1	cup buttermilk
2	teaspoons cinnamon		

Mix butter, brown sugar, and flour together. Add soda, cinnamon, nutmeg, ginger, and eggs in buttermilk and mix all ingredients well. Pour into a bundt pan sprayed with Baker's Joy and bake at 350° for 45 minutes or until toothpick comes out clean.

Sue Anderson, Federation Officer
Kirk Anderson '91
Amy Adamson Anderson '93

Nana's Gingerbread

½ cup butter or margarine, softened
½ cup sugar
1 egg
⅔ cup sorghum molasses

1 teaspoon baking soda
¼ teaspoon ginger
¼ teaspoon cinnamon
2 cups flour
¾ cup boiling water

Cream butter and sugar; add egg. Add molasses and mix well. Stir in dry ingredients. Add boiling water. Mix well. Bake in greased and floured 9×9-inch pan at 325° for 45 minutes or until toothpick inserted in middle comes out clean. Serve warm with butter or whipped cream. Serves 9-12.

Susie Donahue
Megan Donahue '99
Ryan Donahue '02

Poppy Seed Bread

2½ cups sugar
3 eggs
1¼ cups oil
1½ cups milk or evaporated milk
1½ teaspoons baking powder

1½ teaspoons poppy seed
1½ teaspoons salt
1½ teaspoons vanilla
1½ teaspoons almond flavoring
3 cups flour

GLAZE-
¾ cup sugar
¼ cup orange juice
2 tablespoons butter

½ teaspoon vanilla
½ teaspoon almond flavoring

Cream eggs and sugar. Blend in all ingredients except flour. Stir in flour. Batter will be thin. Pour into 4 greased 8×4×3-inch loaf pans. Bake at 325° for 1 hour and 10 minutes. Let cool 5 minutes. Glaze: Mix all ingredients together and cook over low heat until sugar is dissolved. Pour over bread. Yield - 4 loaves.

Martha Tucker
Jennifer Tucker '97

VARIATION-
Increase eggs to 4. Decrease sugar to 2 cups. Increase oil to 1⅔ cups. Increase poppy seed to 3 tablespoons and baking powder to 4 teaspoons. Omit salt, vanilla, and almond flavoring. Do not glaze. May use 2 (9×5×3-inch) loaf pans. Increase oven to 350° and bake for 1 hour.

Phyllis Condit
Matthew Clifton '01

Pumpkin Bread

3½ cups flour	2 teaspoons allspice
3 cups sugar	1 cup oil
2 teaspoons baking soda	1 (16-ounce) can pumpkin
1½ teaspoons salt	⅔ cup water
1 teaspoon nutmeg	4 eggs
2 teaspoons cinnamon	1 cup raisins

Put all ingredients into a large mixing bowl and mix together. Pour into 2 greased (9×5×3-inch) loaf pans. Bake at 350° for 1 hour. Yield - 2 loaves.

Sharon Reid
Ethan Reid '96

Strawberry Bread with Spread

1½ cups flour	1 (10-ounce) package frozen
½ teaspoon baking soda	strawberries, reserving
½ teaspoon cinnamon	¼ cup strawberry juice
1 cup sugar	½ cup plus 2 tablespoons oil
	2 eggs, well beaten
	½ teaspoon red food coloring

SPREAD-

¼ cup strawberry juice	4 ounces cream cheese, softened

Mix all dry ingredients together. Make a well in the center of the mixture. Pour strawberries, oil, and eggs into the well. Mix until all ingredients are combined. Add food coloring. Pour into a greased and floured 9×5×3-inch loaf pan. Bake at 350° for 1 hour or until done. Cool in pan for 10 minutes. Remove and cool completely.

Spread: Mix strawberry juice and cream cheese until spreading consistency. Serve with bread. Yield - 1 loaf.

Cindy Rodriguez '95

VARIATION-
Double all ingredients, except cinnamon. Increase cinnamon to 2 teaspoons and add 1 teaspoon salt. Add all strawberry juice to batter. Omit food coloring. Add 1½ cups chopped pecans. Yield - 2 loaves. May use 3 smaller pans or 5 to 6 mini-pans. Adjust temperature and time for smaller loaves.

Mary Husa
Ben Husa '00

Zucchini Bread

3 eggs	2 teaspoons baking powder
1½ cups sugar	2 teaspoons baking soda
1 cup oil	3 teaspoons cinnamon
2 cups zucchini, grated and well drained (3 medium)	1 teaspoon salt
2 teaspoons vanilla	1 cup raisins
2 cups flour	1 cup walnuts, chopped

Beat eggs lightly in large bowl. Stir in oil, sugar, zucchini, and vanilla. Sift dry ingredients together and stir into egg mixture until well blended. Stir in raisins and nuts. Spoon batter into 2 well greased (9×5×3-inch) loaf pans. Bake at 375° for 1 hour. Cool in pan 10 minutes. Remove from pan and cool completely. Yield - 2 loaves.

JaNahn Rodriguez, President ('97-'98)
David Rodriguez '94
Cindy Rodriguez '95
Dan Rodriguez '99

Pineapple Zucchini Bread

3 eggs	1 teaspoon baking powder
2 cups sugar	1 teaspoon baking soda
1 cup oil	1 teaspoon salt
2 teaspoons vanilla	1 cup crushed pineapple
2 cups zucchini, grated and well drained (3 medium)	½ cup golden raisins
3 cups flour	1 cup nuts, chopped

Combine eggs, sugar, oil, and vanilla, and beat until fluffy. Add zucchini and dry ingredients, mixing well. Stir in pineapple, raisins, and nuts. Pour into 2 greased and floured (9×5×3-inch) loaf pans. Bake at 350° for 1 hour. Yield - 2 loaves.

Bread should be kept refrigerated as the pineapple ferments.

Maria Dellinger

Zannie's Zucchini Bread

1 cup oil	½ teaspoon baking powder
1 cup sugar	2 teaspoons cinnamon
½ cup molasses	½ teaspoon nutmeg
2 teaspoons vanilla	¼ teaspoon ground cloves
2 eggs	¼ teaspoon allspice
2½ cups flour	2 cups zucchini, grated (3 medium)
1 teaspoon salt	1 cup raisins
1 teaspoon baking soda	1 cup pecans, chopped

Mix the first 5 ingredients. Sift together the dry ingredients. Add to the egg mixture and stir well. Add zucchini, raisin, and pecans, stirring well. Pour into 2 greased and floured (9×5×3-inch) loaf pans. Bake at 350° for 1 hour. Yield - 2 loaves.

Suzanne Blaney
Erin Blaney '01

Fresh Apple Coffeecake

½ cup margarine, softened	5 cups apple, peeled and chopped (about 4 large apples)
2 cups sugar	
4 eggs	1 teaspoon vanilla
2 cups flour	1½ tablespoons sugar
2 teaspoons baking powder	½ teaspoon cinnamon
½ teaspoon salt	

Beat margarine at medium speed. Gradually add sugar and beat well. Add eggs, one at a time, beating after each addition. Combine flour, baking powder, and salt and add to creamed mixture. Stir in apple and vanilla. Spoon batter into a greased and floured 13×9-inch pan. Combine the remaining sugar and cinnamon and sprinkle over the cake batter. Bake at 350° for 45 minutes or until done. Yield - 15 servings.

JaNahn Rodriguez, President ('97-'98)
David Rodriguez '94
Cindy Rodriguez '95
Dan Rodriguez '99

Christmas Coffeecake

1 (0.25-ounce) package dry
  yeast
3 cups flour (divided)
3 ounces cream cheese
½ cup milk
¼ cup sugar
2 tablespoons butter

1 teaspoon salt
1 egg
1 (8.25-ounce) can crushed
  pineapple, drained, reserving
  liquid
1 cup powdered sugar, sifted
Maraschino cherries

Combine yeast and 1 cup flour. In saucepan, combine cream cheese, milk, sugar, butter, and salt. Heat, stirring often, until cream cheese melts. Add to dry ingredients. Add the egg. Using an electric mixer, beat 30 seconds on low speed, then 3 minutes on high speed. Add pineapple and remaining flour to make soft dough. Turn out on floured surface. Knead 3 to 5 minutes. Place in greased bowl, turning to grease all surfaces. Cover and let rise until double. Punch down. Shape dough into 22 balls. Arrange in tree shape on greased baking sheet using 2 balls for the tree trunk. Let rise until nearly double. Bake at 350° for 30-35 minutes. Combine powdered sugar and 3-4 teaspoons of reserved pineapple juice. Drizzle on top of cake. Garnish with cherries. Yield - 1 loaf.

JaNahn Rodriguez, President ('97-'98)
David Rodriguez '94
Cindy Rodriguez '95
Dan Rodriguez '99

Heath Brickle Coffeecake

½ cup butter
2 cups flour
1 cup brown sugar
½ cup sugar
1 cup buttermilk

1 egg
1 teaspoon baking soda
1 teaspoon vanilla
1 cup Heath Brickle (divided)
¼ cup pecans or almonds, chopped

Blend flour, butter, and sugars. Remove ½ cup of mixture and set aside. To the rest, add the buttermilk, baking soda, egg, vanilla, and ½ cup Heath Brickle. Pour into greased and floured 10×14-inch pan. Mix remaining Heath Brickle, nuts, and the set aside flour/sugar mixture. Sprinkle over the top of the batter. Bake at 350° for 30 minutes. Serves 15-20.

Karen Reynolds
Paige Reynolds '00

Sour Cream Coffeecake

2	sticks margarine	2	cups flour
2	cups sugar	1	teaspoon baking powder
2	eggs	½	teaspoon salt
1	cup sour cream	4	teaspoons brown sugar
1	teaspoon vanilla	1	teaspoon cinnamon

By hand, beat together margarine, sugar, eggs, sour cream, and vanilla. Stir in flour, baking powder, and salt. Pour ½ of the mixture into a greased and floured bundt pan. Mix brown sugar and cinnamon and sprinkle on top of batter. Pour the remaining batter into the pan. Bake at 350° for 1 hour. Yield - 1 coffeecake.

Cindy Etier
Emily Etier '01

Easy Drop Danish

¼	cup margarine, softened	¼	cup jam or preserves of your choice
2	tablespoons sugar		
2	cups dry baking mix	⅔	cup powdered sugar
⅔	cup milk	¼	teaspoon vanilla
		1	tablespoon warm water

Mix margarine, sugar, and baking mix. Stir in milk and beat 15 strokes. Drop by tablespoon, 2 inches apart, on greased baking sheet. Make a shallow well in each and add 1 teaspoon jam. Bake at 450° for 10-15 minutes. Make a glaze of the powdered sugar, vanilla, and water. Spread on top of each while warm. Yield - 12 rolls.

Susie Donahue
Megan Donahue '99
Ryan Donahue '02

Monkey Breakfast Bread

½   cup pecans, chopped
3   (10-ounce) cans buttermilk
    biscuits
½   cup sugar

1   teaspoon cinnamon
1   cup brown sugar
½   cup margarine, melted

Sprinkle pecans evenly in bottom of well greased bundt or tube pan. Cut the biscuits into quarters and dip the pieces into a mixture of cinnamon and sugar. Layer the biscuits into the pan. Combine the brown sugar and margarine and pour over the biscuits. Bake at 350° for 30-40 minutes. Cool 10 minutes and invert onto serving plate. Serves 8-10.

I make this every Christmas morning for my Aggie.

Phyllis Condit
Matthew Clifton '01

Overnight Breakfast Ring

¾   cup margarine (divided)
½   cup brown sugar

1   (24-ounce) package frozen rolls
1   cup sugar
1   tablespoon cinnamon

Combine ¼ cup margarine and brown sugar. Pour into ungreased bundt or tube pan. Dip rolls in ½ cup melted margarine. Combine cinnamon and sugar and roll the rolls in the mixture. Place the rolls in the pan. Pour remaining butter and sugar mixture over the rolls. Cover and let rise overnight. Bake at 325° for 40-45 minutes. Let cool 10 minutes. Remove from pan by inverting on a plate. Serves 8 to 10.

Cindy Etier
Emily Etier '01

Hallah Bread

½   cup warm water
2   (0.25-ounce) packages
    dry yeast
1¼ cups warm milk
2   tablespoons sugar
1   tablespoon salt

3   tablespoons margarine
3   eggs, whole
1   egg, separated
6¾ to 7¼ cups flour
Peanut oil

Sprinkle yeast into warm water. Stir until yeast is dissolved. Set aside. Stir sugar, salt, and margarine into the warm milk. Add the yeast to the milk mixture and stir. Stir in 3 eggs and 1 egg yolk and beat well. Add ½ of the flour and beat until smooth. Add enough additional flour to make a soft dough. Allow the dough to rest for 20 minutes. Divide the dough into 2 pieces. Divide each piece into ⅔ and ⅓ pieces. Divide each of these pieces into thirds and Braid. Braid the larger piece for the bottom braid. Repeat with the smaller piece and place on top of the large braid, tucking under and pressing them slightly together. Repeat with the remaining piece. Brush the tops of both braids with oil. Cover and refrigerate 3 to 24 hours. Let stand at room temperature for 10 minutes before baking. Brush top with reserved egg white. Bake at 375° for 30 minutes. Yield - 2 loaves.

These loaves are beautiful and make a special homemade gift.

JaNahn Rodriguez, President ('97-'98)
David Rodriguez '94
Cindy Rodriguez '95
Dan Rodriguez '99

Quick Cheddar Bread

3⅓ cups dry baking mix
2½ cups sharp cheddar cheese,
    grated

2   eggs, slightly beaten
1¼ cups milk

Combine dry baking mix and cheese. Stir eggs and milk into cheese mixture. Mix only enough to moisten. Pour batter into greased and floured 9×5×3-inch loaf pan. Bake at 350° for 55 minutes. Cool slightly in pan. Yield - 1 loaf.

Cindy Etier
Emily Etier '01

Oatmeal Batter Bread

3 cups flour (divided)	¼ cup shortening
1 cup, plus 3 tablespoons rolled oats (divided)	¼ cup honey
	2 teaspoons salt
1 (0.25-ounce) package dry yeast	1 egg, whole
	1 egg, separated
1¼ cups milk	

In large mixer bowl, combine 1½ cups flour, 1 cup oats, and yeast. In sauce-pan, heat the milk, shortening, honey, and salt until warm (115-120°), stirring constantly. Add to the dry mixture. Add the egg and egg yolk to the mixture. Beat at low speed for ½ minute, scraping the sides of the bowl constantly. Beat 3 minutes at high speed. Stir in remaining flour by hand to make a soft dough. Beat until smooth. Cover and let rise in a warm place until double. Stir dough down. Sprinkle a greased 2-quart casserole dish with 2 tablespoons oats. Turn dough into the dish. Cover and let rise again in a warm place until double. Brush the top with the beaten, reserved, egg white and sprinkle with the remaining oats. Bake at 350° for 45-50 minutes. Let cool for 15 minutes and remove from pan. Yield - 1 loaf.

Helen Moese
Linda Moese '97

Beer Bread

3 cups self-rising flour	1 (12-ounce) beer, room temperature
3 tablespoons sugar	¼ cup butter, melted

Combine flour, sugar, and beer and pour in a greased 9×5×3-inch loaf pan. Bake at 350° for 40 minutes. Pour the melted butter over bread and return to oven for 10 minutes or until brown.

May add grated cheese, dill, onion flakes, or any choice of herbs to dry ingredients. Yield-1 loaf.

Nancy Pfrommer
Natasha Pfrommer '95
Nicole Pfrommer '97
Nerissa Pfrommer '99

Stollen (German Christmas Bread)

4 cups flour
3 teaspoons baking powder
1 cup sugar
2 eggs
1 teaspoon vanilla
Pinch of salt
¼ teaspoon almond flavoring
¼ teaspoon lemon flavoring
2 tablespoons rum OR
  ¼ teaspoon rum flavoring
¼ teaspoon ground cardamom
¼ teaspoon nutmeg

½ cup margarine or butter, softened
4 ounces sour cream
8 ounces cream cheese, softened
1½ cups raisins, washed and drained
¾ cup currants, washed and drained
1 cup almonds OR hazelnuts, ground or chopped
½ cup citron, candied (available during holiday season)

Mix flour and baking powder together and sift onto clean smooth counter top. Make an indention in center. Put sugar, eggs, spices, and flavorings into center and mix with some of the flour to form a thick mixture. Cream together butter, sour cream, and cream cheese. Add sour cream mixture, raisins, currants, nuts, and citron to the mixture. Knead to form a smooth dough. If too sticky, add more flour. Form into stollen or loaf making an indention on the top. Place onto a greased and floured cookie sheet and bake at 350° for 50-60 minutes or until toothpick comes out clean. Brush warm loaf with butter and dust with powdered sugar. Yield - 1 loaf.

Eberhart Moese, Aggie Dad
Linda Moese '97

159

German Christmas Bread (Easy Method)

1 (16-ounce) loaf frozen bread dough
½ cup pecans, chopped
½ cup candied cherries (any color), halved

½ cup raisins
1½ teaspoons rum flavoring
1 tablespoon butter, melted
Powdered sugar

Thaw bread at room temperature until pliable. Mix together pecans, cherries, raisins and rum flavoring. Roll dough on lightly floured surface to 1 inch thickness. Spoon cherry mixture onto dough. Knead dough to fold in cherry mixture. Roll dough into ½-inch thick oval. Lightly crease dough just off center. Fold small section over larger section. Place on greased baking sheet, rolling the dough to maintain shape. Brush top with butter. Allow to rise in warm place until doubled. Bake at 375° for 20-25 minutes. Cool on rack. Sprinkle with powdered sugar. Yield - 1 loaf.

Don't bake bread? Try this one! Recipe came off of Christmas wrapping paper.

Sue Owen
Michael Owen '95

Cheesy Bread

1 round loaf sourdough bread
1 stick margarine, melted
1 teaspoon poppy seed

1 teaspoon dried parsley
1 tablespoon onion, finely minced
Mozzarella cheese, very thin slices

Cut loaf into 1½-inch diamonds, almost to bottom of loaf. Place the loaf on a large piece of foil. Mix remaining ingredients, except for cheese, and drizzle into cuts of the bread. Take the cheese slices and place into the cuts. Wrap the loaf in foil, sealing tightly. Bake at 350° for 15 minutes. Open the foil, exposing the top, and bake another 15 minutes. Yield - 1 loaf.

Good with vegetable soup.

Lillian Gips
Bruce Holmes '78
Jeff Broaddus '98

Cheese Garlic Biscuits

2 cups dry baking mix	¼ cup butter or margarine, melted
½ cup cheddar cheese, grated	¼ teaspoon garlic powder
⅔ cup milk	

Combine dry baking mix, cheese, and milk and mix thoroughly. Drop by spoonfuls onto lightly greased cookie sheet. Bake at 450° for 8-10 minutes. Remove from oven and brush with mixture of butter and garlic powder. Serve warm. Yield - 9 biscuits.

Anna Sheffield
Ann Sheffield Kuebler '97
Kevin Kuebler '97

Black-Eyed Pea Cornbread

1 cup cornmeal	1 onion, chopped
½ cup flour	1 jalapeño, chopped
1 teaspoon salt	¾ cup cut corn, drained
½ teaspoon baking soda	1 pound sausage, browned
2 eggs, slightly beaten	1 cup cooked black-eyed peas,
1 cup buttermilk	drained
½ cup vegetable oil	8 ounces cheese, grated

Mix together cornmeal, flour, salt, and soda. Add eggs, buttermilk, and oil, mixing well. Stir in remaining ingredients. Pour into a well greased 9×13-inch pan. Bake at 350° for 45 minutes. Serves 8-10.

Betty Pennington
Shelley Lenamond '98
Mitchell Lenamond '99

Broccoli Cornbread

1 (10-ounce) package frozen chopped broccoli, thawed	1½ sticks margarine
1 medium onion, chopped	12 ounces cottage cheese
4 eggs	2 (8.5-ounce) boxes cornbread mix

Mix all ingredients together. Pour into a greased 9×13-inch pan. Bake at 350° for 35 minutes. Serves 8-10.

Too much cottage cheese will ruin the cornbread. A cookie pan may be placed under the pan to protect the bottom from getting too brown.

Lynda Jackson, Federation Officer

Mama's Cornbread

1 egg	½ teaspoon salt
1 cup buttermilk	½ teaspoon baking soda
1½ cups cornmeal	2 teaspoons baking powder
½ cup flour	2 tablespoons oil

Mix egg and buttermilk. Add other ingredients and stir only until moistened. Pour into 9×9-inch greased pan. Bake at 450° for 15-20 minutes. Serves 4.

For best results, put oil in cast iron skillet and heat. Add the hot oil to the batter and mix well. Pour the batter into the hot skillet and put in oven. This makes the cornbread bottom crisp.

Suzanne Blaney
Erin Blaney '01

Easy Focaccia Bread

1 (10-ounce) can refrigerated
  pizza crust
¼ cup Caesar salad dressing
  (divided)

3 tablespoons oil-packed,
  sun-dried tomatoes, drained
  and chopped
¼ cup ripe olives, sliced
¼ cup green olives, sliced
2 teaspoons fresh basil, chopped

Preheat oven to 425°. Unroll dough and place on greased cookie sheet. Press dough to form 10×11-inch rectangle. Brush dough with 3 tablespoons salad dressing. In a small bowl, combine tomatoes, olives, basil, and 1 tablespoon salad dressing. Mix well and spread over crust. Bake for 8-10 minutes. Serves 4-6.

Judy Boldt (Bob '68)
Laura Boldt '94
David Boldt '97

Onion-Cheese Supper Bread

½ cup onion, chopped
1 teaspoon oil
1 egg, beaten
½ cup milk
1½ cups dry baking mix

1 cup cheddar cheese, grated
  (divided)
1 tablespoon poppy seed, optional
2 tablespoons butter, melted

Preheat oven to 400°. Sauté onion in oil until tender and lightly browned. Combine egg and milk and add to the baking mix. Stir only until dry ingredients are moistened. Add onion and ½ cup cheese. Spread dough into greased 8-inch round baking pan. Sprinkle top with remaining cheese and poppy seed. Drizzle melted butter over all. Bake 20-25 minutes. Serve hot. Yield - 6-8 servings.

Janie Wallace
Rachel Wallace '01

Pork 'n' Bean Bread

2 cups sugar	1 teaspoon cinnamon
1 cup oil	½ teaspoon baking powder
3 eggs	½ teaspoon baking soda
1 (16-ounce) can pork and beans, drained	1 cup raisins
2 cups flour	1 teaspoon vanilla

Mix sugar, oil, eggs, and beans, beating until smooth. In a separate bowl, combine dry ingredients. Add to bean mixture, stirring just until combined. Stir in raisins and vanilla. Pour into 2 (8½×4½×3-inch) greased and floured loaf pans. Bake at 325° for 50-55 minutes. May also bake in 5 greased and floured (16-ounce) cans, filled ²/₃ full. Place on baking sheet. Bake 45-50 minutes, testing for doneness with a toothpick. Cook both cans or loaves completely before removing from pans. Yield - 2 loaves or 5 cans.

Mary Aasterud, President ('94-'95)
Valerie Aasterud McLaughlin '94

Applesauce Muffins

²/₃ cup margarine, melted	1 teaspoon cinnamon
1 cup sugar	½ teaspoon cloves
1½ cups applesauce, heated	½ teaspoon allspice
2 teaspoons baking soda, added to applesauce	¼ teaspoon salt
	1 cup raisins or dates
2 cups cake flour	2 cups nuts, chopped

Combine margarine, sugar, and applesauce/soda mixture. Mix together dry ingredients. Add the applesauce mixture to the dry ingredients, mixing until just moistened. Add raisins and nuts. Fill greased mini-muffin cups ²/₃ full. Bake at 350° for 12-15 minutes. Yield - 3-4 dozen mini-muffins.

Mary Aasterud, President ('94-'95)
Valerie Aasterud McLaughlin '94

All Bran Muffins

3	cups All Bran cereal (divided)	½	cup margarine, melted
1	cup boiling water	2½	cups flour
1½	cups sugar	2½	teaspoons baking soda
2	eggs, beaten	1	teaspoon salt
2	cups buttermilk	1	cup raisins

Put 1 cup cereal in large bowl. Pour boiling water over the cereal and let stand. Mix remainder of cereal with sugar, eggs, and buttermilk. Mix in melted margarine, sifted flour, soda, and salt. Combine all ingredients. Cover and store in refrigerator overnight. Fill greased muffin tins ⅔ full. Bake at 400° for 15-20 minutes. Yield - 3½ dozen.

Batter will keep in refrigerator for 6 weeks. The baked muffins freeze well.

Helen Beasley, President ('91-'92)
Nancy Beasley '90

VARIATION-
Use 1 cup All Bran cereal and 2 cups 100% Bran cereal. Decrease sugar to 1¼ cups and salt to ½ teaspoon. Omit raisins.

Sally Rasmussen
Matthew Rasmussen '01

Fudgy Picnic Muffins

4	squares semisweet chocolate	4	eggs
1	cup butter or margarine	1-2	cups pecans, chopped
1	cup flour	1	teaspoon vanilla
1¾	cups sugar		

Melt chocolate with butter. Combine flour and sugar. Add eggs and chocolate mixture to flour. Stir well. Batter will be heavy. Add pecans and vanilla. Pour into paper-lined muffin pans. Bake at 300° for 40-45 minutes. Yield - 24 muffins.

Muffins freeze well.

Martha Tucker
Jennifer Tucker '97

Pumpkin Walnut Muffins

2	cups flour	2	eggs
2	teaspoons baking powder	1	cup pumpkin
½	teaspoon baking soda	1	cup sugar (white or brown)
1	teaspoon salt	½	cup milk
1	teaspoon cinnamon	½	cup butter, melted
½	teaspoon nutmeg	1	cup walnuts or pecans, chopped

Sift together dry ingredients and set aside. Lightly beat eggs. Stir in pumpkin, sugar, milk, and butter, mixing well. Add dry ingredients to egg mixture and mix well. Stir in nuts. Pour into paper-lined muffin tins. Bake at 350° for 25 minutes or until done. Yield - 12-15 muffins.

For easy removal of paper liners, spray with vegetable oil before filling. This was a blue-ribbon winner in 4-H food shows.

Sue Owen
Michael Owen '95

Sour Cream Muffins

1	stick margarine	1½	cups sour cream
1½	cups sugar	1	teaspoon baking soda
½	teaspoon salt	2¾	cups flour
4	eggs, beaten		

Mix all ingredients thoroughly. Pour into buttered muffin tins. Sprinkle with sugar. Bake at 450° for 15 minutes. Yield - 12 muffins.

May use mini-muffin pans; reduce baking time to 9 minutes.

Cindy Etier
Emily Etier '01

Oven-Baked Apple Pancake

3	eggs, at room temperature	2	large apples, peeled and cored
¼	teaspoon salt	3	tablespoons lemon juice
½	cup flour	⅔	cup sugar
½	cup milk	1	teaspoon cinnamon
7	tablespoons butter (divided)	5	tablespoons powdered sugar

Combine eggs, salt, flour, and milk. Melt 2 tablespoons of butter. Add to batter and beat until smooth. Let rest for 1 hour. Preheat oven to 425°. Thinly slice the apples and toss with lemon juice. Melt remaining butter in a 10-inch oven-proof skillet; add the sugar while shaking the skillet. Sprinkle the cinnamon into the skillet and arrange the apples in the skillet. Cook 3 to 4 minutes. Add the batter and bake, without opening the oven, for 18 minutes. Place a plate over the skillet and invert the pancake. The apples will be on top. Dust with powdered sugar. Serves 2.

Martha Tucker
Jennifer Tucker '97

Blender Popovers

2	large eggs	1	cup flour
1	cup milk	¼	teaspoon salt

Place eggs and milk in blender. Blend until bubbly. Add flour and salt. Blend until smooth. Fill 10 well-greased muffin cups ½ full. Bake at 450° for 20 minutes; reduce heat to 350° and bake for 10 more minutes. Cool slightly before removing from pan. Yield - 10 popovers

Cindy Etier
Emily Etier '01

Quick Dinner Rolls

1 cup warm water (110-115°)	2¼ cups flour (divided)
1 (0.25-ounce) package dry yeast	1 teaspoon salt
	1 egg
2 tablespoons sugar	2 tablespoons margarine, melted

In mixing bowl, dissolve yeast in warm water. Add sugar, 1 cup flour, and salt to the yeast and beat until smooth. Add egg and margarine, stirring well. Stir in remaining flour and mix until smooth. Scrape sides of bowl and cover with a damp cloth. Let rise in warm place until double. Stir down dough. Grease 12 large muffin cups. Spoon batter into cups, filling ½ full. Let rise 20-30 minutes. Bake at 400° for 15-20 minutes. Yield - 12 rolls.

Janice Myers, President ('95-'96) (Tony '65)
Greg Myers '92
Cindy Myers Crook '96

Flour Tortillas

4 cups flour	2 teaspoons shortening
1 tablespoon baking powder	1¼ cups warm water
1 teaspoon salt	

Mix flour, baking powder, and salt. Add shortening and enough water to make a soft dough. Knead about 5 minutes. Form round balls. With rolling pin, roll out round shape about ⅛-inch thick. Cook both sides on hot ungreased griddle. Yield - 24 medium tortillas.

Dominga Algarin, Aggie Grandmother
Linda Moese '97

Soft Oaty Pretzels

3 to 3½ cups flour (divided)	1½ teaspoons salt
1½ cups rolled oats (divided)	¾ cup milk
2 tablespoons sugar	¾ cup water
1 (0.25-ounce) package rapid-rise yeast	2 tablespoons margarine
	1 egg, slightly beaten

In a large mixing bowl, combine 2 cups flour, 1¼ cups oats, sugar, yeast, and salt. Mix well. Heat milk, water, and margarine until very warm (120°). Add to flour mixture. Blend together on low, then beat 3 minutes on medium speed. By hand, stir in remaining flour to make a soft dough. Turn out on a floured surface and knead until smooth and elastic (about 5 minutes). Add more flour if too sticky. Cover and let rest 10 minutes. Heat oven to 350°. Divide dough into 24 equal pieces. Roll each piece into 12-inch long rolls and place on greased cookie sheet. Shape into pretzels or letters. Brush tops with beaten egg and sprinkle with ¼ cup oats. Bake for 15-18 minutes until golden brown. Remove from cookie sheet and cool on wire racks. Store in tightly covered container. Yield - 24 pretzels.

Sharon Reid
Ethan Reid '96

Easy Cinnamon Rolls

2 (10-count) cans refrigerator biscuits	²/₃ cup sugar
¾ cup margarine, melted	1 tablespoon cinnamon

Dip each biscuit in melted margarine. Mix cinnamon and sugar. Dip the buttered biscuits in the sugar mixture. Stand biscuits on edge in a greased round cake pan. Sprinkle any remaining sugar on top of the biscuits. Pour any remaining margarine on the top. Bake at 375° for 15-20 minutes. Serves 8-10.

Drizzle a glaze of powdered sugar and water or milk on top, if desired.

Nina Cox, President ('96-'97)
Chris Cox '92

Cranberry Orange Twists

1   (8-count) can orange Danish rolls
¼   cup sugar

1   package Ocean Spray Cran-Fruit for Chicken (cranberry-raspberry flavor)

Separate dough into eight rolls. Unwind each and coat with sugar. Twist and form into a coil and place on ungreased baking sheet. Spoon 1½ teaspoons Cran-Fruit on each roll. Bake at 400° for 8-12 minutes until golden brown. Thin the orange icing that comes with the rolls with 1 teaspoon warm water. Drizzle over rolls. Serve warm. Serves 4.

This is a Christmas tradition in our home. It has been served on Christmas morning, along with scrambled eggs, sausage, juice, and hot chocolate, for 22 years!

Martha Tucker
Jennifer Tucker '97

Apple French Toast

½   (16-ounce) loaf French bread
5   large eggs
1½ cups milk
1   teaspoon vanilla
1   cup brown sugar, packed

½   cup butter or margarine
2   tablespoons light corn syrup
3   Granny Smith apples, peeled and sliced

Cut bread into ¾-inch thick slices. Place in a single layer in a lightly greased 9×13-inch baking pan. Whisk together eggs, milk, and vanilla. Pour over bread. Cover and chill 8 hours. Remove bread from dish and set aside. Wipe dish clean and spray with cooking oil. Heat brown sugar, butter, and syrup in a saucepan until mixture is smooth. Pour sugar mixture into baking dish. Top with apples. Arrange bread slices over apples. Bake at 350° for 40 minutes. Loosen edges with a knife and invert onto platter. Yield - 8 servings.

Betty Pennington
Shelley Lenamond '98
Mitchell Lenamond '99

Philadelphia Sticky Buns

⅓	cup milk	2½	cups flour (divided)
¼	cup sugar	1	egg
½	teaspoon salt	¼	cup brown sugar
¾	cup butter or margarine (divided)	½	cup pecan or walnut halves
		½	teaspoon cinnamon
¼	cup warm water (105-115°)	½	cup raisins, chopped
1	(0.25-ounce) package dry yeast		

In small pan, heat milk just until bubbles form at edge of pan. Remove from heat and add sugar, salt, and ¼ cup butter, stirring to melt. Cool to lukewarm. Sprinkle yeast over water in large bowl; stir to dissolve. Stir in lukewarm milk mixture. Add egg and 2 cups flour. Beat with mixer until smooth. Add remaining flour; mix by hand until dough is smooth and leaves the side of bowl. Turn out dough onto lightly floured surface. Knead until dough is smooth. Place in lightly greased large bowl, turning to bring up the greased side. Cover with a cloth and let rise in warm place until double.

TOPPING-
In small bowl, cream ¼ cup butter and brown sugar. Spread on bottom and sides of a 9-inch square pan. Sprinkle with nuts.

Turn dough onto lightly floured cloth and roll into a 16×12-inch rectangle. Spread the dough with the remaining melted butter. Mix the cinnamon and raisins and sprinkle over the dough. Roll up from long side, jelly-roll fashion. Pinch edge to seal. Cut crosswise into 12 pieces. Place cut side down in pan. Cover and let rise in warm place until doubled. Preheat oven to 375°. Bake 25-30 minutes or until golden brown. Invert on board or plate; let stand 1 minute and remove pan. Serve warm. Yield - 12 buns.

Jane Schimmer

Janie's Stuffed French Toast

8	ounces cream cheese, softened	1	teaspoon cinnamon
1	cup sugar	10	slices thick-sliced bread
½	teaspoon vanilla	5	tablespoons jam of choice
		½	cup pecans, chopped

FILLING-

12	eggs	½	teaspoon salt
2	cups milk	¼	cup butter, melted and cooled
4	ounces cream cheese	½	cup pecans, chopped
½	cup sugar		

Mix cream cheese, sugar, vanilla, and cinnamon together. Spread on 5 slices of bread. Spread 1 tablespoon of jam on each slice. Cover each slice with another slice of bread. Tear the sandwiches into pieces and place in a greased 9×13-inch pan. Sprinkle chopped pecans over the torn sandwiches.

FILLING-

Mix all ingredients, except pecans, and pour over bread. Cover, and refrigerate over night. Next morning, sprinkle pecans over the top. Bake at 375° for 45 minutes. Yield - 12 servings.

SAUCE-

¾	cup sour cream	¾	cup brown sugar
¾	cup non-dairy whipped topping	1	tablespoon Kahlua or amaretto

Mix together and refrigerate over night. Serve separately with Stuffed French Toast.

Eileen Buis
Josh Buis '97
Jordan Buis '99

Heavenly Waffles

2	cups dry baking mix	⅓	cup cooking oil
1	egg	1⅓	cups club soda

Mix all ingredients well and bake in a preheated waffle iron. Serves 4.

Roe Kardell
David Kardell '83
Amy Kardell '85

172

Vegetables and Side Dishes

Asparagus/English Pea Casserole

½ stick butter or margarine	32 ounces Velveeta cheese
3 tablespoons flour	Salt and pepper to taste
1 (16-ounce) can English peas (reserve juice)	1 (9-ounce) can French-fried onions
2 (15-ounce) cans asparagus (reserve juice)	

Make cream sauce with butter, flour, and vegetable juices. Cook over medium heat until thick, stirring constantly. Add Velveeta cheese. Layer peas and asparagus in a 9×13-inch casserole dish. Sprinkle with salt and pepper. Cover with cream sauce. Bake at 350° for 20-30 minutes. Top with French-fried onions. Return to oven until onions begin to brown. Serves 6-8.

Helen Beasley, President ('91-'92)
Nancy Beasley '90

Barbecue Beans

1 pound Italian sausage links	1 (16-ounce) can green beans, drained
1 (21-ounce) can pork and beans, undrained	1 (15½-ounce) can chili beans, undrained
1 (15-ounce) can kidney beans, drained	1 (10½-ounce) can tomato soup
1 (15-ounce) can lima beans, drained	1 (6-ounce) can tomato paste
	1 cup brown sugar
	½ cup hickory barbecue sauce

Cook sausage according to package directions. Drain fat. When cool, slice into thin slices. Combine beans, tomato soup, tomato paste, brown sugar, and barbecue sauce. Stir to mix and add sausage slices. Pour into 4-quart casserole dish. Bake 1½ hours at 225°. Check and cover or uncover as needed for thickness. Serves 8-10.

This is a favorite of the entire family, especially the three Aggie sons-in-law. And it is a quick and easy casserole to make.

Shirley Neal, Federation President ('87-'88)
Linda Neal Goad '79
Beth Neal Peck '81
Juli Neal Baldwin '86

Green Beans and Artichoke Hearts

1 (14½-ounce) can green
beans, drained
1 onion, chopped
1 tablespoon olive oil
1 (8-ounce) can tomato sauce

1 (15-ounce) can artichoke hearts,
drained (not marinated type)
Salt and pepper to taste
⅛ teaspoon cumin
⅛ teaspoon paprika
1 bay leaf

Place drained green beans in a 9×13×2-inch greased casserole dish. Sauté onion in olive oil. Add tomato sauce, artichokes, and all seasonings. Simmer 10 minutes. Add this mixture to green beans and mix well. Bake 15 minutes in 350° oven, uncovered.

Sharon Corry
Trey Corry, '01

Barbecued Green Beans

SAUCE-
¾ cup sugar

¾ cup vinegar

2 (14 ½-ounce) cans
green beans, drained
1 large onion, sliced

10 pieces of bacon, fried crisp, and
crumbled (save bacon
drippings)

Combine sauce ingredients and cook until sugar dissolves. Put drained beans in a 9×13-inch casserole dish. Pour sauce over beans. Place onion slices on top of beans. Sprinkle bacon on top and pour bacon drippings over ingredients. Cover and bake at 350° about one hour. Serves 6-8.

Peggy Erickson, President ('85-'86), Federation President ('95-'96)
Kelle Erickson Shanks '85
Traci Erickson Thomas '89
Ashlee Erickson '95

Green Bean Bundles

1 (15-ounce) can whole green beans
4-5 slices breakfast bacon

2 tablespoons cider vinegar or wine vinegar
Coarse ground black pepper to taste

Drain beans. Arrange beans into 4-5 bundles, and place each bundle on a slice of bacon. Wrap bacon diagonally around beans and tuck ends under, or secure with toothpicks. Arrange the bundles in a shallow baking dish. Drizzle vinegar over bacon and grind coarse pepper over the bacon. Bake at 350° for 20-30 minutes until bacon is brown. Serves 4-5.

Debbie Cauthen
Christopher Cauthen '00

Green Bean Casserole

2 (14 ½-ounce) cans cut green beans, drained
1 (10 ½-ounce) can cream of mushroom soup

1 cup cheddar cheese, grated
¼ cup slivered almonds
1 (2.8-ounce) can French-fried onion rings (optional)

Spray 8×8-inch baking dish with cooking spray. Stir first 4 ingredients together gently. Heat in 350° oven until bubbly—about 20 minutes. Can be topped with onion rings the last 10 minutes. Serves 6-8. Can easily be doubled and cooked in 9×13-inch baking dish.

Judy Boldt (Bob '68)
Laura Boldt '94
David Boldt '97

Also submitted by Rachel Gonzales, Federation President ('83-'84)
(Ralph '53)
Col. Robert F. Gonzales '68 (son)

THE GEORGE BUSH
PRESIDENTIAL LIBRARY CENTER

The George Bush Presidential Library Center, dedicated in November, 1997, makes Texas A&M University the home of the tenth presidential library in the nation.

Operated by the National Archives, the library serves as a museum seeking to preserve and teach accumulated wisdom of the past. It houses artifacts and audio-visual presentations. It also houses the personal records of George Bush's presidency and the history of his time.

The Center for Presidential Studies is the leading center in the United States on the American presidency. It also conducts research on the office of the President of the United States.

This page provided by the generous support of

Blue Bell Creameries
Blue Bell Homemade Ice Cream
from The Little Creamery in Brenham
"The Best Ice Cream in the Country"

Photo from
The George Bush Presidential
Library and Museum

Green Beans and Celery

2	cups celery	2	teaspoons sesame seeds, toasted
2	tablespoons margarine		
1	tablespoon cornstarch	¹/₈	teaspoon garlic salt
¾	cup chicken bouillon	2	(16-ounce) cans cut green beans, drained
2	tablespoons soy sauce		

Cut celery into ½-inch pieces. Sauté celery in margarine until tender. Combine cornstarch, bouillon, soy sauce, sesame seeds, and garlic salt. Add to celery and stir constantly on medium heat until thick. Add green beans and heat thoroughly. Serves 8.

Janice Myers, President ('95-'96) (Tony '65)
Greg Myers '92
Cindy Myers Crook '96

Green Beans au Gratin

4	tablespoons butter or margarine	4	cups (canned or frozen) cut green beans, cooked
5	tablespoons flour	¼	cup Parmesan cheese
1	teaspoon dry mustard		Paprika
1½	cups milk	½	cup blanched almonds, slivered
½	cup cheddar cheese, grated		

Melt butter in saucepan. Add flour and stir. Cook several minutes on low heat. Add mustard. Gradually add milk and stir until smooth and thickened. Add grated cheese and blend until melted. Put green beans into 9×9-inch baking dish and pour sauce over them. Mix gently. Top with grated Parmesan, paprika, and almonds. Bake 30 minutes at 350°. Serves 6-8.

This has pleased three generations of Aggies and my Longhorn son-in-law!

Lillian Gips
Bruce Holmes '78 (son)
Jeffrey Broaddus '98 (grandson)

Sweet and Sour Green Beans

3	strips bacon (reserve bacon drippings)	1	tablespoon brown sugar
1	small onion, sliced	1	tablespoon vinegar
2	teaspoons cornstarch	1	(16-ounce) can cut green beans, drained, reserving ½ cup liquid
¼	teaspoon dry mustard		

Fry bacon until crisp. Drain and crumble. Add the onion to the bacon drippings, and cook until clear. Stir into onions the cornstarch and mustard. Add the reserved liquid. Cook, stirring, until mixture boils. Add the brown sugar, vinegar, and green beans. Blend together and heat thoroughly. Serves 3.

Janice Myers, President ('95-'96) (Tony '65)
Greg Myers '92
Cindy Myers Crook '96

Killer Beans

(Good for any holiday or non-holiday occasion)

1	pound bacon	3	cans Rotel tomatoes
1	large 1015 onion (or other sweet onion), chopped	1	can beer (preferably Bud Light for George)
1	clove garlic, minced		Chopped jalapeño peppers
1	gallon Ranch Style beans		(optional or for garnish)

Cut bacon into small pieces and fry until crisp. Add chopped onion and garlic and sauté until transparent. Add all other ingredients and bring to a boil. Reduce heat and cook until beer cooks off. Serves about 20.

We like to add jalapeño peppers while cooking. May be too lethal for some, so peppers may be reserved for garnish and for those who love the heat just a little bit!

Pat Johnston, President ('79-'80)
Federation President ('82-'83)
Carol Nicholas '80
Robert Johnston '83

South Louisiana Red Beans

1 pound small red beans	2 cloves garlic, chopped
1 pound smoked sausage	1 bay leaf
1 rib celery, chopped	1 large onion, chopped
Cayenne pepper to taste	

Sort and wash beans. Put in large pot with enough water to cover beans. Bring to a quick boil. Cover and remove from heat. Let sit for one hour. Cut smoked sausage into bite-sized pieces. Place all ingredients in a crock pot. Add enough water to cover beans and cook on low for 10-12 hours. (If beans are cooked on top of the stove, cook for two hours.) Serve over rice. Recipe may be doubled, using only 1 pound of sausage.

Anna Sheffield
Ann Sheffield Kuebler '97
Kevin Kuebler '97

"Boilermaker's" Broccoli Onion Deluxe

1 pound fresh broccoli or 1 (10-ounce) package frozen cut broccoli	¼ teaspoon salt
	1 cup milk
	1 (3-ounce) package cream cheese
2 cups frozen small whole onions	½ cup sharp cheddar cheese, shredded
4 tablespoons butter (divided)	
2 tablespoons flour	1 cup soft bread crumbs

Cook 1-inch pieces of broccoli and onions in salted water until tender. Drain. Put broccoli and onions in 1½-quart casserole. In another saucepan, melt 2 tablespoons butter, blend in flour and salt. Add milk. Cook, stirring constantly, until bubbly. Reduce heat. Blend in cream cheese until smooth. Pour sauce over the vegetables and mix lightly. Top with ½ cup sharp cheddar cheese, shredded. Cover. Chill. Bake casserole, covered, at 350° for 30 minutes. Melt 2 tablespoons butter and toss with 1 cup soft bread crumbs. Sprinkle crumbs around edge. Bake uncovered until heated through, about 30 more minutes. Serves 6-8.

June Bradfield, Grandmother
Raquisha Albert '00

179

Broccoli and Corn Scallop

2 tablespoons onion, chopped
2 tablespoons margarine (divided)
1 tablespoon flour
1 ¼ cups milk
8 ounces Monterey Jack cheese, shredded

1 (12-ounce) can whole kernel corn, drained
½ cup cracker crumbs (divided)
2 (10-ounce) packages frozen broccoli spears, cooked and drained

Sauté onion in 1 tablespoon margarine. Blend in flour. Gradually add milk. Cook over medium heat, stirring constantly until thickened. Add cheese, stirring until melted. Stir in corn and ¼ cup crumbs. Arrange broccoli in 9×9-inch baking dish. Pour sauce over broccoli. Toss remaining crumbs with 1 tablespoon melted margarine and sprinkle over top. Bake at 350° for 45 minutes.

Nina Cox, President ('96-'97)
Chris Cox '92

Broccoli Rice Casserole

2 cups cooked rice
1 (10-ounce) package frozen chopped broccoli, cooked and drained
8 ounces cheddar cheese, Velveeta cheese, or Cheese Whiz

1 (10½-ounce) can cream of mushroom soup
1 cup celery, chopped
½ cup onion, chopped

Mix cooked rice and broccoli. Combine cheese and mushroom soup. Mix rice and broccoli with cheese mixture, celery, and onion. Pour into greased 9-inch square baking dish. Bake in a 350° oven for 30 minutes. Serves 4-6.

Trudy Lewis, President, (El Paso A&M Mothers' Club '87-'88)
Stan Lewis '88

Company Broccoli

2 (10-ounce) packages frozen chopped broccoli
½ pound Velveeta cheese, melted
1 stick margarine, melted
2 cups crushed Ritz crackers
2 tablespoons margarine, melted

Cook and drain broccoli. Add cheese and margarine and mix. Spray 9×13-inch dish with no-stick cooking spray, then pour in mixture. Top with mixture of crushed crackers and margarine. Bake at 350° for 20-30 minutes. Serves 8-10.

Marion Crawford (Don '64)
Kristin Crawford '91
Julie Crawford '95

Prize-Winning Broccoli

1 (16-ounce) package frozen broccoli spears
2 tablespoons oil
¹/₃ cup pine nuts
1 medium yellow bell pepper, cut into strips
½ cup Parmesan cheese, freshly grated

SAUCE-
1 cup ranch salad dressing
1 teaspoon dill weed
1 teaspoon prepared horseradish
1 teaspoon honey
¼ teaspoon garlic powder

Cook broccoli according to package directions. Heat oil in large skillet over medium heat. Add pine nuts and bell pepper strips. Cook while stirring for 5 minutes, until nuts are golden brown and pepper is tender-crisp. In small saucepan combine sauce ingredients. Cook over medium heat, stirring constantly (do not boil). Drain broccoli and arrange on serving platter. Drain nuts and peppers. Pour over broccoli. Spoon sauce over top. Sprinkle with fresh Parmesan.

Judy Boldt (Bob '68)
Laura Boldt '94
David Boldt '97

Copper Pennies

MARINADE-

1-2 (10½-ounce) cans tomato soup
½ cup salad oil
1 cup sugar

¾ cup vinegar
1 teaspoon Worcestershire sauce
1 teaspoon prepared mustard

CARROTS-

2 pounds carrots, cooked, cooled, and sliced (or use frozen crinkle-cut carrots)
1 purple onion, cut in thin rings

1 small green bell pepper, cut in rings (about ¼ of a large pepper)
1-2 jalapeño peppers, thinly sliced

Mix all marinade ingredients. Place the following items in layers in a large container with a lid - carrots, peppers, and onions. Pour marinade mixture over each layer. Refrigerate 24 hours. Turn container every 4-6 hours to allow carrots to marinate evenly. Keep refrigerated. Serves 10-12.

Zelma Washington
Michelyn Washington '98

Also submitted by Marian Crawford (Don '64)
Kristin Crawford '91
Julie Crawford '95

VARIATION-

Decrease oil to ¼ cup. Increase Worcestershire sauce to 1 tablespoon. Add 2 stalks celery, diced. Omit jalapeño peppers.

Pat Perez
Jose Perez '99

Baked Corn Soufflé

1 onion, minced	1 (15-ounce) can whole kernel
1 medium green bell pepper,	corn, drained
minced	1 (8.5-ounce) package corn
4 tablespoons butter	muffin mix
2 eggs	½ teaspoon salt
1 (15-ounce) can cream-style	1 cup sour cream
corn	4 ounces cheddar cheese, grated

Sauté onion and green pepper in butter. Set aside. Mix together eggs, corn, muffin mix, and salt. Pour corn mixture into greased 9×13-inch casserole dish. Blend onion and green pepper with sour cream. Spoon over corn mixture. Top with grated cheese. Bake at 400° for 30 minutes or until firm.

Wonderful! Our family loves this one. Adie always asks for this when she comes home in the winter months.

Vara Buchanan
Adie Buchanan '01

Butter Cream Corn

8 medium ears of corn or	¾ cup milk
4 cups canned corn	6 tablespoons butter (divided)
1 teaspoon salt	¼ teaspoon paprika
2 tablespoons water	Dash of pepper

If using fresh corn, cut kernels off the cob with a sharp knife. Mix corn with salt and water in a 1½-quart baking dish. Cover with foil and bake at 400° for 25 minutes. Remove foil and pour in milk. Add 2 tablespoons butter, paprika, and pepper. Return to oven 10 minutes longer. Stir corn mixture, and just before serving, dot with 4 tablespoons butter. Optional: sprinkle with chopped parsley.

Nina Cox, President ('96-'97)
Chris Cox '92

Pam Campbell's Green Chilies and Corn

1   stick butter
8   ounces cream cheese
2   pounds frozen corn

1   (4.5-ounce) can chopped green chilies

Melt butter and cream cheese together in a crock pot on High. Add corn, one pound at a time while stirring. Stir in green chilies. When bubbly, turn to Low.

This is great to take to an office luncheon or a holiday or family get-together. Delicious!

Phyllis Condit
Matthew Clifton '01

Corn Casserole

3   eggs
1   (16-ounce) can creamed corn
1   (10-ounce) package frozen whole kernel corn, thawed and drained
¼   pound margarine, melted
½   cup yellow corn meal
1   cup sour cream

4   ounces Monterey Jack cheese, grated
4   ounces sharp cheddar cheese, grated
1   (4-ounce) can chopped green chilies
¼   teaspoon Worcestershire sauce

Beat eggs. Add rest of ingredients. Stir well. Pour in greased 9×13-inch casserole. Bake at 350° for 50-60 minutes. Let set 10 minutes before serving. Yield - 6-8 servings.

Martha Tucker
Jennifer Tucker '97

Corn Pudding

1   (15-ounce) can cream-style corn
2   tablespoons sugar
2   tablespoons flour
½   cup milk

1   teaspoon salt
¼   teaspoon nutmeg
2   eggs
2   tablespoons butter, melted

Mix all ingredients except butter, and pour into a greased 1-quart baking dish. Pour melted butter on top. Sprinkle with extra nutmeg, if desired. Bake in 350° oven for 1 hour or until set.

Cindie Deasey
Beth Williamson '02

Indian Baked Corn

¼	pound uncooked bacon, chopped	1	(13.5-ounce) can whole kernel corn, drained
⅓	cup onion, chopped	2	tablespoons jalapeños, finely chopped
⅓	cup celery, chopped		
⅓	cup green bell pepper, chopped	2	tablespoons chopped pimientos
½	cup butter	1	teaspoon salt
¼	cup milk	1	tablespoon sugar
1	(13.5-ounce) can cream-style corn	2	cups corn bread, crumbled (divided)
		2	tablespoons butter, melted

Preheat oven to 350°. In skillet over medium heat, cook bacon until crisp. Add onion, celery, and green pepper. Cook about 2 minutes. Set aside. Place butter in medium saucepan over medium heat. Melt butter and add milk, corn, jalapeños, pimientos, salt, and sugar. Heat through. Stir bacon and sautéed vegetables into saucepan, along with 1 cup crumbs. Stir frequently, and heat until mixture bubbles. Transfer to 8×8×2-inch baking dish sprayed with cooking spray. Combine remaining 1 cup crumbs with melted butter. Sprinkle crumbs over casserole. Bake until crumbs are light brown, about 8-12 minutes. Serves 8-10.

This dish is a Thanksgiving tradition at our house.

Janie Wallace
Rachel Wallace '01

Jalapeño Corn

¼	cup butter	3	(11-ounce) cans niblet corn, drained
1	(8-ounce) package cream cheese		
½	cup milk	⅔	cup canned jalapeños, sliced

Melt butter, cream cheese, and milk together in a medium saucepan. Mix in corn and jalapeños. Pour into 8×8-inch baking dish. Bake at 350° for 20 minutes, or until bubbly. Serves 6.

This recipe is the answer to "What do you want me to fix when you come home this weekend?"

Kathy Welty
Mark Welty '99

Scalloped Corn and Tomatoes

2   (14 ½-ounce) cans of
    chopped tomatoes, drained
1   (15-ounce) can whole kernel
    corn, drained
1   (15-ounce) can cream-style
    corn
2   eggs, slightly beaten
¼   cup flour

2   teaspoons sugar
½-1 teaspoon pepper
1   medium onion, chopped
½   teaspoon garlic powder
⅓   cup butter or margarine
4   cups soft bread crumbs
½   cup Parmesan cheese, grated

In a 2-quart casserole stir together tomatoes, whole kernel corn, cream-style corn, eggs, flour, sugar, and pepper. For topping cook onion and garlic powder in hot butter until tender. Stir in crumbs and cheese. Sprinkle topping over corn mixture. Bake uncovered in a 350° oven for 1 hour or until brown and set. Makes 12 servings.

Carla Bergstrom (Paul '63)

Eggplant Casserole

1   large eggplant
1   small onion, chopped
2   tablespoons margarine
1   egg, beaten

1   (10½-ounce) can cream of
    mushroom soup
½   cup bread crumbs
½   cup cheddar cheese, grated

Peel and slice eggplant. Soak in cold, salty water. Sauté onion in margarine until clear. Drain eggplant and place in boiling water (small amount). Cook on low until tender. Drain thoroughly. Mix lightly with beaten egg, cream of mushroom soup, and sautéed onion. Pour into a greased 9×13-inch casserole dish. Sprinkle top with bread crumbs and grated cheese. Bake at 325° for approximately 35 minutes or until firm.

Anna Sheffield
Ann Sheffield Kuebler '97
Kevin Kuebler '97

Aggie Onion Casserole

4 pounds sweet 1015 onions	1 cup evaporated skim milk
2-4 tablespoons butter or margarine	1 cup shredded cheddar cheese
1 (10¾-ounce) can cream of mushroom soup, undiluted	8 thick slices French bread
	Butter or margarine, melted

Slice onions in half lengthwise, then into ½-inch slices crosswise. Sauté in butter until tender-crisp. Spoon into vegetable oil-sprayed 9×13-inch baking dish. Top with a mixture of soup and milk. Sprinkle with cheese and arrange bread slices on top. Brush bread with butter. Bake 30-35 minutes at 350°. Serves 6 - 8.

We call the 1015 Onions, "Aggie Onions"!

Kay Broaddus
Jeffrey Broaddus '98

1015 Sweet Onions Stuffed with Broccoli

3 medium 1015 onions	2 tablespoons margarine
1 (10-ounce) package frozen chopped broccoli	2 tablespoons flour
⅔ cup Parmesan cheese	¼ teaspoon salt
¼ cup mayonnaise	⅓ cup milk
2 teaspoons lemon juice	1 (3-ounce) package cream cheese, softened

Peel and halve onions. Parboil in salted water 12 minutes. Drain. Remove centers leaving ¾-inch edges. Chop center portions to equal one cup. Set aside. Cook broccoli according to package directions. Drain. Combine chopped onions, broccoli, Parmesan cheese, mayonnaise, and lemon juice. Spoon into centers of onion halves. Place in casserole dish. Melt margarine in saucepan over medium heat. Blend in flour and salt. Add milk and cook until thick, stirring constantly. Remove from heat and blend in cream cheese. Spoon sauce over onion halves and bake uncovered for 20 minutes at 375°. Makes 6 servings.

Julie Thedford (Marvin '65)
Mary Helen Thedford Ramsey '93
Clay Ramsey '93
Katherine Thedford '98

Potato Casserole

2 pounds hash brown potatoes (frozen)	1 cup cheddar cheese, shredded
1 (10½-ounce) can cream of mushroom or cream of chicken soup	½ cup onion, grated
	½ cup margarine, melted
	1 (2.8-ounce) can fried onion rings OR
1 pint sour cream	2 cups crushed corn flakes

Mix first six ingredients directly in a greased 9×13-inch baking dish. Bake at 425° for 40 minutes. Top with fried onion rings or crushed corn flakes the last 5 minutes. Serves 10-12.

This is a hit wherever you go! Great for company. It's easy to make and delicious!

Gail Stevenson
Jeff Rogers '97
Greg Rogers '99
Also submitted by Donna Taylor
Bryan Taylor '93
Andy Taylor '97
Katie Taylor '01

VARIATION 1-
Reduce sour cream to 1 cup. Combine cereal with ¼ cup margarine before sprinkling over casserole.

Pat Hardi, President ('93-'94)
Steven Hardi, '91

VARIATION 2-
Add 1 teaspoon salt, ½ teaspoon pepper, and ½ cup bacon bits to the original recipe. Omit onion rings or corn flakes.

Nancy Tong
Paul Tong '99

VARIATION 3-
Reduce onion and margarine to ¼ cup each. Use 1 cup bread crumbs in place of onion rings or corn flakes.

Terry Moomaw
Adam Moomaw '01

VARIATION 4-
Add 1 teaspoon salt, ¼ teaspoon pepper, 1 soup can milk. Increase cheese to 2 cups. Reduce sour cream to 1 cup.

Marion Crawford (Don '64)
Kristin Crawford '91
Julie Crawford '95

Herb Smoked Potatoes

2 tablespoons olive oil	¼ teaspoon salt
¼ teaspoon liquid smoke	Freshly ground pepper to taste
16 tiny new potatoes, scrubbed and halved	1 tablespoon fresh rosemary leaves, minced

Preheat oven to 400°. Combine all ingredients. Stir until potatoes are coated. Wrap potatoes in foil and place on baking sheet. Bake for 25 minutes until tender. Makes 4 servings. Can be cooked on a covered grill for 40 minutes.

Sue Owen
Michael Owen '95

Party Stuffed Potatoes

6 baking potatoes	½ (1.15-ounce) package onion soup mix
½ cup butter	
8 ounces sour cream	1 cup cheddar cheese, shredded
	Salt, pepper, paprika to taste

Bake potatoes; allow to cool to touch. Scoop pulp out, leaving shells intact. Combine potato pulp, butter, sour cream, soup mix, cheese, salt, and pepper. Whip until smooth. Stuff shells with mixture. Sprinkle with paprika. Bake at 350° for 25 minutes.

Martha Tucker
Jennifer Tucker '97

Potato Cheese Bake

6 russet potatoes, boiled and grated	2½ cups cheddar cheese, grated (divided)
1 pint sour cream	6 green onions, chopped
½ cup milk	3 tablespoons margarine or butter
	Salt and pepper to taste

Parboil potatoes then peel and grate them. Mix potatoes with all ingredients, saving ½ cup cheese for top. Put mixture in 9×13-inch casserole; cover. Bake at 350° for about 45 minutes to 1 hour. Top with ½ cup cheese.

Diane Gray, Federation Officer

Potato Soufflé

8	large baking potatoes (4½ – 5 pounds)
1	(8-ounce) package cream cheese, at room temperature
1	cup sour cream
2	teaspoons garlic salt
½	teaspoon pepper
2	teaspoons green chives, chopped
4	tablespoons butter
	Paprika

Peel potatoes and cook, covered, in 5-quart pan with 1 inch of boiling water for 40 minutes, or until potatoes are tender. Drain, then mash well. With electric mixer, beat together cream cheese, and sour cream. Gradually add mashed potatoes until smooth. Beat in garlic salt, pepper, and chives. Turn into buttered 3-quart soufflé dish. Dot with butter and sprinkle lightly with paprika. Bake at 400° for 1 hour, or until hot and crusty.

May be made up to 3 days ahead. Just cover and chill. To bake, bring to room temperature and bake as above.

Eileen Buis
Josh Buis '97
Jordan Buis '99

Sour Cream Potato Casserole

10	medium-sized potatoes
12	ounces cream cheese
8	ounces sour cream
2	tablespoons chives
	Salt and pepper to taste
¼	cup butter or margarine

Boil potatoes until tender. Mash. Add cream cheese, sour cream, chives, salt, and pepper. Mix thoroughly. Mixture will be thin. Pour into buttered 9×13-inch casserole dish. Dot with butter over top. Bake at 350° for 1 hour.

Cindy Etier
Emily Etier '01

Spicy Steak Fries

2	egg whites	1	tablespoon paprika
2	tablespoons water	1	teaspoon salt
1	(18-ounce) package frozen potato wedges	½	teaspoon garlic powder
½	cup seasoned dry bread crumbs	½	teaspoon ground cayenne pepper

Preheat oven according to potato package directions. In large bowl whisk together egg whites and water. Toss potato wedges in mixture until coated. In plastic bag mix the remaining ingredients. Add the potatoes and shake well. Bake on greased baking sheet in a single layer. Serves 6-8.

Cindy Etier
Emily Etier '01

Ratatouille

2	large onions, chopped	4	zucchini, sliced
2	cloves garlic, minced		Salt and pepper to taste
½	cup oil	6	ripe tomatoes, chopped
2	green bell peppers, chopped	2	tablespoons parsley
2	eggplants or yellow squash, peeled and cut in bite-sized pieces	¼	teaspoon marjoram
		¼	teaspoon basil
		½	teaspoon oregano

Sauté onion and garlic in oil. Add green pepper and eggplant. Cook 5 minutes. Stir in zucchini, salt, and pepper. Cover and simmer for 30 minutes or until tender. Uncover and add chopped tomatoes and seasonings. Cook for an additional 15 minutes.

Eileen Buis
Josh Buis '97
Jordan Buis '99

Rice and Corn Casserole

1 (6.8-ounce) package chicken Rice-a-Roni	1 (10½-ounce) can cream of chicken soup
1 onion, chopped	1 (8-ounce) jar Jalapeño Cheese Whiz
2 (11-ounce) cans Mexicorn, drained	

Prepare rice and pasta mix as directed on package. Add remaining ingredients. Pour into 9×13-inch greased casserole pan and bake at 350° for about 30 minutes or until hot. Serves 8-10.

Can be heated in microwave. Add cooked chicken for main course casserole.

Linda Murphy
Kristina Murphy '91
Karin Murphy Harbour '93
Sean Harbour '92

Dirty Rice

1 pound pork sausage	1 bunch green onions, chopped
1 cup onion, chopped	4½ cups chicken stock
2-3 garlic cloves, minced	2 cups uncooked rice
½ cup celery, chopped	Crushed red pepper to taste
½ cup green bell pepper, chopped	Salt to taste

Brown sausage and drain. Add onion, garlic, celery, bell pepper, and green onions. Cook until vegetables are sautéed. Add remaining ingredients. Simmer until rice is cooked and liquid is absorbed (about 20 minutes). Serves 10-12.

Betty Pennington
Shelley Lenamond '98
Mitchell Lenamond '99

East Texas Corn Bread Dressing

2 (6-ounce) packages yellow corn bread mix, prepared and crumbled
8 slices day old wheat bread, torn into bite-sized pieces
4 eggs, beaten
1 medium onion, grated fine

2 ribs celery, sliced
¼ cup oil
2 teaspoons salt
1 teaspoon black pepper
1 teaspoon poultry seasoning
2 (14-ounce) cans chicken broth

Cook onions and celery in a little water until tender. Drain. Thoroughly mix all ingredients together in a large bowl until well blended. It will be very moist. Pour into greased 9×13-inch pan. Bake at 350° for 1 hour. Serves 8 - 10.

This dressing was served at our house every Thanksgiving. It can be frozen and reheated.

Thelma Taylor, Grandmother
Laura Boldt '94
David Boldt '97

Mexican Fried Rice

1 cup rice
1½ tablespoons oil
1 medium tomato, chopped, OR ½ cup canned tomatoes, drained
1 slice of onion, chopped

2 cups boiling water
2 chicken bouillon cubes
½ teaspoon garlic powder
½ teaspoon comino powder or cumin

Brown rice in oil over medium heat. Stir often. When brown, add chopped vegetables and stir some more. Add water, bouillon cubes, garlic powder, and comino. Bring to a boil. Turn heat down and simmer for 15 minutes, covered. Turn off heat and leave covered for 5 minutes. Stir with a 2-pronged fork to fluff. Ready to serve.

Dominga Algarin, Grandmother
Linda Moese '97

Rice and Green Chili Casserole

4 cups cooked rice	2 teaspoons salt
4 tablespoons butter	1 onion, chopped
6 ounces chopped green chilies	3 (12-ounce) packages Monterey
1 (16-ounce) carton sour cream	Jack cheese, grated

Combine cooked rice, butter, green chilies, sour cream, salt, onion, and 2 packages of cheese, and pour into greased 9×13-inch casserole dish. Top with remaining package of cheese. Bake at 350° for 30 minutes or until bubbly.

Aggie Mom

Saffron Rice

¼ cup pine nuts	¼ cup raisins
3 tablespoons olive oil	1 teaspoon salt
1 cup onions, finely chopped	Pinch of saffron to color
1½ cups rice	¾ cup water

Lightly brown pine nuts in oil. Add onions and sauté until soft and yellow. Add remaining ingredients and simmer 15-20 minutes until rice is tender.

Lillian Gips
Bruce Holmes '78
Jeff Broaddus '98

Marinated Black-Eyed Peas

3 (17-ounce) cans blackeyed peas, drained	1 cup salad oil
½ cup onion, chopped	1 tablespoon chili powder
1 cup green olives with pimiento, sliced	½ cup wine vinegar
	1 clove garlic, minced

Mix all ingredients together. Marinate 24 hours.

Great to serve on a warm New Year's Day!

Judy Boldt (Bob '68)
Laura Boldt '94
David Boldt '97

Wild Rice

½ teaspoon salt	½ (10 ½-ounce) can cream of
1½ cups boiling water	mushroom soup, undiluted
½ cup uncooked wild rice	½ cup heavy cream
1 tablespoon butter or	⅛ teaspoon dried marjoram
margarine	Dash dried basil
2 tablespoons onion, minced	Dash dried tarragon
1 tablespoon green bell pepper,	¼ teaspoon curry powder
minced	¼ teaspoon salt
1 (3-ounce) can sliced	⅛ teaspoon pepper
mushrooms, drained	

Add ½ teaspoon salt to boiling water in saucepan. Stir in rice. Simmer, covered, 30 minutes, or until rice is tender and water is absorbed. While rice cooks, melt 1 tablespoon of butter in another saucepan. Sauté onion, green pepper, and drained mushrooms in butter for 5 minutes. Stir in cream of mushroom soup, cream, marjoram, basil, tarragon, curry powder, salt, and pepper. Heat 10 minutes. Then add cooked wild rice to this mixture and heat on low, stirring occasionally.

This is a Christmas tradition in our family. I always serve it with Rock Cornish game hens.

Martha Tucker
Jennifer Tucker '97

Creamed Spinach

3 (10-ounce) packages frozen	4 tablespoons margarine (divided)
spinach	Salt and pepper to taste
2 (3-ounce) packages cream	Generous dash of nutmeg
cheese	1 cup Pepperidge Farm Herb
	Dressing

Cook and drain spinach. Return to hot pan and add all other ingredients except 2 tablespoons margarine and dressing. Place in buttered casserole. Sprinkle dressing on top and drizzle 2 tablespoons melted margarine on top. Bake at 350° for 25 minutes. Serves 8-10.

Sarah Jacob Kielty '94

Spinach Casserole

2   (10-ounce) packages spinach,   1   cup mayonnaise
    cooked and strained   1   cup cheddar cheese, grated
1   cup cream of mushroom soup,   1   onion, chopped
    undiluted   Bread crumbs

To the cooked spinach, add the soup, mayonnaise, cheese, and onion. Pour into greased 9×9-inch casserole. Top with bread crumbs. Cook in oven for 45 minutes at 350°.

Anna Sheffield
Ann Sheffield Kuebler '97
Kevin Kuebler '97

Baked Acorn Squash with Sausage

4   acorn squash, halved, and   4   tablespoons butter, melted
    seeds removed   Dash of salt
12 links pork sausage   ½   cup honey

Preheat oven to 350°. Place squash, cut side down, in a shallow pan. Bake for 35 minutes. Cook sausage until brown and chop into small pieces. Brush cut side of squash with melted butter. Sprinkle salt and drizzle honey over the inside. Divide chopped, cooked sausage among the squash halves. Bake another 25 minutes. Serves 6-8.

Sue Owen
Michael Owen '95

Hot Mexican Rice

2   (13.5-ounce) cans whole   3   cups cooked rice
    kernel corn, drained   10 ounces Monterey Jack cheese,
8   ounces sour cream   grated
1   teaspoon cumin   2   jalapeño peppers, finely
                                        chopped

Mix all ingredients. Pour into 9×13-inch casserole. Bake at 350° for 30 minutes, or until bubbly. You may cook it in the microwave for 15-20 minutes. Serves 8-10.

Nancy Tong
Paul Tong '99

Cranberry-Acorn Squash OR
"The Only Decent Way to Fix Squash"

2	medium acorn squash	¼	cup brown sugar
1	cup fresh or frozen cranberries	3	tablespoons butter, melted
1	cup chopped apple	½	teaspoon orange peel

Preheat oven to 350°. Cut squash in half and remove seeds. Place cut side down on greased baking pan. Bake for 40 minutes. Turn cut side up. Mix remaining ingredients and spoon into squash. Return to oven and bake 30 minutes or until done. Makes 4 servings.

One of Michael's 4-H food show prize winners!

Michael Owen '95

Cheese-Squash-Corn Casserole

6	medium yellow squash	2	(4.5-ounce) cans chopped green chilies, drained
1	medium onion, chopped		
1	8-ounce block Velveeta	1	(16-ounce) can shoe peg corn, drained
1	(3-ounce) package cream cheese		

Slice squash ¼ inch thick. Cook squash and onion until tender. Drain well. While hot, add Velveeta, cream cheese, green chilies, and corn. Pour into greased casserole dish. Bake at 350° for 30 minutes.

Optional: sprinkle buttered bread crumbs on top before baking.

Cindy Etier
Emily Etier '01

197

Squash Casserole with Herb Stuffing Mix

2 pounds fresh yellow squash, sliced
1 small onion, chopped
Salt to taste
Pepper to taste
1 tablespoon butter, melted

1 (10-ounce) can cream of chicken soup
1 cup sour cream
2 tablespoons diced pimientos
½ cup butter, melted
8 ounces herb seasoned stuffing mix

Cook squash and onion in water until tender. Drain and mash. Blend in salt, pepper, 1 tablespoon butter, soup, sour cream, and pimiento. Set aside. Mix ½ cup butter with stuffing mix. Stir ½ of the stuffing mix into squash mixture. Pour into greased 1½-quart baking dish and top with remaining stuffing. Bake at 375° for 30 minutes. Serves 8.

Susan Saiter
Rob Saiter '90
David Saiter '98

Yellow Squash Casserole

¼ cup butter or margarine, melted
1 pound yellow squash, thinly sliced
½ teaspoon salt
¼ teaspoon pepper
1 egg, beaten

½ cup mayonnaise
¼ cup green bell pepper, chopped
⅓ cup onion, chopped
1 tablespoon pimiento, chopped (optional)
1 teaspoon sugar
½ cup mild cheddar cheese, shredded

Preheat oven to 350°. Pour melted butter into 1½-quart casserole. Add squash and toss. Sprinkle with salt and pepper. Combine egg, mayonnaise, green pepper, onion, pimiento, and sugar. Mix well and spread over squash. Sprinkle evenly with cheese. Bake at 350° for 35-40 minutes. Makes 4-6 servings.

Carla Bergstrom (Paul '63)

Bourbon Sweet Potato Casserole

1 cup sugar	1 cup chopped nuts
3 eggs	½ cup butter or margarine, melted
2 cups half-and-half	1 teaspoon cinnamon
2 cups grated sweet potato	½ teaspoon cloves
2 teaspoons bourbon	½ teaspoon nutmeg

Mix all ingredients. Pour into a greased 9×13-inch casserole and bake at 350° for 1 hour.

I have substituted liquid creamer for the half-and-half and brandy for the bourbon, but I prefer the bourbon. Nuts should not be too finely chopped.

Terry Ramsey
Clayton Ramsey '93
Mary T. Ramsey '93

Hawaiian Sweet Potato Casserole

6-7 medium sweet potatoes	1 cup sugar
1 stick margarine, softened	2 eggs, beaten

TOPPING-

½ cup flour	1 (8-ounce) can crushed pineapple
1 cup brown sugar	1 cup chopped nuts
1 teaspoon vanilla	1 stick margarine, melted
¼ cup milk	2 tablespoons boiling water
1 cup coconut	

Cook potatoes. Peel and mash. Combine potatoes with next three ingredients and mix well. Pour into greased casserole dish. Combine topping ingredients and spread over potato mixture. Bake 30 minutes at 350°. Yield-8-10 servings.

Janice Dowlearn
Scott W. Dowlearn '01

Orange-Glazed Sweet Potatoes

6	medium sweet potatoes	3	tablespoons butter or margarine
1	cup orange juice	¹/₃	cup brown sugar
1	tablespoon cornstarch	¹/₃	cup granulated sugar

Cook unpeeled sweet potatoes 30 minutes in boiling, salted water until tender. Drain, peel, slice and place in greased 9×13-inch pan. Combine orange juice, cornstarch, margarine, and both sugars in saucepan. Cook, stirring constantly, until thickened. Pour glaze over potatoes. Bake at 350° for 30 minutes. Serves 6.

Janice Myers, President ('95-'96) (Tony '65)
Greg Myers '92
Cindy Myers Crook '96

Sweet Potatoes with Marshmallow Topping

4	large sweet potatoes	¼	cup brown sugar
4	tablespoons butter	¼	cup maple syrup
¼	cup milk	8	large marshmallows

Bake four large sweet potatoes at 350° for 1½ hours. Remove skins and mash potatoes. Add butter. Blend in milk, brown sugar, and maple syrup. Pour into a 9×13-inch casserole dish. Top with marshmallows. Bake at 350° for 1 hour.

Ann Caronna
Ruth Caronna Schuman '89
Ken Schuman '88
Mark Caronna '96

Italian Tomatoes

4	large tomatoes, peeled and halved	1	cup dry bread crumbs or cracker crumbs
8	ounce bottle of Italian salad dressing	2	teaspoons basil
16	ounces marinated artichoke hearts, sliced	½	cup Parmesan cheese, grated
		4	tablespoons butter

Place tomato halves in 7×11-inch baking dish. Pour dressing over tomatoes and refrigerate. One hour before serving, arrange artichokes over tomatoes. Sprinkle with crumbs, basil, and cheese. Dot with butter and bake at 350° for 20 minutes. Must be prepared ahead. Serves 8.

Susan Saiter
Rob Saiter '90
David Saiter '98

Greek Spaghetti Casserole

1	(16-ounce) package thin spaghetti, cooked	1	(28-ounce) can tomatoes, drained and chopped
1	medium onion, chopped	1	(14-ounce) can chopped ripe olives, drained
1	medium green bell pepper, chopped	4	ounces sharp cheddar cheese, grated
½	cup margarine, melted	1	(10½-ounce) can cream of mushroom soup
1	(14-ounce) can sliced mushrooms, drained	¼	cup water

Sauté onion and bell pepper in margarine. Stir in olives, tomatoes, and mushrooms. Simmer for 10 minutes. Spread half of the cooked spaghetti in a well-greased 9×13-inch casserole dish. Top with half of the sauce and half of the cheese. Repeat layers. Combine soup and water. Spread over casserole. Cover with foil and bake at 350° for 25-30 minutes or until bubbly. This freezes well. Serves 6-8.

Martha Tucker
Jennifer Tucker '97

Jennifer's Favorite Vegetable Dish

1	(20-ounce) package frozen mixed vegetables	¼	pound Velveeta cheese
			Dash of garlic salt
1	(10¾-ounce) can golden mushroom soup	1	(4-ounce) can mushrooms (optional)
1	stick margarine	1	(6-ounce) box seasoned croutons

Cook vegetables according to package directions and drain well. Heat soup, margarine, cheese, garlic salt, and mushrooms until mixture is thick and melted. Add to the vegetables in a greased 9×13-inch casserole dish. Stir in a few croutons, then cover top with croutons. Bake at 350° for 15-20 minutes. Serves 8.

Robin Luffy
Jennifer Luffy '00
Brian Luffy '02

Vegetable Casserole

1	(16-ounce) can shoe peg corn, drained	1	(10¾-ounce) can cream of mushroom soup
1	(16-ounce) can French-style green beans, drained	1	cup sour cream
½	cup onion, chopped	¾	cup cheddar cheese, grated
¼	cup green bell pepper, chopped		Almond slices, optional
		4	tablespoons butter
		½	cup Ritz crackers, crushed

Mix together the corn and beans. Stir in onion, pepper, soup, sour cream, cheese, and almond slices. Pour into a greased 9×13-inch baking dish and dot with butter. Top with crushed Ritz crackers and bake at 375° for 30 minutes. Serves 8.

Aggie Mom

Vegetables and Pasta

4	ounces bow tie or corkscrew pasta	1	(8-ounce) package cream cheese, softened
1	(8¾-ounce) can whole kernel sweet corn, drained (reserve 3 tablespoons of liquid)	1	(16-ounce) can sweet peas, drained
		½	cup sliced green onions
		¼	cup Parmesan cheese, grated

Cook pasta according to package directions; drain. Blend reserved corn liquid with cream cheese. Combine all ingredients, and spoon into 1½-quart baking dish. Cover and bake at 375° for 20 minutes or until heated through. Serves 6-8.

Helen Beasley, President ('91-'92)
Nancy Beasley '90

Double Cheese and Zucchini Bake

½	cup butter (divided)	½	cup dry bread crumbs (divided)
1	medium onion, chopped	1	teaspoon Italian seasoning
2	garlic cloves, minced		Salt to taste
8	medium zucchini, sliced		Freshly ground pepper to taste
2	cups Monterey Jack cheese, shredded (divided)	3	eggs, beaten to blend
		½	cup whipping cream
1	cup Parmesan cheese, freshly grated (divided)	12	small Roma tomato slices

Grease 9×13 glass baking dish. Sauté onion and garlic in ¼ cup butter in heavy large skillet over medium heat. Cook until softened, stirring occasionally, 4-5 minutes. Add zucchini and cook until just tender, stirring frequently, about 6 minutes. Remove from heat. Stir in 1 cup Monterey Jack cheese, ½ cup Parmesan cheese, ¼ cup bread crumbs, and Italian seasoning. Season with salt and pepper. Transfer mixture to prepared dish. Sprinkle remaining Monterey Jack cheese over this mixture. Combine eggs and cream. Pour over zucchini. Sprinkle on remaining Parmesan cheese and bread crumbs. Top with 12 tomato slices. Dot with remaining ¼ cup butter. Bake at 350°, about 35 minutes, or until golden brown. Serves 10-12. Can be prepared 1 day ahead. Cover and refrigerate. Rewarm thoroughly in regular oven before serving. Use as a main dish for brunch or as a vegetable dish.

Gloria Gilpin, President ('98-'99) (Bobby '62)
Wes Gilpin '93
Katherine Gilpin '97

Zippy Zucchini and Tomatoes

3	medium zucchini	4	ounces zesty Italian salad dressing
2	Roma tomatoes	¼	cup Parmesan cheese, grated

Slice zucchini and tomatoes thin. Layer in a shallow glass baking dish (1-quart or 9×9). Pour dressing over vegetables. Allow to marinate until just before serving. Cover loosely and microwave on High for 10 minutes. Sprinkle with cheese and serve piping hot. For variation in flavor, try Caesar dressing.

Judy Boldt (Bob '68)
Laura Boldt '94
David Boldt '97

Hearty Poultry Stuffing

½ cup unsalted butter or margarine

1 medium onion, chopped

1 large bell pepper, chopped

¼ cup celery, chopped

4 bacon slices, diced

1 teaspoon rubbed sage OR 1 tablespoon fresh sage, chopped

1 teaspoon thyme, dried OR 1 tablespoon fresh thyme, chopped

1 teaspoon dried rosemary, minced OR 1 tablespoon fresh rosemary, minced

1 teaspoon dried leaf oregano OR 1 tablespoon fresh oregano, chopped

1 teaspoon salt

½ teaspoon freshly ground pepper

¼ pound smoked ham, coarsely ground

4 cups (about 4 ounces) corn bread, crumbled and lightly packed

6 cups (about 6 ounces) French bread cubes, lightly packed

2 eggs, slightly beaten

About 1 ¼ cups brown poultry stock OR canned chicken stock

Melt butter or margarine in a heavy 10-inch skillet over medium heat. Add onion, bell pepper, celery, bacon, seasonings, and ham. Sauté, stirring often, until vegetables are wilted and bacon is cooked, but not brown, about 10 minutes. Place corn bread and French bread in a bowl. Pour vegetable mixture over bread. Toss to combine, and stir in eggs. Add enough stock or broth to make a moist dressing, stirring to break up corn bread and French bread. Pour into greased 9×13-inch pan. Bake in preheated 350° oven for 1 hour. Makes about 1 pound or 8 servings.

Artie J. Jenkins
Altie Jenkins '00

Main Dishes
and
Casseroles

Breakfast Tacos

2 pounds breakfast-style sausage	18 flour tortillas
	½ onion, chopped
1 green pepper, chopped	4 eggs

SAUCE-
1 pound cheddar cheese, grated   ¼ cup flour
2 tablespoons butter

Cook sausage, onion, and green pepper. Drain. Stir in eggs. Fill tortillas. Roll, place in pan sprayed with vegetable spray. Can get 9 in a pan. Top with sauce made by melting butter, stirring in flour and then stirring in cheese until melted. Bake at 350° for 30 minutes. Serves 8-10

Cora Nell Sneary, Grandmother
Shannon Sneary '00

Broccoli-Ham Casserole

8 slices white bread	2 cups (½ pound) sharp cheddar cheese, shredded
¾ cup butter, melted	
2 cups ham, cooked and cubed	4 eggs
2 cups broccoli, cooked and chopped	2 cups milk
	1 teaspoon salt
	½ teaspoon pepper

Cube bread. Add melted butter and toss well. In buttered 9×13-inch casserole, layer the ingredients in the following order - half of the bread cubes, half of the shredded cheese, half of the broccoli, all of the ham, then remaining broccoli, remaining cheese, and remaining bread cubes. Beat eggs and milk thoroughly with seasonings. Pour over all the layers. Refrigerate overnight or at least 2 hours. Bake in 350° oven until puffy and nicely brown for one hour. Serves 8-10.

JaNahn Rodriguez, President, ('97-'98)
David Rodriguez '94
Cindy Rodriguez '95
Dan Rodriguez '99

Brunch Enchiladas

12 ounces (2 cups) Danish
    canned ham, chopped
2½ cups cheddar Cheese,
    shredded and divided
½ cup green onions, sliced
8 (7- or 8-inch) flour tortillas

Corn meal
4 eggs, beaten
2 cups half-and-half
1 tablespoon flour
¼ teaspoon garlic powder
Few drops bottled "hot pepper
    sauce"

Combine ham, 1½ cups cheese, and onion. Place ⅛ of mixture (about 1/3 cup) at one end of each tortilla. Roll up. Arrange tortillas, seam side down, in a greased and corn meal sprinkled 9×13-inch casserole dish. Combine eggs, half-and-half, flour, garlic powder, and hot sauce. Pour over tortillas. Cover and refrigerate overnight. Bake, covered, in 350° oven for 55 - 60 minutes until set. Sprinkle with 1 cup cheese. Let stand 10 minutes. Makes 8 servings.

Diane Gray, Federation Officer

Chili/Cheese/Egg Casserole

10 eggs, beaten until light
½ cup flour
1 teaspoon baking powder
½ teaspoon salt
1 (16-ounce) carton small
    curd cottage cheese

1 pound Monterey Jack cheese,
    grated
½ cup melted butter
1 (4.5-ounce) can chopped
    green chilies

Combine all ingredients. Pour into 9×13-inch buttered pan and bake at 350° for 35 minutes or until firm in center. Serves 12.

Susan Saiter
Rob Saiter '90
David Saiter '98

Four Cheese Sausage Casserole

1	pound breakfast sausage	3	ounces cream cheese, cubed
1	bunch green onions, chopped	1	(8 ounce) carton cottage cheese
2	(6-ounce) cans mushrooms	10	ounces Monterey Jack cheese
6	eggs	6	ounces mild cheddar
½	cup flour		cheese, grated
1	teaspoon baking powder	6	tablespoons butter
⅛	teaspoon salt		Paprika
1	cup milk		

Brown crumbled sausage and set aside. Chop green onions and mushrooms and set aside. In a large bowl, beat eggs with wire whisk, add flour, baking powder, salt, and milk. Cut cream cheese into small cubes. Add cream cheese and cottage cheese to egg mixture. Add grated Monterey Jack and cheddar cheese, along with cooked sausage, chopped onions, and mushrooms. Butter a 9×13-inch casserole and pour mixture into dish. Dot with butter. Top with sprinkling of paprika. Cover and refrigerate overnight. Next day, bring to room temperature and bake 350° for 45 minutes. Serves 6-8. For a variation, you may toast 6 slices of bread lightly and place in bottom of casserole before adding mixture.

Martha Tucker
Jennifer Tucker '97

Sausage/Rotel/Egg Bake

12	eggs, beaten	1	pint sour cream
1	green pepper, chopped fine	¾	pound cheddar cheese, shredded
1	onion, chopped fine	1	(10-ounce) can Rotel tomatoes
1	pound sausage, browned,		and chilies, drained
	crumbled and drained OR		
	2 cups ham, chopped fine		

Mix everything with beaten eggs in large bowl. Pour into greased 9×13-inch pan. Bake at 350° until set - about 45 minutes. Serves 12.

Sue Owen
Michael Owen '95

REVEILLE

Reveille is the First Lady of Texas A&M. Contrary to usual custom, the wife of the President of Texas A&M willingly relinquishes that title to the Collie mascot. With five stars, Reveille is the highest ranking member of the Corps of Cadets. Cadets must greet her saying, "Howdy, Miss Reveille, Ma'am." You must never say "dog" in her presence. She was the only female in the Corps for many decades.

Today, Reveille is maintained by Company E-2, with a sophomore cadet responsible for her care. She attends classes with the Mascot Corporal and is always welcomed in restaurants and businesses in Bryan-College Station, often garnering a free meal for her keeper!

The page provided by the generous support of

Reveille Photo
By
Richard Korcyznski

Seasonal Baked Eggs

1 dozen eggs
1 pound Monterey Jack
cheese, grated
2 cups cottage cheese
¼ cup flour
1 teaspoon baking powder
1 stick butter (not margarine),
melted
Salt and pepper to taste
Seasonal Ingredient (one or
more of the following
according to the season
or local preference)

Green chili pepper
Fresh Mexican salsa, chopped
Sweet onions, chopped
Smoked salmon
Fresh sweet basil and tomato,
chopped
Red bell pepper, chopped
Smoked oysters
Fresh asparagus tips

Briskly mix all ingredients (except seasonal ingredient) in a large bowl. The dish is very good without ANY seasonal ingredient. If you want to vary the recipe, stir in one of the "seasonal" items after the basic ingredients are thoroughly mixed and fluffy. Pour into a 9×13-inch pan. Bake at 350° for 35 to 40 minutes until eggs are set and top is light brown. May serve as a single entreé or with breakfast meats. Garnish with fresh sliced tomatoes, herbs from the garden, or with fruit compote. Serves 12.

This recipe is one that we use frequently at Mansion on Main and the guests always enjoy. The recipe is quite versatile, in that it can be adapted to the season or to local tastes, according to what is in season or available at the market.

Peggy Taylor (owner, Mansion on Main Bed and Breakfast
in Texarkana and McKay House Bed and Breakfast in Jefferson)
Janna Gilbert '82
Jennifer Hogg '85
Steve Taylor '89

Bacon-Ham Quiche

1 egg, beaten
1 cup evaporated milk
½ teaspoon salt
½ teaspoon Worcestershire
   sauce
½ cup Swiss cheese, grated
½ cup Monterey Jack cheese,
   grated

1 (3-ounce) can French
   fried onions
6 slices bacon, cooked
   and crumbled
½ cup ham, chopped
1 pie shell, unbaked

Beat egg. Add milk, salt, sauce, and cheese. Sprinkle ⅓ cup onions over pie shell. Pour egg mixture into pie shell. Sprinkle bacon and ham over that. Sprinkle ⅓ cup onions on top. Bake at 325° for 50-55 minutes. Serves 6-8.

Terry Moomaw
Adam Moomaw '01

Ham and Cheddar Quiche

2 9-inch deep-dish pie shells
1 cup baked deli ham, shaved

½ cup green onions, thinly sliced
12 ounces (3 cups) cheddar cheese,
    grated

CUSTARD-
12 eggs
2 cups whipping cream

1 teaspoon salt
1 pinch red pepper

Spread half of ham in bottom of each pie shell. It should crumble apart easily if it has been thinly shaved. Add half of green onions and ¾ cup of cheese to each pie shell. Combine eggs, cream, salt, and pepper, mixing well. Pour half of mixture into each shell and top each with ¾ cup of cheese. Place quiches on a cookie sheet and bake at 350° for 35-40 minutes, until the middle has set. Each quiche can be wrapped with plastic wrap and placed in a 1-gallon plastic bag to be frozen. To heat - thaw completely and bake at 325° for 10 minutes, or until warmed. Serves 12-16.

Sandra Bruns
France Bruns Yoder '94
John Yoder '93
Charlotte Bruns Franta '96

Crustless Spinach Quiche

2	(10-ounce) packages frozen spinach	10	eggs
2	tablespoons butter	2	(10-ounce) packages Muenster cheese, grated
1	bunch green onions, chopped		Salt and pepper to taste

Cook spinach. Drain and put in skillet containing butter and onions. Cook until all water is absorbed. In large bowl, beat eggs and add cheese, salt, and pepper. Mix all ingredients together. Pour or spoon into 9×13-inch greased baking dish. Bake 1 hour at 350° or until knife comes out clean. Serves 10-12.

Pat Johnston, President ('79-'80),
Federation President ('82-'83)
Carol Nicholas '80
Robert Johnson '83

Onion Quiche

1	9-inch unbaked pie crust	3	eggs, beaten
2	large onions, thinly sliced	1	cup milk
2	tablespoons margarine	½	teaspoon salt
½	pound Swiss cheese, grated	⅛	teaspoon pepper
1	tablespoon flour		

Heat oven to 400°. Sauté onion in margarine until tender. Turn into pie crust. Toss cheese with flour, sprinkle over onion. Beat eggs well, stir in milk, salt, and pepper. Pour over cheese. Bake 20 minutes. Reduce heat to 300° and bake 25 more minutes or until done. Serves 6-8.

Sue Duncan
Nikki Duncan '97
Stephen Duncan '99

Quiche Brotagne

½ cup mayonnaise	3 ounces small shrimp, cooked and peeled
2 tablespoons flour	
2 eggs, beaten	2 cups Swiss cheese, grated
½ cup white wine	1 small celery rib, sliced
6 ounces crab meat, drained	5 green onions, chopped
	1 9-inch pie crust, baked

Blend mayonnaise, flour, eggs, and wine. Stir in crab meat, shrimp, cheese, celery, and onion. Pour into crust and bake at 350° for 35 minutes or until done. Serves 6.

Susan Saiter
Rob Saiter '90
David Saiter '98

Barley Casserole

½ cup butter or margarine	1 (1-ounce) package onion soup mix
16 ounces fine pearl barley (Quick Quaker is good)	
2 medium onions, chopped	2 cups water
1 cup slivered almonds	1 (8-ounce) can sliced mushrooms (or fresh, sliced)
2 (14½-ounce) cans chicken broth	1 (8-ounce) can water chestnuts, sliced

Melt butter in large saucepan. Add the barley and onions. Sauté until light golden. Add almonds, chicken broth, and onion soup mix. Sauté mushrooms in a little butter, adding to barley with water and water chestnuts. Stir well. Turn into a 9×11-inch greased casserole; cover and bake one hour at 350°. This may be prepared ahead of time and reheated. Freezes well. Serves 12. For a main entreé, add bite-sized baked or sauteéd chicken breast.

Lillian Gips
Bruce Holmes '78 (son)
Jeff Broaddus '98 (grandson)

Hearty Crock Pot Beans

1	(16-ounce) can pork and beans	8	slices bacon, chopped
1	(16-ounce) can navy beans, drained and washed	1	onion, chopped
		¾	cup ketchup
1	(16 ounce) can kidney beans, drained and washed	½	cup brown sugar
		2	tablespoons vinegar
½	pound hamburger	1	tablespoon prepared mustard
		2	tablespoons oil

Brown hamburger, bacon, and onion in oil. Combine with ketchup, brown sugar, vinegar, and mustard. Put all the beans in a crock pot. Add all other ingredients. Cook 1½ hours on high heat, no longer than 6½ hours on low heat. Serves 12.

Our family usually serves it as a main dish. Bread and a green salad complete the meal.

Martha Tucker
Jennifer Tucker '97

Garlic Cheese Grits

1	cup uncooked grits	2	eggs, beaten
1	(6-ounce) roll garlic-flavored processed cheese food, cubed	¾	cup milk
		¼	teaspoon white pepper
1	stick margarine	¾	cup cheddar cheese, grated

Cook grits as directed on package in 3-quart saucepan. While still hot, add garlic cheese and margarine. Stir well. Let cool slightly, and then add eggs, milk, and pepper. Pour into greased 8×8-inch pan. Bake at 325° for 35 minutes. Top with grated cheese and return to oven for 20 more minutes. Great accompaniment to ham!

Judy Boldt (Bob '68)
Laura Boldt '94
David Boldt '97

Favorite Macaroni and Cheese

½ pound (about 2 cups) macaroni
1 tablespoon butter
1 egg, beaten
1 teaspoon salt
1 teaspoon dry mustard
3 cups sharp cheddar cheese, grated
1 cup milk

Boil macaroni in water until tender. Drain thoroughly. Stir in butter and egg. Mix mustard and salt with 1 tablespoon hot water and add to milk. Add cheese to macaroni leaving enough to sprinkle on top. Pour into buttered casserole dish. Pour on milk and sprinkle with remaining cheese. Bake at 350° for about 45 minutes or until custard is set and top is crusty. Serves 4.

May serve as a meat substitute. Try this with stewed tomatoes.

Lynne Charbonneau
Scott Charbonneau '98
Mark Charbonneau '01

Spinach Burritos

16 ounces sour cream
2 (10½-ounce) cans cream of mushroom soup
2 (10-ounce) boxes chopped spinach, thawed and drained
2 pounds Monterey Jack cheese, grated
16 flour tortillas

Combine soup and spinach. Spread ½ mixture in a 9×13-inch casserole dish. Fill tortillas with cheese and lay on top. Cover with remaining spinach mixture. Top with remaining cheese. Bake at 350° until brown and bubbling. Marlene's Hot Sauce is a must with these burritos! Makes 12 servings.

Fabulous!

Paula Lively
Jim Lively '96
Carrie Lively Patterson '96
Troy Patterson '93

Away All Day Stew

2	pounds beef for stew	1	cup carrots, sliced
1	(10 ½-ounce) can	2	onions, chopped
	condensed tomato soup	1	teaspoon salt
½	soup can water		Dash pepper
1	potato, diced		Bay leaf (optional)
1	(16-ounce) can peas		
	(liquid included)		

Cover tightly, and put in a 300° oven for about 4 hours. Stir now and then if convenient. Remove bay leaf before serving. Serves 6-8.

Beverly Vespa
Jennifer Vespa '95

Beef and Green Beans

2	tablespoons soy sauce	½	pound French cut green beans,
1	teaspoon sugar		fresh or frozen
1	tablespoon cornstarch	1½	cups boiling water
1	tablespoon cooking sherry		
½	pound tender beef		
	(top round, sirloin),		
	thinly sliced, Chinese style		

Dredge beef in mixture of soy sauce, sugar, cornstarch, and sherry. Bring green beans and water to boil and cook several minutes. (Do not overcook - beans should be tender, but crisp.) Drain. Heat skillet (sprayed with oil). You may want a little oil, but it is not essential. Sauté the beef a few minutes, until almost done. Add drained beans and cook and stir until "juice" is thickened. Serve with rice. Serves 4. If there isn't enough liquid, add a mixture of ½ cup water, 1 tablespoon cornstarch, and 1 tablespoon soy sauce to the skillet. If you like it, next time add these ingredients when you add the green beans.

Kay Broaddus
Jeffrey Broaddus '98

Aggie Tree Sale Brisket

5-6 pound brisket	1 (3-ounce) bottle liquid smoke
Celery salt	Salt and pepper
Garlic salt	Worcestershire sauce
Onion salt	1 (6-ounce) bottle barbecue sauce

Pour liquid smoke over beef. Sprinkle on celery, onion, and garlic salt to taste. Cover with foil. Refrigerate overnight. Cover brisket with salt, pepper, and Worcestershire sauce (1-2 ounces). Bake, covered at 275° for 5 hours. Cover brisket with barbecue sauce. Bake 1 hour, uncovered. When done, pour all liquid in pan, add rest of barbecue sauce. Cook until reduced some. Serves 12-15.

Carol Smith, President ('92-'93) (Wilburn '60)
Stephanie Smith McVay '85
Martin McVay '83
Darryl Smith '90

Also submitted by Martha Tucker
Jennifer Tucker '97

Easy Pepper Steak

1 (0.87-ounce) package brown gravy mix	1 tablespoon oil
¾ cup water	1 medium onion, sliced
1 tablespoon soy sauce	2 bell peppers, cut in thin strips
1½ - 2 pounds flank steak or sirloin steak, thinly sliced diagonally	

Combine brown gravy mix, water, and soy sauce. Set aside. Heat oil in large skillet. Sauté meat 8-10 minutes, or until brown. Stir in brown gravy mixture, bring to a boil, and simmer 10 minutes. Add onion and bell peppers, simmer 10 minutes. Serve over rice, if desired. Serves 4.

Debbie Gilmore
Jimmy Gilmore '00

Rocky Mountain Brisket with Barbecue Sauce

4 pounds beef brisket, trimmed	2 tablespoons chili powder
1½ teaspoons salt	1 teaspoon crushed bay leaves
1½ teaspoons pepper	2 tablespoons liquid smoke

BARBECUE SAUCE-

3 tablespoons brown sugar	4 tablespoons Worcestershire sauce
1 (14-ounce) bottle ketchup	3 teaspoons dry mustard
½ cup water	2 teaspoons celery seed
2 tablespoons liquid smoke	6 tablespoons margarine
Salt and pepper to taste	¼ teaspoon cayenne pepper

Combine salt, pepper, chili powder, and bay leaves. Rub meat completely with liquid smoke. Place meat, fat side up, in a large roasting pan. Sprinkle dry seasoning mixture on top. Cover tightly and bake for 4 hours at 325°. Scrape seasoning off meat and serve with barbecue sauce.

Sauce - Combine all ingredients and bring to a boil, stirring occasionally. Cook for 10 minutes. Serves 10-12.

Susie Donahue
Megan Donahue '99
Ryan Donahue '02

Mandarin Steak

1 pound round steak, cut in 1-inch cubes	1 soup can of water
1 (10½-ounce) can cream of mushroom soup	⅛ cup soy sauce
	Pepper to taste

Brown meat in large skillet. Stir in remaining ingredients. Cover and simmer on low 1-2 hours. Serve over rice or noodles. Serves 2-3.

Judy Boldt (Bob '68)
Laura Boldt '94
David Boldt '97

Grillades and Grits

GRILLADES-

1¾ pounds veal or beef round, thinly sliced

2 teaspoons salt

1 teaspoon black pepper

¼ teaspoon cayenne pepper

5 cloves garlic, finely chopped

2 tablespoons butter

1 tablespoon olive oil

1 ½cups onions, coarsely chopped

1 cup celery (more or less to taste), chopped

½ cup bell pepper (red, if available), chopped

1 (16-ounce) can tomatoes

1¼ cups beef stock

2 tablespoons flour

GRITS-

3 cups cooked grits, not instant type

5 ⅓ tablespoons butter (not margarine)

1 egg

Salt and pepper to taste

Trim excess fat off the meat, cut into 2-inch squares. Pound each square of meat until almost double in size. Then, dip both sides of meat into spice mixture, then pound meat again until very tender. Brown the meat with the butter and oil in a hot skillet, add flour and turn heat down, brown VERY slowly, making a dark roux (like making gravy, but cooked more slowly and darker - not burned). Add the onions, celery, and bell pepper. Cook, stirring constantly until the vegetables are beginning to be tender. Add the tomatoes and stock, cover and simmer for about 30 minutes until the meat is tender and the entire dish (grillades) is a rich brown. Cook grits according to directions on package. When grits are done, and while still hot, add butter and one raw egg. Beat or stir well. Salt and pepper to taste. Serve with grillades. Most often, grillades are served over grits, but may be served as two dishes. Serves 6

A great Cajun breakfast or brunch entreé!! Enjoy! This recipe is often served at brunch in the French or Cajun region of Louisiana, especially in New Orleans.

Peggy Taylor (owner - Mansion on Main Bed and Breakfast in Texarkana and McKay House Bed and Breakfast in Jefferson)
Janna Gilbert '82
Jennifer Hogg '85
Steve Taylor '89

Pepper Steak (Crock Pot)

1½ pounds round steak	¼ cup soy sauce
½ teaspoon ginger	1 cup beef broth
½ teaspoon garlic salt	1 bell pepper, cut into strips

Cut round steak into ½-inch strips. Add meat to crock pot with the above ingredients. Cook on low, according to crock pot directions. Excellent served with rice.

Sharon Corry
Trey Corry '01

Enchiladas Dos (For Two)

½ pound hamburger	2 tablespoons flour
¼ cup onion, chopped	1 teaspoon chicken
½ teaspoon salt	bouillon granules
4 ounces taco sauce	²/₃ cup water
4 flour tortillas	2 tablespoons chopped
½ cup cheddar cheese,	green chilies
shredded and divided	¹/₃ cup sour cream
2 tablespoons margarine	

Brown hamburger and onion. Drain and stir in salt and taco sauce. Divide meat onto tortillas and top with ¼ cup cheese. Roll up and place in 8-inch square baking dish. Melt margarine and add flour and bouillon. Stir in water and cook until thickened. Add chilies and sour cream. Pour over tortillas and bake uncovered at 350° for 20-30 minutes. Sprinkle with cheese and return to oven for 5 minutes. Serves 2.

Susie Donahue
Megan Donahue '99
Ryan Donahue '02

Green Chili Enchiladas

1 large onion, chopped	1 (10½-ounce) can cream of
2 cloves garlic, minced	chicken soup
2 pounds ground beef	1 cup water
2 (4.5-ounce) cans chopped	1 cup milk
green chilies	1 (12-count) package corn tortillas,
1 pound Velveeta cheese	torn in piece.

Sauté onions, garlic, and ground beef. Remove from heat and drain. Add green chilies. In saucepan, combine cheese, soup, water, and milk. Heat until cheese melts. Alternate layers of tortillas (torn apart), meat mixture, and cheese mixture in 9×13-inch greased casserole dish. Bake at 400° until bubbly (15-20 minutes). Yield - 8 servings

Janice Dowlearn
Scott W. Dowlearn '01

Trudy's Easy Enchilada Casserole

1 (12-count) package corn	1 pound ground beef
tortillas	1 cup onion, minced
1 (10-ounce) can	3 cups American cheese, grated
enchilada sauce	

Brown ground meat, drain and set aside. Line a 1½-quart baking dish with tortillas. Sprinkle with onion. Cover with ½ of meat and ½ of cheese. Pour half of the enchilada sauce over the layers. Repeat the procedure. Bake in 350° oven for about 15 minutes, or until cheese melts. Serves 6-8 and is easily increased.

Trudy Lewis, President (El Paso Mothers' Club '87 - '88)
Stan Lewis '88

Hamburger and Baked Beans

1½ pounds lean ground beef
1 cup onion, finely chopped
1 (16-ounce) can pork and
beans

1 (8-ounce) can tomato sauce
¼ cup brown sugar
¼ cup ketchup
Salt and pepper to taste

In a large skillet, brown ground beef and sauté onions until tender. Mix in remaining ingredients. Cover and cook approximately 20-30 minutes. Can be frozen. To prepare for serving, thaw and bake in a 9×13-inch baking dish in a 350° oven 30-45 minutes. Serve with a vegetable, salad, and garlic toast. Serves 8-10.

Nina Cox, President ('96-'97)
Chris Cox '92

Hamburger Quiche

1 unbaked 9-inch pastry shell
½ pound ground beef
½ cup mayonnaise
½ cup milk
Dash of pepper

2 eggs
1 tablespoon cornstarch
1½ cups (½ pound) cheddar cheese,
chopped
½ cup green onion, chopped

Brown beef and drain. Set aside. Blend mayonnaise, milk, eggs, and cornstarch until smooth. Stir in beef, cheese, onion, and pepper. Pour into pastry shell and bake at 350° for 35-40 minutes, or until knife inserted in center comes out clean. Serves 6.

Susie Donahue
Megan Donahue '99
Ryan Donahue '02

Lasagna

1 pound ground beef	3 cups creamy cottage cheese
1 clove garlic, minced	OR ricotta cheese
2½ teaspoons salt	½ cup Parmesan cheese, grated
1 (16-ounce) can tomatoes	2 tablespoons parsley flakes
2 (6-ounce) cans tomato paste	2 eggs, beaten
1 (10-ounce) package	½ teaspoon pepper
lasagna noodles	16 ounces mozzarella cheese,
	sliced thin

Brown meat. Drain. Add garlic, 1 teaspoon salt, tomatoes, and tomato paste. Simmer uncovered 30 minutes, stirring occasionally. Cook noodles according to package directions. Drain. Rinse with cold water. Combine cottage cheese, Parmesan cheese, parsley flakes, eggs, 1½ teaspoon salt and pepper. Place half the noodles in greased 9×13-inch baking dish. Spread with half the cottage cheese filling. Add half the mozzarella cheese and half the meat sauce. Repeat layers. Bake at 375° for 30 minutes. Let stand 10 minutes before cutting. Serves 12.

Pat Hardi, President ('93-'94)
Steven Hardi '91

Also submitted by Anne Turano '84

VARIATION 1- Add 1 (10-ounce) package frozen spinach thawed, and drained to the cheese-egg mixture.

Betty Donahue, Grandmother
Megan Donahue '99
Ryan Donahue '02

VARIATION 2- Use 1 (32-ounce) jar of spicy spaghetti sauce instead of tomatoes/tomato paste sauce.

Mary Ellen Blankenship, President ('88-'89)
Clay Blankenship '82
Ruth Ellen Blankenship Heaton '90

Easy Spinach Lasagna (Low Fat)

1 (8-ounce) carton
  ricotta cheese
1 (10-ounce) box frozen
  chopped spinach,
  thawed and drained
1 egg
1 (26-ounce) jar spaghetti
  sauce

3 cups fat free mozzarella cheese,
  grated
1 (8-ounce) package lasagna
  noodles
1 cup water

Spray 9×13-inch baking dish with cooking spray. Mix together ricotta, spinach, and egg. In baking dish, layer $^1/_3$ jar spaghetti sauce, $^1/_3$ mozzarella, uncooked noodles, $^1/_3$ ricotta mixture, $^1/_3$ spaghetti sauce, $^1/_3$ mozzarella, uncooked noodles, remaining ricotta mixture, remaining spaghetti sauce, and remaining mozzarella cheese. Then pour 1 cup water all the way around the edge of the pan. Cover with foil. Bake at 350° for 1 hour, 15 minutes. Uncover for last 15 minutes. Serves 8-10.

Can be put together one day, refrigerated, and baked the next day. Don't forget to put the 1 cup of water around the edge just before baking.

Judy Boldt (Bob '68)
Laura Boldt '94
David Boldt '97

Cadet-Pleasing Meat Loaf

1½ pounds ground beef
  (chuck or ground round)
1 cup V-8 juice
¾ cup oats
1 egg, beaten

¼ cup onion, grated
½ teaspoon salt
1 teaspoon pepper
Ketchup to garnish

Mix all ingredients well. Turn into greased loaf pan. Bake at 350° for 1 hour. Decorate top with ketchup (either before or after baking). Serves 6-8. Even those who don't like meat loaf like this one. Can be cooked in the microwave for 30 minutes on 70% power (roast).

Judy Boldt (Bob '68)
Laura Boldt '94
David Boldt '97

Simple Manicotti

1 pound ground beef	2 (8-ounce) boxes
1 medium onion, diced	manicotti shells
Salt and pepper to taste	1 egg, beaten
1 (10-ounce) package frozen,	½ cup Parmesan cheese
chopped spinach, cooked	1 (8-ounce) package mozzarella
2 (26-ounce) jars spaghetti	cheese, shredded
sauce	

Brown meat with onion. Add salt and pepper to taste. Drain well. Press out as much liquid as possible from the spinach and mix with ground beef, egg, and Parmesan cheese. Fill shells and place in a 9×13-inch casserole dish, cover with sauce, top with Mozzarella, and bake covered at 350° about 30-45 minutes or until hot and bubbly. Serves 8.

Anna Sheffield
Ann Sheffield Kuebler '97
Kevin Kuebler '97

Rice/V-8 Meat Loaf

2 pounds ground meat	2 slices bread, soaked in milk
2 tablespoons Worcestershire	1 (12-ounce) can V-8 juice
sauce	2 cups instant rice
1 tablespoon Accent	1 (6-ounce) can tomato sauce
2 eggs	

Mix first 4 ingredients. Soak bread slices in milk, pull apart and add to meat mixture. Add V-8 juice and rice. Mix by hand and mold in loaf pan. Cover with tomato sauce. Bake at 325° for 1½ to 2 hours. Add potatoes in oven to bake for complete meal. Serves 6-8.

Dianne Mayfield, Federation Officer
Mitch Cogbill '93
Donna Cogbill '94

Sauce Topped Meat Loaf

4	slices stale bread, cubed	1	teaspoon salt
2	tablespoons Worcestershire sauce	1	teaspoon onion powder or minced onions
2	eggs, beaten	1½	pounds ground beef, crumbled
⅓	cup milk		

SAUCE-
½	cup ketchup	¼	teaspoon dry mustard
½	cup brown sugar		Dash nutmeg

Put bread cubes in a large bowl. Stir in Worcestershire, eggs, milk, salt, and onion powder. Stir in the ground beef. Put into a loaf pan. Bake at 350° for 55 minutes. Drain off the grease. Mix sauce and spoon over meat loaf. Bake an additional 10-15 minutes. Serves 6-8.

Nina Cox, President ('96-'97)
Chris Cox '92

Stuffed Meat Loaf

2	pounds ground beef	1	medium onion, diced
½	cup ketchup	1	cup celery, diced
1	(16-ounce) can whole kernel corn, drained		Salt and pepper to taste

Press or roll beef on waxed paper to ½ to ¾ inches thick. Combine ketchup and vegetables. Spread evenly over meat, then season. Roll meat up jelly roll style. Place roll on heavy aluminum foil and seal. Bake at 350° for 1 hour. Serves 6.

Super for camping. Bake on slow to medium coals, turning frequently for 1 hour.

Mrs. Alyne Smith

Mexican Casserole

1 (6.8-ounce) package chicken Rice-a-Roni	1 (10½-ounce) can cream of chicken soup
1 onion, chopped	1 (8-ounce) jar Jalapeño Cheese Whiz
2 (11-ounce) cans Mexicorn, drained	

Prepare rice and pasta mix as directed on package. Add remaining ingredients. Pour into 9×13-inch greased casserole pan and bake at 350° for about 30 minutes or until hot. Serves 8-10.

Can be heated in microwave. Add cooked chicken for main course casserole.

Linda Murphy
Kristina Murphy '91
Karin Murphy Harbour '93
Sean Harbour '92

Mexican Casserole with Cheese

1 pound uncooked ground round	1 onion, chopped
1 cup Doritos, crushed	1 cup Doritos, crushed
1 (15 ounce) can Ranch Style beans	1 (10 1/2-ounce) can cream of chicken soup
½ pound cheddar cheese, grated	1 (10-ounce) can Rotel tomatoes and green chilies

Layer ingredients in the order listed in a 9×13-inch casserole pan. Bake at 350° for 1 hour.

Sue Anderson, Federation Officer
Kirk Anderson '91
Amy Adamson Anderson '93

Super Mexican Casserole

1 (12-count) package
   flour tortillas
1½ pounds hamburger
1 onion, chopped
1 tablespoon chili powder
Salt and pepper

1 (15-ounce) can Ranch Style
   beans, undrained
1 pound Velveeta cheese, sliced
1 (10½-ounce) can cream of
   chicken soup
1 (10-ounce) can Rotel tomatoes
   and green chilies

Line bottom of greased 9×13-inch baking pan with 6 tortillas. In skillet, brown hamburger with onion, chili powder, and salt and pepper to taste. Drain and spread over tortillas. Cover with beans and slices of Velveeta. Top with 6 remaining tortillas. Combine soup and Rotel and pour over casserole. Cover with foil and bake at 350° for 1 hour. Serves 10-12.

Susie Donahue
Megan Donahue '99
Ryan Donahue '02

Tamale Vegetable Mexican Casserole

1 pound lean ground beef
½ medium onion, chopped
1 (8½-ounce) can
   green peas (drained)
1 (16-ounce) can whole
   kernel corn (drained)

1 (16-ounce) can chili with beans
1 (15-ounce) can tamales with
   liquid, unwrapped and cut up
1 cup cheddar cheese, grated
1 (15-ounce) can black olives,
   chopped

Brown ground meat and onion. Stir together peas, corn, chili, and tamales. Combine with meat. In 9×13-inch greased casserole dish, layer meat/vegetable mixture, cheese, olives. Bake at 300° for 1½ hours. Serves 6-8.

Helen Beasley, President ('91-'92)
Nancy Beasley '90

Patchwork Casserole

2 pounds ground beef	1 cup water
2 cups green pepper, chopped	1 teaspoon salt
1 cup onion, chopped	½ teaspoon basil
2 pounds frozen hash brown potatoes	¼ teaspoon pepper
	1 pound cheddar cheese, grated
2 (8-ounce) cans tomato sauce	¼ pound cheddar cheese,
2 (6-ounce) cans tomato paste	cut in thin slices

Brown meat. Drain. Add pepper and onion. Cook till tender. Add remaining ingredients, except cheese. Mix well. Spoon half of meat and potato mixture into 3-quart baking dish. Cover with grated cheese. Top with remaining meat and potato mixture. Cover with aluminum foil. Bake at 350° for 45 minutes. Uncover dish. Cut remaining cheese into decorative shapes and arrange in patchwork design on casserole. Let stand until cheese has melted. Serves 6-8.

Julie Thedford (Marvin '65)
Mary Helen Ramsey '93
Clay Ramsey '93
Katherine Thedford '98

Stuffed Bell Peppers

5 bell peppers	1 teaspoon oregano
1½ to 2 pounds lean ground beef	½ teaspoon crushed sage
1 cup cracker crumbs	Salt
¾ cup instant rice	

SAUCE-

1 (4-ounce) can tomato paste	4-5 tablespoons barbecue sauce
1½ cans water	1 teaspoon sugar
½ cup ketchup	

Combine sauce ingredients and set aside. Cut off tops of peppers and remove seeds. Place the peppers in boiling water for 5 minutes only. Remove from water and let peppers cool. Fill with mixture of beef, cracker crumbs, rice, oregano, and sage. Place in medium baking dish and cover peppers with sauce. Bake at 400° for approximately 1 hour. Do not overcook as peppers will be tough. Serves 5.

Ezell Hunt, Grandmother
Nancy Beasley '90

Italian Rice Casserole

1 cup rice, uncooked	1 cup ricotta cheese
3 egg whites, slightly beaten	1 pound ground beef
²/₃ cup Parmesan cheese, divided	1 (15½-ounce) jar spaghetti sauce
2 cups mozzarella cheese, shredded	1 tablespoon oregano

Cook rice, according to package directions. Cool slightly. Add egg whites and ¹/₃ cup Parmesan cheese to rice. Mix and set aside. Combine mozzarella, ricotta, and ¹/₃ cup Parmesan cheese. Mix and set aside. Brown hamburger meat. Drain fat and set aside. Add spaghetti sauce and oregano. Heat through. Spoon ½ of rice mixture into a greased 3-quart casserole dish. Cover with half the cheese mixture. Top with ½ meat sauce. Repeat layers. Sprinkle Parmesan on top. Bake at 375° for 20 minutes until heated through. Serve 6-8.

Kathy Welty
Mark Welty '99

Shepherd's Pie

1 onion, chopped	½ teaspoon pepper
2 tablespoons margarine	¼ teaspoon thyme
2 carrots, chopped	¼ teaspoon rosemary
1 cup mushrooms, chopped	2 teaspoons soy sauce
1 pound ground lamb	½ cup red cooking wine or sherry
1 pound ground beef	4 servings prepared mashed potatoes
1 (6-ounce) can tomato paste	
1 (14-ounce) can beef broth	1 (15-ounce) can green peas (optional)
1 teaspoon salt	

Sauté onion, carrots, and mushrooms in margarine. Add meats and cook until browned. Add tomato paste, broth, and seasonings. Cover and cook for 2 hours. Drain off liquid or thicken with flour. Put into a 9×13-inch casserole and cover with mashed potatoes. Dot with margarine and place under broiler to brown. (A layer of green peas can be put on top of meat mixture before topping with mashed potatoes.) Serves 12.

Betty Donahue, Grandmother
Megan Donahue '99
Ryan Donahue '02

Spanish Ground Beef and Rice

1 pound ground beef	1 (16-ounce) can Ranch Style
1 (15-ounce) can Spanish rice	beans
	Cheddar cheese, grated (optional)

Brown meat and drain. Add rice and beans and stir. Heat through in skillet.
Serve from pan or put into 8-inch square casserole and top with grated cheese.
Place in 350° oven until cheese is melted. Serves 4.

Gene Jacob
Sarah Jacob Kielty '94

American Stroganoff

1 pound ground beef	1 teaspoon paprika
1 (10½-ounce) can cream of	½ tablespoon dried minced onion
chicken soup	1 cup sour cream
1 (3-ounce) can mushrooms	1 (9-ounce) package noodles,
1 tablespoon flour	cooked

Brown ground beef in large skillet. Drain grease and add flour and onions.
Stir in cream of chicken soup, paprika, and mushrooms. Simmer 6 minutes.
Prepare noodles according to package directions. When ready to serve, stir
sour cream into stroganoff. Pour stroganoff over noodles. Serves 6.

Cindie Deasey
Beth Williamson '02

Tortilla Casserole

2 pounds lean ground beef	1 (10½ -ounce) can mushroom
1 large onion, chopped	soup
1½ pounds mild	1 (10½ -ounce) can cream of
cheddar cheese, grated	chicken soup
1 (10-ounce) can Rotel	1 (12-count) package flour
tomatoes and green chilies	tortillas, broken in small pieces

Brown meat in skillet. Add onion and cook until meat is done. Combine the
rest of the ingredients. Mix together with cooked meat and onion. Pour into
9×13-inch greased casserole. Cover. Bake at 350° for about 30 minutes.
Serves 6.

Debbie Gilmore
Jimmy Gilmore '00

Texas Aggie Casserole
(Ground Beef with Noodles)

1½	pounds ground beef	2	cloves garlic
1	(16-ounce) can tomatoes	1	(6-ounce) package medium
1	(8-ounce) can tomato sauce		egg noodles
Pepper to taste		1	cup sour cream
2	teaspoons salt	1	(3-ounce) package cream cheese
2	teaspoons sugar	6	green onions, chopped
1	tablespoon oregano	1	cup cheddar cheese, grated

In a large pot, cook together beef, tomatoes, tomato sauce, pepper, salt, sugar, oregano, and garlic. Cook noodles and drain. Mix noodles with sour cream, cream cheese, and onions. In greased 9×13-inch casserole, put layers of meat, noodle mixture, and grated cheese. Repeat. Bake at 350° for 35 minutes. Serves 5-6.

I usually triple this recipe. Any not used the first time freezes very well.

Cora Nell Sneary
Loy E. Sneary '72

Baked Chicken with Almonds

1	chicken breast	1	teaspoon parsley, chopped
½	teaspoon curry	1	tablespoon mushrooms, sliced
Dash garlic powder		1	tablespoon slivered almonds
1	teaspoon green onion,	1	tablespoon fresh lemon juice
	chopped	1	tablespoon butter

Place 1 chicken breast in the center of a square of aluminum foil. Season each serving of chicken breast with the rest of the ingredients. Enclose the chicken in the aluminum foil and place in a casserole dish. Bake at 350° for 45 minutes. Unwrap and place mixture on top of a bed of rice.

Sharon Corry
Trey Corry, '01

Chicken Breasts in Phyllo

1½ cups mayonnaise
1 cup green onions, chopped
⅓ cup lemon juice
2 teaspoons dry tarragon
2 cloves garlic, minced
12 chicken breast halves,
   boned, skinned

Salt and pepper to taste
24 sheets phyllo dough
1⅓ cups butter, melted
⅓ cup Parmesan cheese,
   freshly grated

Combine first 5 ingredients to make a sauce. Lightly sprinkle chicken with salt and pepper. Keep package of phyllo covered with a damp cloth. Place a sheet of phyllo on a working surface. Quickly brush with melted butter (about 2 teaspoons). Place second sheet on top of first. Brush with butter. Spread about 1½ tablespoons sauce on each side of breast (3 tablespoons in all). Place breast in one corner of buttered phyllo sheet. Fold corner over breast, then fold sides over and roll breast up in the sheets to form a package. Place in an ungreased 9×13-inch baking dish. Repeat with remaining breasts and phyllo. Brush packets with rest of butter and sprinkle with Parmesan cheese. At this point, the dish may be refrigerated or frozen (tightly sealed). Thaw completely before baking. Bake at 375° for 30-40 minutes, or until golden. Serve hot. Serves 12.

Kay Broaddus
Jeffrey Broaddus '98

Chicken Breasts Roll Ups

4 chicken breasts, boneless
   and skinless,
4 thin slices, Carl Buddig
   deli-style roast beef
2 (10½-ounce) cans cream of
   chicken soup

½ pint sour cream
8 bacon slices
Salt

Wash chicken breasts and salt lightly. Wrap beef slices around chicken breasts. Mix chicken soup and ½ pint sour cream. Pour over chicken breast in casserole dish. Put bacon slices on top. Bake at 275° for 3 hours, uncovered. Serves 4.

Anna Sheffield
Ann Sheffield Kuebler '97
Kevin Kuebler '97

Chicken with Dried Beef

1	(2.25-ounce) jar of sliced, dried beef	1	(10½-ounce) can cream of mushroom soup
6	slices bacon	1	pint sour cream
6	chicken breasts, boned	1	(3-ounce) package cream cheese
Pepper to taste		1	(4-ounce) can sliced mushrooms

Place dried beef (no salt), crumbled, in bottom of buttered 9-inch square casserole dish. Wrap bacon around the chicken breasts and sprinkle with pepper. Lay chicken breasts in casserole. Combine soup, sour cream, and cream cheese in a blender. Stir in mushrooms and pour mixture over chicken breasts in casserole. Cover with foil and cook in 300° oven for 2 hours. Remove foil and cook for 1 more hour. Serves 6.

This is delicious. People who don't care for chicken have told me that they love it!

Martha Tucker
Jennifer Tucker '97

JaNahn's Chicken Broccoli Casserole

1	chicken	1	cup uncooked rice
1	teaspoon oregano	1	(2-ounce) jar pimentos, drained
1	(10½-ounce) can cream of mushroom soup	1	(9-ounce) package frozen broccoli
1	cup Velveeta cheese, cubed		

Cook chicken until it falls off the bone in salt water and oregano. Remove chicken from bones and cube meat. Cook rice in chicken broth. Cook broccoli and drain. Mix all together in 9×13-inch greased pan. Bake 350° for 30 minutes. Serves 8.

JaNahn Rodriguez, President ('97-'98)
David Rodriguez '94
Cindy Rodriguez '95
Dan Rodriguez '99

Chicken Cacciatore

2¹/₃ pounds of chicken pieces	1 (14-ounce) jar spaghetti sauce
1 medium onion, chopped	½ teaspoon dried basil
2 tablespoons margarine	

Brown chicken pieces skin side down over low heat. Cook chicken 10 minutes each side, making sure the chicken is cooked. Sauté onions in margarine until soft. Stir in sauce and basil. Cover and simmer 20 minutes. Serve with spaghetti and garlic bread. Serves 4-6.

Christina Trevino (David '72)
Maria '00

Continental Chicken Casserole

½ cup margarine, melted	10 - 12 corn tortillas, cut in strips
2 bunches green onions (chop all of it)	1 (10½-ounce) can cream of mushroom soup
1 (4-ounce) can green chilies, diced	1 (10½-ounce) can cream of chicken soup
1 (8-ounce) can water chestnuts (sliced)	1 pound Monterey Jack cheese, grated
3 cups cooked chicken, diced	

Sauté onion in melted margarine. Add soups, water chestnuts, chilies, and chicken (including the liquids from chilies and chestnuts). Spray 9×13-inch casserole dish with cooking spray. Layer chicken, tortillas, and cheese, ending with cheese. Bake in 325° oven for 30 minutes. Serves 10.

I serve French's Green Bean Casserole with the above casserole.

Rachel Gonzales, Federation President ('83 - '84) (Ralph '53)
Col. Robert F. Gonzales '68

Swiss Chicken Cutlets

10 boneless chicken breasts	½ teaspoon salt
Salt	⅛ teaspoon pepper
2 eggs, beaten	2½ cups milk
1 cup fine dry bread crumbs	½ cup dry white wine
¼ cup cooking oil	½ cup (4-ounces) processed Swiss
3 tablespoons butter or	cheese, shredded
margarine	Avocado slices and tomato wedges
¼ cup all purpose flour	to garnish

Place each chicken breast between two pieces of waxed paper. Pound to ¼-inch thickness. Sprinkle with salt. Dip into beaten egg, then crumbs. Heat 2 tablespoons oil and brown chicken cutlets a few at a time for about 2 minutes per side and set aside. In a saucepan, melt butter, blend in flour, salt, and pepper. Add milk and cook, stirring until thick and bubbling. Remove from heat. Add the wine. Pour half into 9×13-inch baking dish. Place cutlets on top of sauce and cover with the rest of the sauce. Cover with foil and leave in refrigerator overnight. Bake, covered at 350° for 50 minutes. Remove from oven. Sprinkle with the Swiss cheese and bake 10 minutes, uncovered. Garnish with the avocado and tomato slices. Serves 10.

Sandra Hurley
Jonathan Hurley '98

Chicken Divan

4-5 chicken breasts	1 cup cheddar cheese, grated
2 (10-ounce) boxes of	1 cup bread crumbs
broccoli, chopped	2 teaspoons lemon juice
1 (10½-ounce) can cream	½ teaspoon curry powder
of chicken soup	2 tablespoons butter
1 cup mayonnaise	

Boil chicken in seasoned water. Cut into bite-sized pieces. Cook broccoli in microwave and drain. Spray 9×13-inch pan with cooking spray. Put broccoli in bottom of pan. Cover with chicken. Mix soup, mayonnaise, and cheese together and pour over chicken. Melt butter and pour over bread crumbs. Sprinkle buttered bread crumbs over mixture. Bake at 350° for 45 minutes. Serves 12.

Cindy Rodriguez '95

Chicken Enchilada Casserole

3	cups chicken, cooked	1	tablespoon chili powder
1	(10½-ounce) can cream of chicken soup	1	teaspoon garlic powder
		12	corn tortillas
1	(10-ounce) can Rotel tomatoes with chilies, drained	3	cups Monterey Jack cheese, grated
		8	ounces tortilla chips, crumbled
1	(14½-ounce) can chicken broth		

In a large saucepan, heat together the soup, Rotel tomatoes, broth, and seasonings. Add chicken. Pour a little of this mixture into a 9×13-inch greased baking dish. Layer the tortillas, sauce, and cheese until it is all used. Top with cheese and crumbled tortilla chips. Bake at 350° for 20 minutes, until bubbly. Serves 6-8.

Kathy Welty
Mark Welty '99

Green Salsa Chicken Enchiladas

4	chicken breast halves, cooked, deboned, and cut in 1-inch pieces	1	cup water
		1	(4-ounce) can green salsa
1	(8-ounce) package cream cheese, softened	1	cup whipping cream
		15 - 18	corn tortillas
1	small onion, finely chopped	2	tablespoons oil
Salt		8	ounces Monterey Jack cheese, grated
1	pound tomatillos		

Preheat oven to 350°. In a large bowl, mix chicken, cream cheese, and onion. Season to taste with salt and set aside. In a large saucepan, cook tomatillos in water over low heat until tender, about 10 minutes. Cool. Drain. Then liquefy in blender for approximately 1 minute. Transfer to medium bowl. Add salsa and cream. Whisk until well blended. Set aside. In a medium skillet, soften tortillas in hot oil. Drain well. Place one tablespoon tomatillo sauce in a tortilla with 1 tablespoon chicken mixture. Roll and place in 9×13-inch baking dish, seam side down. Repeat with remaining tortillas. Pour remaining sauce over enchiladas and top with grated cheese. Bake for 30 minutes. Serves 6 - 8.

Vara Buchanan
Adie Buchanan '01

Sour Cream Chicken Enchiladas

12 flour tortillas

FILLING-

3 cups cooked chicken, chopped	¼ to ½ cup onions, chopped (may be cooked with chicken)
1 (4-ounce) can green chilies, chopped	1 cup Monterey Jack cheese, grated

SAUCE-

3 tablespoons margarine	2 cups sour cream
3 tablespoons flour	1 cup Monterey Jack cheese
1 cup chicken broth (may use broth from cooking chicken)	

Mix first 4 ingredients and set aside. Melt margarine in saucepan. Add flour and salt. Add chicken broth and stir until thickened. Remove from heat and add cheese. Stir until melted. Add sour cream. Preheat oven to 350°. Grease 9×13-inch casserole pan. Soften tortillas by heating in microwave. Place approximately ¼ cup filling in each tortilla and roll. Place seam side down in pan. Top with sauce. Separate filled tortillas so that the sauce fills between the tortillas. Sprinkle top with cayenne pepper, paprika, or place sliced jalapeño peppers on top. Bake 20-30 minutes until slightly brown and cheese is melted. Serves 6

Janice Myers, President ('95-'96) (Tony '65)
Greg Myers '92
Cindy Myers Crook '96

Oven Fried Spicy Chicken

4-6 chicken breasts, skinless and boneless	¼ teaspoon oregano
½ cup mayonnaise	½ teaspoon garlic salt
1 cup crushed corn flakes	¼ teaspoon pepper
	¼ cup Parmesan, grated

Mix dry ingredients together. Brush both sides of chicken breasts with mayonnaise. Coat chicken with corn flake mixture. Bake, uncovered in a 9×13-inch baking dish at 350° for 50-60 minutes until golden brown. Serves 4-6.

Marilyn McBride
Shannon McBride '98

Garden Herb Roasted Chicken

1 whole chicken	Onion powder
Garlic powder	Seasoning salt

FRESH HERBS-

1 large sprig rosemary	1 small sprig oregano
1 large sprig basil	1 small sprig thyme
1 small sprig parsley	

Prepare chicken for baking. Remove and discard innards. Rinse chicken. Pat dry. Sprinkle generously inside and out with garlic powder, onion powder, and seasoning salt. Place sprigs of herbs inside chicken. Bake in baking pan in 350° oven for 1 hour, till juices run clear. Serves 4.

Gloria Gilpin, President ('98-'99), (Bobby '62)
Wes Gilpin '93
Katherine Gilpin '97

Chicken Italiano

2½ - 3 pounds chicken	1 cup water
1 (0.5-ounce) envelope	Salt
spaghetti sauce mix	3 tablespoons shortening or oil
1 (8-ounce) can seasoned	
tomato sauce	

Sprinkle chicken with salt. Brown slowly in shortening. Drain. Combine everything else and pour on top of chicken. Cover and cook very slowly for 20 - 30 minutes until chicken is tender. Serve with noodles. If you want more sauce, add more tomato sauce and/or water, but not more of the spaghetti sauce mix.

JaNahn Rodriguez, President ('97-'98)
David Rodriguez '94
Cindy Rodriguez '95
Dan Rodriguez '99

Mexican Chicken With Salsa

SALSA-

1   small avocado, peeled, pitted, and coarsely chopped

Juice of 1 lime

1   small tomato, coarsely chopped

2   tablespoons cooking oil (best with sesame oil)

½   cup chopped red Spanish onion

2   tablespoons fresh cilantro (chopped)

Salt and red pepper flakes to taste

MEAT-

2   whole chicken breasts

1   lime

2   tablespoons cooking oil (best with sesame oil)

2   cloves garlic, cut in half

½   cup chicken stock

Salt and red pepper flakes to taste

GARNISH-

1   head of leaf lettuce, separated into leaves and sliced into long thin strips

4   fresh cilantro sprigs

8   corn tortillas, warmed

1   lime

To make salsa, combine the avocado, lime juice, tomato, oil, onion, cilantro, salt, and pepper flakes in a bowl. Stir to mix well. Set aside. To make chicken, half the chicken breasts, skin, and debone them. Trim off excess fat. Cut into 1-inch lengthwise strips. Place in separate bowl, squeeze juice of 1 lime over the chicken. Toss gently. To cook, warm the oil in a large sauté pan over medium heat. Add the garlic and sauté until soft, about 1-2 minutes. Discard the garlic. Add the chicken and sauté, turning the pieces, about 1 minute on each side. Place on a warmed plate, and keep warm. Pour off the oil from the pan. Add chicken stock to the pan, bring to a boil over high heat. Deglaze the pan by stirring gently to dislodge any browned bits. Cook to reduce liquid by about ½. Add salt and pepper flakes. Presentation - Arrange lettuce strips on individual plates, top with chicken strips. Pour the warm sauce over the chicken, then add some salsa to each plate. Cut 1 lime into quarters. Garnish each plate with a quarter of a lime and a cilantro sprig. Serve with warm tortillas. Serves 4.

Quisha Albert '00

Jamaican Chicken

6   chicken breasts,
    boneless and skinless
1   tablespoon butter or
    margarine
1-2 tablespoons brown sugar
1   large onion, chopped
1   medium green pepper,
    chopped
1   (16-ounce) can whole
    tomatoes with juice
1   tablespoon red wine
    vinegar
½   pound mushrooms, thinly sliced
2   teaspoons salt
1   teaspoon pepper
½   teaspoon dried thyme
1   bay leaf
1   tablespoon cornstarch

In a large, heavy skillet, heat butter. Add sugar and stir until bubbly. Add chicken and brown on both sides. Adjust heat so butter won't scorch. Add onion and cook until transparent. Stir in remaining ingredients. Cover and simmer, turning chicken occasionally, until chicken is tender. Cook 35-40 minutes. To thicken sauce, mix 1 tablespoon cornstarch with a little water and stir into sauce. Serve with rice. Serves 4-6.

Helen Beasley, President ('91-'92)
Nancy Beasley '90

Microwave Chicken

6   chicken breast halves,
    boneless and skinless
4   tablespoons butter, melted
2   teaspoons lemon pepper
1   (2.5-ounce) jar sliced
    mushrooms, drained
1   (2.8-ounce) can French-fried
    onion rings
½   cup Swiss cheese, grated

Roll chicken in a mixture of butter and lemon pepper. Place in a microwaveable dish, cover, and cook on high for 5-6 minutes. Turn the chicken over and top with mushrooms. Cook on high 6 minutes more. Pour over with onion rings and grated cheese. Cook on high for 3 minutes. Serves 6.

Mary Aasterud, President ('94-'95)
Valerie Aasterud McLaughlin '94

CORPS QUILT

Texas A&M Mothers' Clubs were established to lend a "mother's touch" to the lives of the students. Reminiscent of the days when each child was given a handmade quilt upon leaving home, the Corps of Cadets Quilt represents the love Aggie Moms have for all Texas A&M students.

Major General Thomas G. Darling approached the Dallas County Aggie Moms in 1993 with the idea of a Corps quilt representing the Spirit of the Corps and highlighting its major traditions. The Moms gave the idea life and presented the quilt to the Sanders Corps Center in October, 1994.

The quilt is designed using eighteen emblems, with the brick patterned arches of the entrance to the Corps housing area as the border. The center design is of the Corps brass. The quilt is 76 inches square, commemorating Texas A&M's beginning in 1876. Patches worn by cadets signifying the branches of the Corps plus the drill and ceremony patch anchor the four corners.

Other details include the diamonds filling the center square, representing the commanding officers of each Corps unit, and Texas stars in each arch. Fur from Reveille V and Reveille VI was used as stuffing under the square showing the mascot. Hearts, representing Aggie Mom love, are entwined into the tiny stitches of the quilting pattern.

Each square was made by a Mom with special family ties to each emblem. Tireless effort by Texas A&M students, dads, and grandparents makes the work of the Aggie Moms truly family-oriented. Even Major General Darling spent several hours quilting!

"Everyone knows the important role that
Aggie Moms have played in the support of the Corps in
Aggieland, but this latest gift from the
Dallas Aggie Moms shows that support in a very special way."

Joe Fenton, '58, curator of the
Sanders Corps of Cadets Center

Corps Quilt Photo
By
Richard Korcynznski

No Work Baked Chicken

3 tablespoons plus
1 teaspoon apricot or peach jam
2 tablespoons prepared mustard
¼ cup nuts, chopped (cashews, pecans, macadamias)

¼ cup plain dry bread crumbs
2 tablespoons flour
4 large chicken breasts, boneless and skinless

Combine 2 tablespoons jam, mustard, nuts, and bread crumbs to form a thick paste. Lightly flour chicken and spread 1 teaspoon jam on each chicken breast, covering both sides. Place in baking dish and spread seasoned paste on top. Bake at 350° for 30 minutes. Place under broiler to crisp and brown, 1-2 minutes. Serves 4.

Susie Donahue
Megan Donahue '99
Ryan Donahue '02

Chicken Parmesan

4 chicken breasts (boneless, skinless)
2 eggs, slightly beaten
¼ teaspoon salt
⅛ teaspoon pepper
¾ cup fine dry seasoned bread crumbs
½ cup oil
2 cups tomato sauce

¼ teaspoon sweet basil
⅛ teaspoon garlic powder (if garlic salt is used, omit ¼ teaspoon salt)
1 tablespoon butter
1 (8-ounce) package mozzarella cheese slices
½ cup Parmesan cheese

Pound chicken until about ¼-inch thick. Mix egg, salt, and pepper, and dip chicken in egg and then in crumbs. Heat oil in skillet and brown chicken on both sides. Place chicken in a large 9×13-inch baking dish. Heat tomato sauce, basil, and garlic in pan (about 10 minutes). Stir in butter and pour over chicken. Sprinkle with Parmesan cheese. Cover and bake at 350° for 30 minutes. Uncover and place mozzarella cheese over chicken. Return to oven uncovered and bake until the cheese melts. Serves 6-8.

Sandra Bruns
Frances Bruns Yoder '94
John Yoder '93
Charlotte Bruns Franta '96

Chicken Pasta Parmesan

2	tablespoons vegetable oil	2	tablespoons milk
1	pound skinless, boneless chicken breasts, cut into cubes	1	tablespoon dry sherry
		1	cup fresh mushrooms, sliced
¼	cup onion, chopped	1	cup broccoli flowerets, cooked
1	(10½-ounce) can cream of broccoli OR cream of chicken soup	½	cup Parmesan cheese, grated
		1	(7-ounce) package spaghetti, cooked

In 10-inch skillet over medium heat, in hot oil, cook chicken and onion until chicken is browned and onion is tender. Stir in soup, milk, and sherry. Add mushrooms, broccoli, and ½ cup cheese. Reduce heat to low. Cover, cook 10 minutes or until chicken is no longer pink, stirring occasionally. Serve over spaghetti. Serve with additional cheese, if desired. Serves 6.

One-half cup thinly sliced green and sweet red peppers can be substituted for the broccoli.

> *Julie Thedford (Marvin '65)*
> *Mary Helen Ramsey '93*
> *Clay Ramsey '93*
> *Katherine Thedford '98*

Perfect Chicken Casserole

1	cup rice, cooked	1	medium onion, diced
3	cups chicken, cooked and diced	1	(10 ½-ounce) can cream of celery soup
1	(3-ounce) jar pimentos, chopped	1	cup mayonnaise
			Salt and pepper to taste
½	cup ripe olives, diced	2	cups green peas, cooked
1	(8-ounce) can sliced water chestnuts	½	cup cheddar cheese, grated

Combine chicken, pimentos, olives, water chestnuts, and onion with cooked rice and blend well. Combine soup and mayonnaise and stir into rice mixture. Add salt and pepper. Stir in green peas. Pour into a 2½ - 3-quart casserole. Bake at 350° for 30 minutes. Sprinkle grated cheese over top of casserole and bake long enough to melt cheese. Serves 6-8.

> *Anna Sheffield*
> *Ann Sheffield Kuebler '97*
> *Kevin Kuebler '97*

Poppy Seed Chicken

2	tubes Ritz crackers, crushed	2	(10½-ounce) cans cream of
1¾	sticks margarine, melted		chicken soup
2	tablespoons poppy seed	1	cup sour cream
4-6	chicken breasts, boneless, cooked, and cut into bite-sized pieces		

Mix crackers, margarine, and poppy seed. Press half of mixture into greased 9-inch square casserole dish. Mix chicken, soup, and sour cream. Pour over crust. Top with remaining crust mixture. Bake at 350° for 35 minutes or until golden brown. Serves 6.

Pat Hardi, President ('93-'94)
Steven Hardi '91, '94

Also submitted by Cindy Rodriguez '95

Easy Chicken Pot Pie

4	chicken breasts, cooked and diced	2	(10½-ounce) cans creamy chicken mushroom soup
1	(20-ounce) bag frozen vegetables, cooked and drained	2	deep dish pie crusts, thawed
			Garlic powder to taste
			Salt and pepper to taste

Boil chicken breasts until tender. Drain and dice. Mix vegetables and soup. Season with garlic powder, salt, and pepper. Pour into pie shell and top with second shell. Seal edges and cut slits to let out steam. Bake at 375° until crust is golden brown (30-45 minutes) and pie is bubbly.

Anna Sheffield
Ann Sheffield Kuebler '97
Kevin Kuebler '97

Lebanese Chicken and Rice

2 pounds chicken breasts, boneless and skinless	¼ teaspoon black pepper
5-6 cups water	2 tablespoons lemon juice
1 yellow onion, sliced	1 tablespoon oil
¼ teaspoon ground cinnamon	¼ pound slivered almonds or pine nuts
¼ teaspoon ground allspice	½ cup butter
¼ teaspoon ground cloves	2 cups rice
1 tablespoon salt	

Wash the chicken. Place it in a Dutch oven. Add water to cover the chicken. Add peeled and sliced yellow onion, cinnamon, allspice, cloves, salt, pepper, and lemon juice. Cook over medium heat for 35 minutes. Remove from heat. Strain and save some of the chicken stock. You may add some salt and pepper and other spices if you wish. Drain and place chicken aside. In a small skillet, heat oil. Add the almonds and stir until golden. In a medium pan, heat the butter. Add rice, salt, pepper, and water. (For extra flavor, you could save the strained stock and use instead of water to cook the rice.) Cover and cook 20-30 minutes. Serve on a large round or oval platter. Place the rice, then add the chicken. You may break each chicken breast into 2 or 3 pieces and place in the center or spread all around platter. Garnish with browned almonds or pine nuts, small sprigs of fresh parsley, and whole radish in center. Makes 12-15 servings.

Nu Helal
Hunter Helal '96

Chicken and Rice Casserole

2 cups Minute Rice	1 (7-ounce) can mushrooms
1 (10½-ounce) can cream of chicken soup	1 (2-ounce) jar pimentos
	1 (15-ounce) can green peas
1 (10½-ounce) can cream of mushroom soup	1 (12-ounce) can chicken chunks
1 (10½-ounce) can cream of celery soup	

Stir all ingredients together. Pour into a greased 9×13-inch casserole dish. Bake at 350° for 30 minutes. Serves 6-8.

Cindy Etier
Emily Etier '01

Chicken/Sausage and Rice Casserole

2½-3-pounds chicken	1 cup onion, chopped
2 tablespoons olive oil	2 large garlic cloves, minced
½ pound smoked sausage, cut into ½-inch pieces	1 teaspoon salt
	¼ teaspoon saffron or turmeric
2 (10½-ounce) cans condensed chicken broth	¼ teaspoon crushed red pepper
	1 bay leaf
1 (14½-ounce) can tomatoes, undrained and cut up	1 (10-ounce) package frozen peas
	2 cups rice
⅔ cup water	⅓ cup black olives

Brown chicken in oil. Spoon off all but 2 tablespoons drippings. Add sausage, tomatoes, water, onion, garlic, salt, saffron, pepper, and bay leaf. Cover and cook over low heat 30 minutes. Add remaining ingredients and cook 30 minutes longer. Yield - 8 servings.

JaNahn Rodriguez, President ('97-'98)
David Rodriguez '94
Cindy Rodriguez '95
Dan Rodriguez '99

Chicken and Wild Rice Casserole

8 slices bacon, uncooked	2 (10½-ounce) cans golden mushroom soup
8 chicken breasts, boneless and skinless	1½ cups water
2 (6.2-ounce) boxes Uncle Ben's Long Grain and Wild Rice Mix with seasoning	Salt and pepper to taste

Place bacon in bottom of 9×13-inch baking dish. Sprinkle wild rice over bacon. Place seasoned chicken breasts over rice. Mix 1½ cups water with the soup and pour over chicken breasts. Top with seasoning packets from the rice. Cover. Cook at 350° for 1½ hours. Serves 8.

This was served at an Aggie Mom Luncheon.

Maria Wagner
Linda Wagner '96

Chicken Spaghetti

1 whole chicken	½ cup green bell pepper, chopped
Salt to taste	2 cups celery, chopped
½ teaspoon pepper	1 (28-ounce) can diced tomatoes
1 teaspoon seasoned salt	1 (8-ounce) can mushrooms
¾ teaspoon garlic powder	1 (4-ounce) jar pimento, drained
½ teaspoon oregano	and chopped
1 cup onion, chopped	1 pound thin spaghetti
	1 cup cheese, grated (optional)

Cover chicken with water. Add seasonings and cook until well done. Debone and cut in small pieces. Cook stock down to about 4-5 cups and save. In large skillet, sauté onions, pepper, and celery in small amount of oil until soft. Add tomatoes and simmer 25 minutes. Add mushrooms and pimentos. Cook spaghetti (broken into small lengths) according to directions on package. Add onion-celery mixture to spaghetti. Add chicken and enough broth to make slightly soupy. Add cheese and heat, stirring until cheese melts. Serves 12-15.

Janice Myers, President ('95-'96) (Tony '65)
Greg Myers '92
Cindy Myers Crook '96

Easy Crock Pot Chicken

⅔ cup flour	1 (2½ - 3-pound) chicken, cut up
1 teaspoon dry sage	and skinned
1 teaspoon dry basil	2-4 tablespoons butter or margarine
1 teaspoon seasoned salt	2 cups chicken broth

Combine flour and seasonings in shallow large bowl. Coat chicken, saving remaining flour. In a large skillet, melt butter and brown chicken on all sides. Transfer to crock pot. Add ¼ cup seasoned flour to the skillet (discard the rest) and stir until smooth. When it bubbles, add chicken broth and bring to boil. Cook 1 minute, then pour over chicken. Cover and cook in crock pot 2-2½ hours on high (300°-340°), until chicken juice is clear. Serves 4-6.

Serve with rice, mashed potatoes, or noodles - the gravy is great!

Kay Broaddus
Jeffrey Broaddus '98

246

Helen's Chicken Spaghetti

1 chicken, whole
1 (7-ounce) package spaghetti
½ cup onions, chopped
½ cup green pepper, chopped
1 (16-ounce) can chopped
    tomatoes, drained

1 (10½-ounce) can cream of
    mushroom soup
Salt and pepper to taste
½-1 cup Monterey Jack cheese,
    grated
½-1 cup cheddar cheese, grated

Cook chicken in a microwave safe covered dish for 15 minutes on high power. Let sit for 10 minutes. Chicken is ready to be deboned and cut up. Cook spaghetti with onions and green pepper. Drain and add chopped tomatoes. Add soup and mix with chopped chicken. Season as desired. Put half mixture in casserole dish and top with Monterey Jack cheese. Add remainder of spaghetti mixture and top with cheddar cheese. Place in microwave on medium power for 7-8 minutes or until cheese is bubbly. Serves 6-8.

Chicken can be steamed in this manner for any recipe which calls for cooked chicken.

Helen Moese
Linda Moese '97

Sweet and Sour Chicken

4-6 chicken breasts
8   ounces French dressing

8   ounces apricot preserves
⅓ cup dry onion soup mix

Arrange chicken in 2-quart shallow casserole. Top with mixture of dressing, preserves, and soup mix. Cover and bake at 350° for 1 hour, 15 minutes. Uncover and bake 15 minutes more. May serve over rice. May be made ahead of time. Serves 4-6.

Susan Saiter
Rob Saiter '90
David Saiter '98

VARIATION- Substitute Russian Salad Dressing for French.

Cindy Etier
Emily Etier '01

Chicken and Vegetables Cooked in Foil

4	(4-ounces each) boneless, skinless chicken breasts	4	teaspoons margarine
2	carrots, cut into 1-inch slices	2	tablespoons cooking sherry
8	ounces fresh mushrooms, sliced ¼-inch thick	¼	teaspoon pepper
1	cup zucchini, sliced	¼	teaspoon seasoned salt
		2	teaspoons rosemary

Preheat oven to 350°. Tear off four 12-inch pieces of foil. Place 1 chicken breast on each piece of foil. Cover each piece of chicken with vegetables, margarine, sherry, and seasonings, dividing ingredients evenly. Fold foil around each breast to make a tight pouch. Place foil package on a cookie sheet. Bake for 30 - 40 minutes. Makes 4 servings.

Lynne Charbonneau
Scott Charbonneau '98
Mark Charbonneau '01

Picadillo

1	pound ground turkey or lean beef	½	cup tomato juice
¾	cup onion, chopped	½	teaspoon cinnamon
3	tablespoons oil	¼	teaspoon ground cumin
1	teaspoon salt		Pinch of cloves
2	tablespoons vinegar	½	cup slivered and blanched almonds
1	teaspoon sugar	1	(4-ounce) can green chilies (optional)
2	tomatoes (or 1 cup canned)		
¼	cup raisins		Chili powder to taste

Brown meat and onions in heated oil. Add all other ingredients, except almonds. Stir to blend. Bring to boil, reduce heat and simmer for 30-45 minutes. Stir in almonds. Serve with tortilla chips.

This is a good filling for tamales, rolled tortillas, empañadas, tacos, enchiladas, chiles relleños, etc. Will freeze well. Serves 6-8.

Kay Broaddus
Jeffrey Broaddus '98

Stuffed Manicotti with Mushroom Sauce

1 package manicotti	2 cups stuffing mix or crushed crackers
1 pound ground turkey or beef	
1 cup onion, chopped	1 cup cottage cheese
2 tablespoons oil	1 (10-ounce) package chopped
4 ounces fresh mushrooms, sliced	spinach, thawed and drained
½ cup celery, finely chopped	2 tablespoons fresh basil, chopped
1½ cups tomatoes, chopped	Salt and pepper to taste
	1 egg

MUSHROOM SAUCE-

3 ounces fresh mushrooms	2½ cups milk
3 tablespoons onion, minced	3-4 tablespoons flour
1 tablespoon oil	Salt and pepper to taste

Cook manicotti according to directions. Brown ground meat and onions in oil. Add mushrooms, celery, and tomatoes and cook a few minutes more. Remove from heat. Add stuffing mix, cottage cheese, spinach, basil, salt, pepper, and egg. Drain manicotti and fill, placing them in a 9×13 baking pan. Cover loosely with foil and heat through at 350° about 30 minutes.

MUSHROOM SAUCE-
Sauté mushrooms and onions in oil. Add milk, flour, salt, and pepper and cook to desired thickness. Pour over manicotti after it is baked.

Lillian Gips
Bruce Holmes '78 (son)
Jeffrey Broaddus '98 (grandson)

Pork Chop Delight

6 pork chops	1 (10½-ounce) can chicken and rice soup
½ cup flour	
¼ cup oil	¾ cup water
	Salt and pepper

Flour pork chops well and fry until brown. Drain off grease and add soup and water. Add salt and pepper to taste. Cover skillet and simmer 30 minutes. Serves 6.

Martha Tucker
Jennifer Tucker '97

Turkey Stroganoff

1	cup onion, chopped	1	(8-ounce) can sliced mushrooms
2	cloves garlic, pressed		(optional)
2	tablespoons vegetable oil	2	(10½-ounce) cans cream of
2	pounds turkey, ground		chicken soup
2	tablespoons flour	2	cups sour cream
Salt and pepper to taste		6	cups cooked rice or egg noodles

In a large skillet, heat oil. Add onion and garlic. Sauté until onions are clear. Add ground turkey and brown, stirring constantly. Add 2 tablespoons flour, salt, and pepper. Stir well. Add mushrooms and soup. Stir thoroughly. Cook over medium heat for 10 minutes. Turn heat off and stir in sour cream. Serve over cooked rice or egg noodles. Serves 6-8.

Judy Boldt (Bob '68)
Laura Boldt '94
David Boldt '97

Orzo and Ham

2	cups uncooked orzo	1	pound cooked ham, diced
	(rice-shaped pasta)	2	(9-ounce) packages frozen
2	tablespoons butter or		sugar snap peas
	margarine	1	teaspoon lemon pepper
1	bunch green onions,		seasoning
	chopped	½	teaspoon salt
½	cup green bell pepper,	1	cup evaporated milk
	chopped	¼	cup Parmesan cheese

Cook orzo according to package directions. Drain and keep warm. In Dutch oven, melt butter. Add onions, bell pepper, and ham. Cook until onion is tender (1-2 minutes). Add peas and cook over medium heat for 2 minutes. Reduce heat to low. Stir in seasonings and milk. Simmer 2 minutes. Stir in cooked orzo. Sprinkle with cheese just before serving. Serves 4-6.

Judy Boldt (Bob '68)
Laura Boldt '94
David Boldt '97

Mexican Pork Chops

4-6 pork chops	1¼ cups water
1 cup uncooked rice	Cheddar cheese, grated
1 (8-ounce) can tomato sauce	Green pepper, sliced
1 package taco seasoning	

Brown pork chops. Spread rice in bottom of 9×13-inch casserole dish. Top with pork chops. Combine tomato sauce, taco seasoning, and water. Pour over rice and pork chops. Cover tightly and bake at 350° for 40 minutes. Sprinkle grated cheese on top with one slice green pepper on each chop. Cover and put back in oven until cheese is melted (approximately 5-7 minutes). Serves 4-6.

Helen Beasley, President ('91-'92)
Nancy Beasley '90

Smothered Quail

6 quail, dressed	Salt and pepper to taste
6 tablespoons butter	1 (3-ounce) can mushrooms,
3 tablespoons flour	chopped
2 cups chicken broth	1 (6-ounce) box Uncle Ben's Long
½ cup sherry	Grain and Wild Rice

Brown quail in butter. Remove to baking dish. Add flour to butter. Stir well. Slowly add broth, sherry, and seasonings. Blend thoroughly. Add mushrooms. Pour over quail. Cover and bake at 350° for 1 hour. Serve over rice, prepared according to package directions. Serves 6.

Bonnie Leissler, President ('84-'85)
Kelly Leissler May '86

Pork Chop Dinner

2-3 pork loin chops, ½-inch thick
Salt and pepper to taste
1   tablespoon vegetable oil
¼   cup onion, diced
¼   cup bell pepper, diced

½   cup uncooked rice
1   (16-ounce) can tomatoes
1   teaspoon salt
½   teaspoon sugar
½   teaspoon prepared mustard

Sprinkle chops with salt and pepper. Brown on both sides in hot oil. Remove chops and drain. Reserve drippings in skillet. Add onion and pepper. Sauté until tender. Stir in rice, tomatoes, salt, sugar, and mustard. Add pork chops. Bring to a boil. Reduce heat. Cover and simmer about 30 minutes until rice and chops are done. Serves 3.

Martha Tucker
Jennifer Tucker '97

Pork Chop Scallop

4   pork chops, ½-inch thick
1   (5-ounce) package
    scalloped potatoes

2   tablespoons margarine
    Milk (amount called for on box of
    potatoes)

In skillet, brown pork chops in margarine until almost done. Remove chops and set aside. Empty potatoes and packet of seasoned sauce mix into skillet. Stir in water and milk called for on package. Heat to boiling. Reduce heat and place chops on top. Cover and simmer 35-45 minutes or until potatoes are tender and chops are thoroughly cooked. Serves 4.

Christina Trevino (David '72)
Maria '00

Country Sausage and Potatoes au Gratin

1   pound smoked sausage,
    cut into ½-inch slices
1   large onion, chopped
    (about 1 cup)
1   tablespoon vegetable oil
1   package au gratin potatoes
2½ cups hot water

¼   teaspoon pepper
4   medium (about 2 cups) carrots,
    cut into 2-inch julienne strips
1   bunch (about 2 cups) fresh
    broccoli
1   cup (4-ounces) cheddar cheese,
    shredded

Cook and stir sausage and onion in oil in 10-12-inch skillet until onion is tender (about 5 minutes). Stir in potatoes, sauce mix, water, and pepper. Heat to boiling, reduce heat. Cover and simmer, stirring occasionally about 10 minutes. Stir in carrot strips. Cover and simmer until carrots are tender-crisp and potatoes are tender (about 10 minutes). Stir in broccoli and cook until tender (5-10 minutes). Add cheese on top. Serves 4-5.

Mary Husa
Ben Husa '00

Sausage and Potato Casserole

1   pound smoked sausage
1   cup onion, chopped
4   cups potatoes, thinly sliced
2½ cups hot water
Salt and pepper to taste

2   cups carrots, thinly sliced
1   (10-ounce) package frozen
    chopped broccoli
1   cup cheddar cheese, shredded
    (optional)

Slice sausage into ½-inch slices. Cook and stir sausage and onion in large skillet until onion is tender. Stir in potatoes, water, and pepper. Bring to a boil and reduce heat to simmer. Cook about 10 minutes. Stir in carrots and simmer until tender-crisp (10 minutes). Stir in broccoli and cheese. Cover and cook until broccoli is heated. Serves 5-6.

Janice Myers, President ('95-'96) (Tony '65)
Greg Myers '92
Cindy Myers Crook '96

Sausage and Rice Casserole

1 pound hot breakfast-style sausage	2 (2.26-ounce) packages chicken noodle soup mix
1 cup celery, chopped	½ cup uncooked rice
1 onion, chopped	Paprika
1 bell pepper, chopped	¼ cup blanched almonds
4½ cups water	

Brown sausage. Drain. Bring water to boil. Add soup mix, rice, and chopped vegetables. Boil uncovered until tender. Add sausage. Pour into 9×13-inch greased casserole. Sprinkle with paprika and almonds. Bake at 350° for about 15 minutes. Serves 6-8.

Martha Tucker
Jennifer Tucker '97

Homemade Salami

2 pounds lean ground beef	¼ teaspoon onion powder
½ teaspoon garlic powder	1 tablespoon mustard seed
1½ teaspoons liquid smoke	2 tablespoons Morton's Tender-
1 crushed peppercorn	Quick curing salt
1 cup water	(do not substitute)

Mix all ingredients. Roll. Wrap in foil and refrigerate 24 hours. Unwrap and bake, uncovered, at 300° for 1½ - 2 hours. Let cool and slice, if desired. You can make several small rolls or one large one.

Dianne Mayfield, Federation Officer
Mitch Cogbill '94
Donna Cogbill '94

Low Fat Salami

4 pounds ground turkey	¾ teaspoon garlic powder
2 tablespoons salt	1 ½ teaspoons black pepper
2 tablespoons liquid smoke	

Mix all ingredients thoroughly. Refrigerate 2-4 hours. Divide into 4-8 equal pieces. Make logs and wrap each in nylon net, tying ends. Bake at 225° for 4 hours on cooking oil-sprayed rack. Cool 10 minutes and wrap in paper towels to remove excess fat. Remove netting and refrigerate or freeze.

Lillian Gips
Bruce Holmes '78 (son)
Jeffrey Broaddus '98 (grandson)

Martha's Spaghetti

½ pound ground veal	½ pound mushrooms, sliced
½ pound ground pork	2½ cups tomato pureè
½ pound ground beef	1 cup ketchup
½ pound ground sausage	½ teaspoon Worcestershire sauce
¼ pound butter or margarine	2 teaspoons lemon juice
1½ pounds onions, chopped	2 teaspoons salt
¼ clove garlic, chopped	¼ teaspoon pepper
1 bell pepper, chopped	8 ounces spaghetti
¼ cup water	Parmesan cheese to taste
2 sprigs parsley, chopped	

Brown meat in butter in large iron skillet. Add onions, garlic, peppers, and parsley. Cook until slightly brown. Add mushrooms, tomato pureè, ketchup, ¼ cup water, Worcestershire sauce, lemon juice, salt, and pepper. Simmer, covered for 1½ hours. Boil 8 ounces spaghetti in salted water until soft. Drain off water. Pour sauce over spaghetti and top with Parmesan cheese. Serves 8.

Martha Tucker
Jennifer Tucker '97

Crab Meat Strata

4   croissants or 1 loaf
     French bread, sliced
2   sticks butter (unsalted)
1   green bell pepper (optional)
2-3 celery ribs, chopped
4   scallions (tops or use chives)
1   pound small fresh
     mushrooms
4   ounces cream cheese,
     softened (lite is ok)
8   ounces ricotta cheese
2 ½ cups milk
1   pound fresh or frozen
     crab meat, flaked

4   ounces Danish Havarti cheese,
     shredded
4   large eggs (2 real plus egg
     substitute can be used)
½   teaspoon salt
½   teaspoon white pepper (to taste)
1   tablespoon fresh parsley
2   tablespoons horseradish
1   (1-ounce) package Knorr dry
     Hollandaise mix.
Parsley and sliced black olives for
garnish

Melt 1 stick butter in skillet. Add onions, bell pepper, and celery, and sauté 10 minutes. Add mushrooms and cook 4 more minutes. Set aside. Soften cream cheese, adding a little milk and ricotta cheese. Add this and crab meat to skillet contents. Line 2-quart buttered oval baking dish with bread and tear any remaining bread into large pieces to use later. Pour skillet contents evenly over bread and top with shredded Havarti cheese and remaining bread. Mix eggs, salt, pepper, parsley, 1½ cups milk, and horseradish with whisk and pour over baking dish contents. Refrigerate covered overnight to allow flavors to blend. Just before baking, drizzle ½ cup melted butter over top. Bake at 375° for 40 minutes. Fifteen minutes before dish comes out of the oven, make the Hollandaise (microwave directions work great). To serve - ladle sauce onto center of each plate, spreading to cover and spoon strata on top. Add a dollop of Hollandaise on top. Garnish with fresh parsley or black olives. Serves 6-8.

This dish is a fabulous buffet dish. Definitely not low fat, but one that shellfish lovers will beg for the recipe.

Connie Marcum Tucker
Rex Tucker '99
Kara Tucker '01

Italian Baked Oysters

SEASONED BREAD CRUMBS-

1½ cups dry bread crumbs
2 teaspoons dried leaf basil
OR 2 tablespoons fresh
basil, chopped
1 teaspoon dried leaf
oregano OR 1 tablespoons
fresh oregano, chopped

1 teaspoon dried rosemary,
minced, OR 1 tablespoon fresh
rosemary, minced

OYSTERS-

½ cup unsalted butter or
margarine
1 large onion, chopped
4 large garlic cloves, minced
½ teaspoon dried leaf thyme
OR 1½ tablespoons fresh
thyme, chopped
¾ teaspoon dried leaf oregano
OR 2¼ teaspoons fresh
oregano, chopped

2 tablespoons parsley,
minced, preferably flat leaf
¼ teaspoon cayenne pepper
¼ teaspoon freshly ground pepper
1 teaspoon salt
48 shucked oysters with their liquor
1 cup (3-ounces) Parmesan cheese,
grated

To prepare seasoned bread crumbs, combine all ingredients in a medium bowl. Set aside. Grease a 3-quart casserole dish. Preheat oven to 375°. In a heavy 10-inch skillet over medium heat, melt butter or margarine. Add onion, garlic, herbs, cayenne, black pepper, and salt. Sauté until onion is wilted and transparent, about 5 minutes. Add oysters and their liquor, stirring gently to blend. Simmer mixture over medium heat just until oysters begin to curl at edges. Stir in seasoned bread crumbs. Spoon mixture onto greased dish. Sprinkle top of casserole evenly with Parmesan cheese. Bake in preheated oven until bubbly and lightly browned on top, about 15 minutes. Serve hot. Makes 6-8 servings.

Artie J. Jenkins
Altie Jenkins '00

Grilled Salmon or Halibut

SALMON
Olive oil
Lemon pepper

Garlic salt
Dill

HALIBUT
Vegetable oil

Basil

Purchase enough fish or fish steaks to serve your family. For whole fish, use ½ cup oil and add the spices and herbs to taste. For fish steaks, use ¼ cup oil. Brush fish with mixture and grill over medium heat about 7 minutes per side for whole fish, 5 minutes per side for 1-inch thick steaks. Test fish for doneness. Flesh should flake easily.

Sue Owen
Michael Owen '95

Boiled Shrimp with Remoulade Sauce

2 pounds shrimp, thawed, boiled, and peeled
½ lemon
1 small onion, cut up
2 bay leaves

1 rib celery, cut up
Pepper corns
¼ cup salt
Shrimp-crab boil can be substituted for above seasonings

REMOULADE SAUCE-
1 cup mayonnaise
½ (5.12-ounce) jar Creole mustard
3 teaspoons onion, grated
1 teaspoon horseradish

1 teaspoon lemon juice
1 teaspoon Worcestershire sauce
Shredded lettuce
Tomatoes, wedges, or whole

To cook 2 pounds of shrimp, bring 2½ quarts of water to a boil. Add lemon, onion, bay leaves, celery, and a few pepper corns. Add shrimp and boil for exactly 10 minutes. Add salt, take off heat, and let set 15 minutes. Drain. For sauce, combine first 6 ingredients. Adjust seasonings to taste. Mix with peeled shrimp and serve over shredded lettuce and tomato wedges or stuff into whole tomatoes for main dish. Makes 4 servings.

Aggie Mom

Shrimp Creole

²/₃	cup vegetable oil	2	teaspoons salt
½	cup flour	¾	teaspoon black pepper
1½	cups green onions, sliced	½	teaspoon red pepper
1	cup onion, chopped	¼	teaspoon dried basil
¾	cup green pepper, chopped	½	teaspoon dried thyme
4	cloves garlic, minced	2	slices fresh lemon
3	tablespoons fresh parsley	2	cups (approximately) water or
1	(16-ounce) can tomatoes		fish stock
1	(8-ounce) can tomato sauce	2	pounds raw shrimp, peeled
4	tablespoons red wine	4	cups cooked rice
2	bay leaves		

In a very heavy kettle, heat oil and flour, stirring constantly. Cook and stir until a medium brown roux is formed. Add onions, peppers, garlic, and parsley to cool the roux, then lower heat and continue cooking until vegetables brown slightly. Mix in tomatoes and tomato sauce. Add wine and seasonings and mix. Bring mixture to a low boil. Add water or stock to desired consistency. When mixture boils, reduce heat and simmer about 1 hour. Add shrimp, cover, and simmer for 20 minutes more. Do not overcook shrimp. Adjust seasonings, if necessary. Serve over boiled rice. Makes 6-8 servings.

Julie Thedford (Marvin '65)
Mary Helen Ramsey '93
Clay Ramsey '93
Katherine Thedford '98

Stan's Tuna Casserole

1	(10½-ounce) can cream of mushroom soup	1	(6½-ounce) can tuna
		1	cup potato chips, crushed
¹/₃	cup milk	1	cup canned peas

Empty can of soup into a 9-inch square casserole dish. Add milk and drained tuna and stir. Stir in ¾ cup of crushed chips and peas. Sprinkle remaining chips over top. Bake for 25 minutes in a 350° oven. Serves 4.

Stan Lewis '88

Garlic Shrimp and Pasta

1 (14½-ounce) can chicken broth
½ cup water
2 tablespoons cornstarch
2 tablespoons olive oil
4 cloves garlic, sliced or minced
¼ cup fresh parsley, chopped

¼ teaspoon lemon peel, grated
⅛ teaspoon cayenne pepper, ground
1½ pounds medium shrimp, shelled and deveined
2 tablespoons lemon juice
4 cups hot cooked spaghetti

In a small bowl, stir together broth, water, and cornstarch until smooth. Set aside. In 10-inch skillet over medium heat in hot oil, cook garlic, parsley, lemon peel, and cayenne pepper 1 minute, stirring constantly. Add shrimp and lemon juice. Cook until shrimp turns pink and opaque, stirring constantly. Gradually add broth mixture to skillet. Cook until mixture boils and thickens, stirring constantly. Toss with spaghetti. Serves 4.

Julie Thedford (Marvin '65)
Mary Helen Ramsey '93
Clay Ramsey '93
Katherine Thedford '98

Shrimp Jambalaya

3 tablespoons shortening or oil
2 tablespoons flour
1½ cups onions, chopped
½ cup green peppers, chopped
1 clove garlic, minced
Salt to taste
Red pepper to taste

2½ cups water
2 pounds raw peeled shrimp
1 (28-ounce) can tomatoes, drained
1 (8-ounce) can tomato sauce
2 cups rice, uncooked
Minced parsley to garnish
Minced green onion tops to garnish

Heat shortening or oil. Add flour and let it cook slowly until golden brown, stirring constantly. Add onions, peppers, garlic, and celery. Cook slowly until transparent, stirring often. Add tomatoes and cook until oil rises to top. Stir in rice, shrimp, and 2½ cups water. Cook covered, over low heat until rice is tender. Add more water and oil if mixture appears a bit too dry. Add minced parsley and onion tops. Serve hot. Serves 6.

Debbie Cauthen
Christopher Cauthen '00

Desserts

Pineapple Angel Food Cake

1 (16-ounce) box angel food cake mix	1 (20-ounce) can crushed pineapple

Dump cake mix and pineapple (undrained) into bowl and mix according to package directions. Pour into ungreased 9×13-inch pan. Bake at 350° for 30-35 minutes. Be careful not to overbake. This is a moist, low-fat cake. Can be topped with whipped topping or no-fat ice cream. A great "emergency" dessert, only two ingredients usually found on the pantry shelf!

Doe Knower
"Aggie Friend"

Apple Cake

3 cups apples, peeled and chopped	¼ teaspoon salt
3 cups flour	1 teaspoon vanilla
2 cups sugar	1¼ cups oil
1 teaspoon baking soda	2 eggs
1 teaspoon cinnamon	1 cup pecans, chopped

Combine all ingredients in large mixer bowl. Mix all together. Bake in 9×13-inch pan for 45-50 minutes at 350°. Serves 12-15.

Deborah Reyes
Dustin Reyes '01

VARIATION- Increase cinnamon to 2 teaspoons, oil to 1½ cups, salt to 1 teaspoon. Bake in a greased and floured tube or bundt pan at 325° for 1½ hours.

Becky McConathy
Julie McConathy '97

Apple Cake in a Jar

²/₃ cup shortening
2²/₃ cups sugar
4   eggs
1   teaspoon cinnamon
2   teaspoons baking soda
1½ teaspoons salt
½   teaspoon baking powder

½   teaspoon nutmeg
3   cups flour
²/₃ cup water
3   cups apple, peeled and grated
²/₃ cup raisins
²/₃ cup nuts, chopped

Sterilize 9 wide-mouthed pint-sized canning jars. Put lids in pan of water to heat. Mix ingredients in order given. Do not add any other ingredients. Grease or spray jars. Fill half full with batter. Bake on wire rack at 325° for 45 minutes. As soon as the cake is done, take out one at a time. Wipe the rim of the jar, put hot lid on and screw on band. As the cake cools, it will seal the lid from the sides and will come out easy when ready to serve. Yield - 9 jars. Shelf life - 3 months.

Mary Bedsole
"Butch" Bedsole '48

Carrot Cake

2   cups sugar
2   cups flour
1   teaspoon baking soda
1½ teaspoons cinnamon
½   teaspoon salt

1½ cups oil
1   teaspoon vanilla
4   eggs
2   cups carrots, grated (packed)
Water

ICING-
1   box powdered sugar
1   (8-ounce) package
    cream cheese

8   ounces margarine
1   cup pecans

Sift dry ingredients together. Add oil, vanilla, and eggs. Add carrots. Adjust enough water to make thick pouring consistency and pour into pans. Bake in 8-inch round pans for 30 minutes or one 9×13-inch cake pan for 45-60 minutes. For icing, mix powdered sugar and cream cheese together. Add margarine and pecans. Spread on warm cake.

JaNahn Rodriguez, President ('97-'98)
David Rodriguez '94
Cindy Rodriguez '95
Dan Rodriguez '99

Boston Cream Pie

CAKE-

2 egg whites	1 teaspoon salt
½ cup sugar	⅓ cup cooking oil
2¼ cups flour	1½ teaspoons vanilla
1 cup sugar	2 egg yolks
3 teaspoons baking powder	1 cup milk

FRENCH CUSTARD FILLING-

⅓ cup sugar	1½ cups milk
1 tablespoon flour	1 egg yolk, slightly beaten
1 tablespoon cornstarch	1 teaspoon vanilla
¼ teaspoon salt	

CHOCOLATE GLOSS-

½ cup sugar	½ cup boiling water
1½ tablespoons cornstarch	1½ tablespoons butter
1 ounce unsweetened chocolate	½ teaspoon vanilla
	Dash salt

CAKE- Beat egg whites until foamy. Gradually beat in ½ cup sugar. Beat until stiff and glossy. Sift dry ingredients into another bowl. Add oil, ½ cup milk, and vanilla. Beat 1 minute at medium speed. Add remaining milk and egg yolks. Beat 1 minute. Gently fold in egg white mixture with down up over motion. Bake in paper-lined 9-inch cake pans at 350° for 25 minutes. Cool.

FILLING- Mix dry ingredients. Gradually stir in milk. Cook and stir until mixture thickens and boils. Cook and stir 2-3 minutes longer. Stir little of hot mixture into egg yolk. Return to hot mixture, stirring constantly. Bring just to boiling. Add vanilla and cool. Beat with wire whisk until smooth. Fill between layers and refrigerate.

GLOSS- Combine sugar, cornstarch, chocolate, salt, and water in small saucepan. Cook and stir until blended and thickened. Remove from heat and add butter and vanilla. Pour over top layer while still hot and let drip down sides.

Aggie Mom

Three Layer Carrot Cake

3 cups flour
3 cups sugar
4½ teaspoons cinnamon
1 tablespoon baking soda
6 eggs

3 cups carrots, grated
2 cups cooking oil
1½ cups pecans or walnuts, chopped.

ICING-
8 ounces cream cheese
1 stick butter
1⅓ cups powdered sugar
1 cup brown sugar

⅛ teaspoon ground cloves
⅛ teaspoon ground nutmeg
⅛ teaspoon cinnamon
1½ teaspoons vanilla

Preheat oven to 350°. Grease and flour 3 9-inch pans (or use Baker's Joy). Mix flour, sugar, cinnamon, and baking soda. Add eggs, carrots, oil, and nuts. Mix well. Pour into 3 pans. Bake 40-50 minutes in 350° oven. For icing, beat cheese, butter, and vanilla. Add sugars, spices, and vanilla gradually. Beat well. Refrigerate until firm before frosting cake.

Gloria Gilpin, President ('98-'99) (Bobby '62)
Wes Gilpin '93
Katherine Gilpin '97

Black Russian Bundt Cake

1 box yellow cake mix with pudding
½ cup sugar
1 (6⅞-ounce) package chocolate instant pudding

1 cup oil
4 eggs
¼ cup vodka
¼ cup Kahlua
¾ cup water

GLAZE-
½ cup powdered sugar

¼ cup Kahlua

In a large bowl, combine all ingredients. Mix at low speed about 1 minute. Beat at medium speed 4 minutes. Pour into floured and greased bundt pan. Bake at 350° for 60-70 minutes. Let cool in pan 10 minutes, then on wire rack. For glaze, mix powdered sugar and Kahlua. Poke holes in cake and pour over. Dust with sugar.

Pat Daly
Christine Daly '00

Also submitted by Kelle Erickson Shanks '85

265

Linda's Chocolate Chip Cake

1   package chocolate cake mix
1   cup water
½   cup cooking oil
1   (12-ounce) package
     chocolate chips

1   (3.4-ounce) package instant
     vanilla pudding mix
1   (3.4-ounce) package instant
     chocolate pudding mix
4   eggs

Mix all ingredients, adding eggs one at a time, and beating well after each. Pour in bundt pan and bake at 350° for 1 hour and 10 minutes. Serves 12-16.

Linda Hill, Federation Officer

Earth Quake Cake

1   cup coconut flakes
1   cup pecan pieces
1   box German Chocolate
     cake mix (mixed as
     directed on box)

1   box powdered sugar
1   (8-ounce) package
     cream cheese
1   stick butter

Mix coconut flakes and pecans. Spread on bottom of 9×11-inch cake pan. Pour mixed cake mix over this. Mix butter, powdered sugar, and cream cheese. Before baking, spread over cake mix. Bake at 350° for about 50 minutes or until done.

Betty Pennington
Shelley Lenamond '98
Mitchell Lenamond '99

266

Aunt Ann's Fudge Cake

2	cups sugar	4	squares baking chocolate
1	cup butter, softened		OR ½ cup cocoa
4	eggs, beaten	1	cup flour
1	teaspoon vanilla	1	cup nuts, chopped

Preheat oven to 300°. Cream sugar and butter. Add beaten eggs. Melt chocolate. Add to sugar, butter, and egg mixture. Add flour gradually while stirring. Fold in nuts. Add vanilla. Bake in greased 9×13-inch pan approximately 40 minutes. DO NOT OVERCOOK! (This is the key to keeping fudge cake "fudgy" instead of dry and crumbly. Check at 30 and 35 minutes. Remove when top has a crust and cake begins to pull away from sides.) Enjoy! Serves 12.

Gloria Gilpin, President ('98-'99) (Bobby '62)
Wes Gilpin '93
Katherine Gilpin '97

Fudge Buttermilk Cake

2	cups sugar	1	cup buttermilk
1	cup oil	5	tablespoons cocoa
2	eggs	1	cup hot water
2½	cups flour	2	teaspoons soda
1	teaspoon baking powder	1	teaspoon vanilla
½	teaspoon salt		

In a large bowl, combine all the ingredients in the order given, and beat until well blended. Batter will be thin. Pour into greased and floured cake pans (2 8-inch round or 1 9×13-inch) and bake at 350° for 25-35 minutes. Frost with your choice of chocolate icing.

This recipe has been in my family for years, passed down from my grandmother to my mother to me, and maybe Jennifer will make it one of these days! It is one of the most moist cakes I have ever eaten.

Martha Tucker
Jennifer Tucker '97

Heath Bar Cake

1	package German Chocolate cake mix	1	(11.75-ounce) jar hot fudge sundae sauce, heated
1	can sweetened condensed milk	6	Heath bars, crushed
		1	(8-ounce) container Cool Whip

Prepare cake mix according to package directions. Bake in 9×13-inch pan. Let cool 10 minutes. Poke holes over entire cake. Pour condensed milk into all holes, then top with heated hot fudge sauce. Make sure fudge gets into all the holes. Mix crushed Heath bars with Cool Whip. When the cake has completely cooled, spread Cool Whip mixture over cake.

Anna Sheffield
Ann Sheffield Kuebler '97
Kevin Kuebler '97

Milky Way Cake

8	Milky Way bars, cut in small pieces	4	eggs
2	sticks butter	½	teaspoon baking soda
2	cups sugar	1½	cups buttermilk
		2½	cups all-purpose flour

FROSTING-

2	cups sugar	1	(13-ounce) can evaporated milk
1	stick butter		
1	cup marshmallow cream	1	(16-ounce) package chocolate chips

Combine cut up candy bars and 1 stick of melted butter. Set aside. Cream sugar and 1 stick butter. Add 4 eggs. Add baking soda and flour to creamed mixture, alternating with buttermilk. Stir in candy mixture. Mix well. Pour into a greased and floured bundt pan. Bake at 325° for 1 hour.

For frosting, combine sugar, milk, and butter. Cook to soft ball stage, stirring frequently. Remove from heat. Add chocolate chips and marshmallow cream. Cool slightly and beat until thick. Spread over cake.

Forget the calories and fat grams! It is definitely worth it!

Francene Sorrell
Brandon Sorrell '99

Mississippi Mud Cake

2	sticks butter	¼	teaspoon salt
4	tablespoons cocoa	1½	teaspoons vanilla
2	cups sugar	1½	cups pecans, chopped
4	eggs (beat one at a time)	2	cups miniature marshmallows
1½	cups flour		

ICING-

½	cup butter	1	box powdered sugar
½	cup evaporated milk	⅓	cup cocoa
Dash salt		1	teaspoon vanilla

Melt butter. Add cocoa and mix well. Add sugar, eggs, flour, salt, vanilla, and pecans. Put in 9×13-inch pan. Bake at 325° for 30 minutes. Put marshmallows on cake as soon as it comes out of the oven. To make icing, melt butter, add cocoa, and mix well until dissolved. Add salt and evaporated milk. Bring to a boil and continue cooking 1 minute. Remove from heat and add sugar and vanilla. Beat until smooth. Pour icing over cake. Have this ready as soon as cake comes out of oven.

Suzanne Blaney
Erin Blaney '01

Chewy Apricot Bars

¾	cup flour	½	cup raisins
¾	cup sugar	2	eggs, beaten
1	teaspoon ground cinnamon	1	tablespoon orange juice
¼	teaspoon baking powder	½	cup coconut, shredded
¼	teaspoon salt		or flaked
6	ounces dried apricots, finely chopped		

Preheat oven to 350°. Line a 9-inch square baking pan with foil and spray with cooking spray. Combine flour, sugar, cinnamon, baking powder, and salt. Add apricots, raisins, eggs, and orange juice, stirring after each addition. Spread batter in prepared pan. Sprinkle with coconut. Bake 25-30 minutes. Cool in pan. Lift out by foil and cut in 1×3-inch bars.

Sue Owen
Michael Owen '95

White Chocolate Cake

¼ pound white chocolate	2½ cups flour
½ cup boiling water	1 teaspoon baking soda
1 cup butter	1 cup buttermilk
2 cups sugar	1 cup pecans, chopped
4 eggs, separated	1 (3½-ounce) can coconut
1 teaspoon vanilla	

ICING-

1 (13-ounce) can	1 teaspoon vanilla
evaporated milk	1 (3½-ounce) can
1 cup sugar	coconut flakes
4 tablespoons butter	1 cup pecans, chopped
3 egg yolks	

WHITE CHOCOLATE CREAM CHEESE FROSTING-

4 ounces white chocolate	1 teaspoon vanilla
2 teaspoons milk	1 cup pecans, chopped
¼ cup butter	1 pound powdered sugar
1 (8-ounce) package	
cream cheese	

Melt white chocolate slivers in boiling water. Set aside to cool. Cream butter and sugar until fluffy. Mix in egg yolks, 1 at a time, beating well after each addition. Add chocolate and vanilla. Sift together flour and baking soda. Add to chocolate mixture alternately with buttermilk. Do not over-cream. Fold in egg whites, beaten but not stiff. Gently stir in pecans and coconut. Makes 3 8-inch or 9-inch layers. Bake at 350° approximately 25 minutes. Frost EITHER with icing or white chocolate cream cheese frosting. For icing, combine milk, sugar, and butter and bring to boil, stirring constantly. Blend beaten egg yolks into cooked mixture. Add vanilla. Cook until thick over low heat, about 15 minutes. Remove from heat and add coconut and pecans. Beat until fluffy and of spreading consistency. For frosting, melt chocolate in double boiler with milk and butter. Add cream cheese, vanilla, pecans, and powdered sugar and beat well. Spread.

Dorothy Starry
Sheree Starry Wagner '80

Italian Cream Cake

½ cup margarine
½ cup shortening
2 cups sugar
5 egg yolks
2 cups flour
1 teaspoon baking soda

1 cup buttermilk
1 teaspoon vanilla
1⅓ cups coconut
1 cup nuts, chopped
5 egg whites, stiffly beaten

ICING-
1 (8-ounce) package
   cream cheese, softened
¼ cup margarine

4 cups powdered sugar
1 teaspoon vanilla
1 cup pecans or walnuts, chopped

Mix all ingredients, folding in egg whites last. Bake in 3 9-inch round greased and floured pans. Bake at 350° for 20-25 minutes.

ICING- Beat cream cheese and margarine until smooth. Add sugar and mix well. Add vanilla and beat until smooth. Add nuts. Frost cake. Serves 16.

Janice Myers, President ('95-'96) (Tony '65)
Greg Myers '92
Cindy Myers Crook '96

Candied Fruitcake
(For Those Who Hate Fruitcake!)

½ pound red candied cherries
½ pound green candied
   cherries
1 pound candied pineapple
   (can be plain or red/green)

1 pound raisins (golden are best)
1 pound coconut
1 pound pecans, chopped
1 can condensed milk

Line a 9×13-inch pan with foil. Spray with cooking spray. Mix all ingredients well. Pack into pan. Bake 1 hour and 20 minutes at 300°. Put foil on a cooling rack and spray. When fruitcake is done, turn out on foiled rack and peel off the "baking foil". Cool

Recipe came from an instructor of food service at El Centro College, Dallas.

Sue Owen
Michael Owen '95

Mae's Fruit Cocktail Cake

2 **cups flour**	2 **eggs**
2 **cups fruit cocktail, drained**	2 **teaspoons baking soda**
	1¼ **cups sugar**

FILLING-

½ **cups sugar**	½ **cup milk**
1½ **sticks margarine**	1 **cup pecans**

Mix first 5 ingredients in a greased and floured 9×13-inch pan. Bake 20-25 minutes in a 350° oven or until brown. Spread filling on top and cook another 5 minutes. For filling, mix sugar, margarine, milk, and pecans in saucepan and boil until mixture forms soft ball when dropped in cold water. Spread on cake.

Ruby Lee Sandars, Federation Officer

Fruity Fiesta Cake

3 **cups flour**	1 **teaspoon almond extract**
2 **cups sugar**	2 **cups (about 5) bananas, mashed**
1 **teaspoon baking soda**	
1 **teaspoon salt**	1 **medium can crushed pineapple, drained**
1 **teaspoon cinnamon**	
1 **cup almonds, chopped**	1 **(3-ounce) can coconut flakes**
3 **eggs**	
1½ **cups vegetable oil**	

FROSTING-

1 **(8-ounce) package cream cheese, softened**	1 **teaspoon vanilla extract**
½ **cup margarine**	1 **pound box powdered sugar**

In large mixing bowl, mix together flour, sugar, soda, salt, cinnamon, and almonds. In separate bowl, mix together beaten eggs, oil, extract, bananas, pineapple, and coconut. Stir both mixtures together. Pour into greased and floured pan. Bake at 350° for 1 hour and 20 minutes for a large tube pan, OR 50 minutes for 2 small bundt pans. For frosting, mix all ingredients and beat until smooth. Spread on cooled cake.

Cindy Etier
Emily Etier '01

ACADEMIC BUILDING
ALBRITTON TOWER

The Academic Building, constructed in 1914, is a vivid focal point for the natural beauty of large surrounding trees gracing the Central Texas campus. Nearby is the familiar bronze statue of Lawrence Sullivan Ross, revered president of Texas A&M in the late 1800's.

Fish (freshmen) in the Corps are required to maintain the statue's shiny patina. And it is here at the flagpole where Aggies gather for Silver Taps, a ceremony honoring students who have died.

The tolling of the bells from atop the 139-foot Albritton Tower. The 49 carillon bells, cast in France, also ring every quarter-hour and play the "Spirit of Aggieland" after home football games.

Academic Building/Albritton Tower Photo
By
Michael Blachly, '99

Kugelhopf Kake

2 cups sugar	1 tablespoon baking powder
¼ cup orange juice	½ teaspoon salt
1 cup salad oil	1 cup walnuts, chopped (optional)
1½ teaspoons vanilla	Powdered sugar for dusting
4 eggs (can use egg substitute plus 1 yolk)	
3 cups all-purpose flour	

FILLING-

2 cups cooking apples, thinly sliced	1 tablespoon sugar
	1 teaspoon cinnamon

Mix filling well and divide into two parts. Combine first five ingredients in large mixing bowl and beat a full 5 minutes on high. No need to sift flour. Measure by lightly spooning into measuring cup and leveling off. In small bowl, combine flour, baking powder, salt, and walnuts. Blend well. Add this to large mixing bowl contents and mix well. Pour ⅓ of batter into generously greased and lightly floured 10-inch Kugelhopf (or bundt/tube) pan. Arrange ½ of apple filling, another ⅓ of batter, remainder of filling and top with remaining ⅓ batter. Bake at 350° for 70 minutes or until toothpick comes out clean. Cool for 15 minutes and remove from pan. Sprinkle generously with powdered sugar while still warm. Place on serving plate after cooling and cover. Cake may be frozen. To do so, wrap tightly in plastic wrap and then in foil. Before serving, let stand at room temperature without unwrapping for 1 hour. Cake reaches full flavor after a day or so.

If using egg substitute, cake won't be as high or as rich.

Connie Marcum Tucker
Rex Tucker '99
Kara Tucker '01

Lemon Velvet Cake

1 package lemon instant pudding mix	4 eggs
1 cup cold water	1 teaspoon lemon extract
1 package lemon cake mix	½ cup cooking oil

LEMON GLAZE-

1½ cups powdered sugar	4 tablespoons fresh lemon juice

Preheat oven to 350°. Prepare bundt cake pan by spraying with Baker's Joy. In mixing bowl, combine pudding mix and water. Add cake mix. Add eggs one at a time, beating on low. Add lemon extract. Add oil. Beat 2 minutes on high. Bake in bundt pan for 45-50 minutes. Turn cake out onto plate. Drizzle lemon glaze over warm cake.

Special Occasion Garnish- Fill center with fresh strawberries and evenly place 8 strawberries around base of cake, alternating with glazed lemon slices. Place lemon slices on cake. Drizzle with more lemon glaze, if needed. Before serving, sift powdered sugar generously over cake. Glazed lemon slices - Slice 2 small lemons into thin rounds. Cook gently in pan with ⅓ cup sugar and 4 tablespoons water until lemon slices are tender and coated with sugar. Serves 12.

Mary Cope, Grandmother
Wes Gilpin '93
Katherine Gilpin '97

Mandarin Orange Cake

1	yellow cake mix	1	(11-ounce) can Mandarin oranges, undrained
4	eggs		
½	cup oil		

ICING-

1	(20-ounce) can crushed pineapple, undrained	1	(3.4-ounce) box vanilla instant pudding
1	(12-ounce) container Cool Whip		

Mix cake mix, eggs, oil, and Mandarin oranges together. Pour into a lightly greased 9×13-inch pan. Bake at 350° about 25 minutes, or until done. Cool thoroughly. For icing, mix all ingredients together. Spread over completely cooled cake. Refrigerate at least 3-4 hours.

This is a great light summer treat.

Patricia Perez
Jose L. Perez '99

Easy Pineapple Cake

1	(20-ounce) can crushed pineapple, undrained	1	cup granulated sugar
2	eggs, beaten until light and fluffy	1	cup brown sugar
		2	teaspoons baking soda
2	cups all-purpose flour	1	cup nuts, chopped

FROSTING-

1	(3-ounce) package softened cream cheese	1	teaspoon vanilla
		2	cups powdered sugar
¼	cup butter, softened	¼	teaspoon ginger

Mix all ingredients well by hand. Pour into ungreased 9×13-inch baking dish. Bake at 350° for 45-50 minutes. For frosting, beat cream cheese, butter, and vanilla. Use electric mixer to blend. Gradually add powdered sugar and ginger. Continue beating until smooth. Spread over pineapple cake.

Anna Sheffield
Ann Sheffield Kuebler '97
Kevin Kuebler '97

Poppy Seed Cake

1 box yellow cake mix	1 teaspoon almond extract
1 (6-ounce) package instant pudding	4 eggs
	4 tablespoons poppy seed
1 cup oil	1 cup hot water

ICING-

1 cup powdered sugar	1 teaspoon almond extract
Juice from 1 lemon	

Mix cake mix, pudding, oil, almond, eggs, poppy seed, and water. Pour into greased and floured bundt pan. Bake at 350° for 40-60 minutes. Remove cake from pan. While cake is warm, punch holes in cake and pour icing mixture over cake.

Marion Crawford (Don '64)
Kristin Crawford '91
Julie Crawford '95

Lemon Poppy Seed Cake

1 cup shortening	¼ teaspoon baking powder
3 cups sugar	1½ cups buttermilk
6 eggs, separated	1 teaspoon vanilla
Pinch cream of tartar	1 teaspoon butter flavoring
3 cups flour	1 teaspoon almond flavoring
¼ teaspoon salt	3 tablespoons poppy seed

LEMON SAUCE-

1½ teaspoons powdered sugar	1 teaspoon butter flavoring
½ cup lemon juice	1 teaspoon vanilla

Preheat oven to 325°. Grease and flour angel food cake pan. Cream sugar and shortening. Add egg yolks, one at a time. Add flour, salt, and baking powder alternately with buttermilk. Add flavorings and poppy seeds. Beat 6 egg whites until stiff (add pinch of cream of tartar). Fold into batter. Bake at 325° for 1 hour, 15 minutes. Remove from oven. Pour lemon sauce over cake while hot. Sauce goes into cake better if small holes are poked around top of cake with toothpick. Cool in pan. To serve, add a dollop of whipped topping and a lemon slice twist.

Gladys Meyer
Aggie Aunt

Pound Cake

3 cups granulated sugar
1 cup margarine
1 cup buttermilk
6 eggs
¼ teaspoon salt

¼ teaspoon baking soda
1 teaspoon vanilla
2 teaspoons lemon extract
3 cups flour

Grease bundt pan and powder with powdered sugar. Mix sugar, margarine, and buttermilk. Add beaten eggs. Mix dry ingredients and add gradually while beating in mixer. Add vanilla and lemon extract. Beat until thoroughly mixed. Bake at 325° for 1 hour. Sift powdered sugar over the top after cake is removed from pan.

Gene Jacob
Sara Jacob Kielty '94

Chocolate Pound Cake

2 sticks butter
1 stick margarine
3 cups sugar
3 cups all-purpose flour, sifted
3 eggs

¼ teaspoon salt
½ teaspoon baking powder
6 tablespoons cocoa
1 cup milk
1 teaspoon vanilla

Cream butter and margarine with sugar. Add eggs, one at a time, blending well after each addition. Sift together dry ingredients and add alternately with milk. Add vanilla. Pour into greased and floured tube or bundt pan. Bake at 325° for 1 hour and 15 minutes. Test for doneness.

Anna Sheffield
Ann Sheffield Kuebler '97
Kevin Kuebler '97

Grandmama's Best Yet
Cream Cheese Pound Cake

3 sticks butter or margarine	1½ teaspoons vanilla or
1 (8-ounce) package	butternut flavoring
cream cheese	3 large eggs
3 cups sugar	3 cups flour, sifted
Dash salt	

Cream butter, cream cheese, and sugar until light and fluffy. Add eggs, one at a time, beating well after each addition. Add flavoring, stir in flour and salt. Spoon mixture into greased 10-inch tube pan. Bake at 300-325° for 1½ hours.

The secret to this delicious cake is all ingredients are to be out of refrigerator for 2 hours before preparing.

Anna Sheffield
Ann Sheffield Kuebler '97
Kevin Kuebler '97

Maroon and White Pound Cake

1 cup butter, softened	1½ cups Ocean Spray
1 cup sugar	Dried Cranberries
2 eggs	2½ cups flour
2 teaspoons vanilla	½ teaspoon baking powder
½ cup sour cream	

Preheat oven to 350°. Grease a medium loaf pan or regular bundt pan. Using electric mixer, beat butter and sugar together until light and fluffy. Add eggs, vanilla, and sour cream. Mix well. Mix in dried cranberries. Combine flour and baking powder. Gradually add to cranberry mixture. Mix well. Pour into pan. Bake for 1 hour and 15 minutes or until toothpick inserted into center of cake comes out clean. Remove from pan. Cool completely. Makes 1 loaf or 1 bundt.

Paula Lively
Jim Lively '96
Carrie Lively Patterson '96
Troy Patterson '93

Pecan Pound Cake

3	cups flour	5	eggs	
3	cups sugar	$1/_8$	teaspoon salt	
1	stick margarine	2	cups pecans, chopped	
1	teaspoon vanilla	½	teaspoon baking powder	
¼	cup shortening	1	cup milk	

Cream shortening, margarine, and sugar. Add eggs and beat. Mix dry ingredients and add to creamed mixture alternately with milk. Beat well. Add vanilla and pecans and stir. Cook in floured and greased bundt pan at 300° for 2 hours, 15 minutes.

Mary Ellen Blankenship, President ('88 -'89)
Clay Blankenship '82
Ruth Ellen Blankenship Heaton '90

Sour Cream Pound Cake

1	cup butter	3	cups flour
3	cups sugar	½	teaspoon salt
6	eggs, separated	1	cup sour cream or buttermilk
¼	teaspoon baking soda		
1	teaspoon vanilla or lemon extract		

Cream sugar and butter. Add 6 egg yolks. Sift together dry ingredients. Alternately add dry ingredients and sour cream to the sugar-shortening mixture. Add vanilla. Beat egg whites stiff and fold into mixture. Grease loaf or bundt pan, but do not flour it. Pour batter into pan and bake 1½ hours in 325° oven. Will be crusty and golden brown.

JaNahn Rodriguez, President ('97-'98)
David Rodriguez '94
Cindy Rodriguez '95
Dan Rodriguez '99

Perfect Prune Cake

2	cups sugar	1	teaspoon baking soda
1	cup oil	1	teaspoon salt
3	eggs, well beaten	1	teaspoon cinnamon
1	cup buttermilk	1	teaspoon ground cloves
1	cup cooked unsweetened	1	teaspoon nutmeg
	prunes	1	teaspoon vanilla
1	cup flour	1	cup pecans, chopped

Prunes should be cooked the day before so they sit in the juice overnight. Mix sugar and oil together. Add eggs and mix well. Blend in buttermilk and drained prunes. Sift together flour, soda, salt, and spices. Mix into above mixture. Stir in vanilla and pecans. Bake in greased and floured bundt pan for 55-60 minutes in a 325° oven.

Beatrice Ray, Grandmother
Kristin Crawford '91
Julie Crawford '95

Pumpkin Pie Cake

2	(16-ounce) cans pumpkin	½	teaspoon ginger
1	cup sugar	½	teaspoon salt
1	(12-ounce) can evaporated	4	eggs
	milk	2	sticks butter or margarine,
3	teaspoons cinnamon		melted
1	teaspoon nutmeg	1½	cups pecans, chopped
½	teaspoon ground cloves	1	box yellow cake mix

Preheat oven to 350°. Mix the first 9 ingredients (not cake mix, butter, or pecans). Pour into buttered and floured 9×13-inch pan. Sprinkle dry cake mix over mixture. Pour butter over cake mix. Top with pecans. Bake for 1 hour and 15 minutes. Cover the last 15 minutes. Top with Cool Whip if desired.

Julie Thedford (Marvin '65)
Mary Helen Ramsey '93
Clay Ramsey '93
Katherine Thedford '98

Brian's Favorite Red Cake

½ cup shortening	1 small bottle of
1½ cups sugar	red food coloring
2 eggs	1 teaspoon vanilla
3 tablespoons cocoa	1 tablespoon vinegar
2 cups pre-sifted flour	1 teaspoon baking soda
1 cup buttermilk	

ICING-

1 cup powdered sugar	½ cup shortening
2 tablespoons flour	2 tablespoons milk
½ teaspoon salt	

Combine shortening, sugar, and eggs in mixing bowl. Add cocoa made into a paste by adding a little water. Alternate adding flour and buttermilk into mixture. Add food coloring and vanilla slowly. Mix well. Add vinegar to baking soda in a small dish, then add this into cake mixture and combine. Pour into 2 greased 9-inch cake pans. Bake at 350° for 30 minutes. Makes 2 round layers or one oblong cake. For icing, cream together in a large bowl powdered sugar, flour, salt, and shortening. Add milk. In a small bowl, beat 1 egg white until stiff, then add 1 cup powdered sugar and 2 teaspoons vanilla. Mix the small and large bowl ingredients together and ice the cake. Makes enough icing for a 2-layer cake.

Robin Luffy
Jennifer '00
Brian '02

Twinkie Cake (No Bake)

1 (10-ounce) box Twinkies	3 bananas, sliced
1 (15-ounce) can crushed	½ cup pecans, finely chopped
pineapple	Cherries, finely chopped (optional)
8 ounces Cool Whip	

Slice twinkies in half lengthwise. Place in 9×13-inch dish, cream side up. Add a layer of bananas, then pour a can of crushed pineapple with juice over bananas. Cover with Cool Whip and top with pecans and cherries. Cover and refrigerate overnight.

Anna Sheffield
Ann Sheffield Kuebler '97
Kevin Kuebler '97

Quick Rum Cake

1	cup pecans, chopped	½	cup water
1	package yellow cake mix	½	cup cooking oil
1	(5½-ounce) package French vanilla instant pudding	½	cup rum
		4	eggs

SAUCE-

1	stick butter	¼	cup water
1	cup sugar	3	ounces rum

Grease and flour tube or bundt pan. Sprinkle chopped pecans on bottom of bundt pan. Mix together cake mix, pudding, water, cooking oil, and rum. Beat in eggs one at a time. Pour batter into pan and bake 1 hour at 325°. Let cool. For sauce, boil butter, sugar, water, and rum together in saucepan. Pour over cake while in pan. This will soak into cake. Let cake completely cool before removing from pan.

Mary Beth Dennehy
Kerry Dennehy '99
Erin Dennehy '01

Strawberry Cake

1	package white cake mix	⅔	cup oil
1	(3-ounce) package strawberry gelatin (save 1 tablespoon for icing)	½	cup water
		4	eggs, well beaten
		½	cup strawberries, fresh or frozen

ICING-

1	box powdered sugar	1	tablespoon strawberry gelatin powder
4	ounces margarine	½	cup strawberries, crushed

Combine cake mix, Gelatin, oil, water, and eggs. Mix well. Add crushed berries and mix well. Pour batter into a greased 9×13-inch pan. Bake at 350° for 25-30 minutes. Cool before icing. For icing, combine powdered sugar, margarine, gelatin powder, and strawberries. Beat well and spread on cooled cake.

JaNahn Rodriguez, President ('97-'98)
David Rodriguez '94
Cindy Rodriguez '95
Dan Rodriguez '99

Strawberry Preserve Cake

1	box white cake mix	1	(12-ounce) carton whipped frozen topping

FILLING-

1	(13¾-ounce) package coconut macaroon cookies	2	(10-ounce) packages of frozen strawberries with sugar
1	(10-ounce) jar strawberry preserves		

Crush macaroon cookies (1½ cups) and mix in strawberries and preserves and set aside for filling. Prepare cake in the usual manner using 8-inch round cake pans. After cake has cooled, split each layer in half to make 4 layers. Spread the filling between 3 layers and on top of the cake. Ice with whipped topping and decorate with strawberry halves. Keep refrigerated and serve cold.

Eileen Buis
Josh Buis '97
Jordan Buis '99

Sweet Potato Bundt Cake

4	medium sweet potatoes	1	cup firmly packed brown sugar
3	cups flour	1	cup margarine
2	teaspoons baking soda	4	eggs, beaten
½	teaspoons baking powder	2	teaspoons orange peel, grated
1	teaspoon allspice	½	cup fresh orange juice
½	teaspoon salt	1	cup pecans, chopped
1½	cups white sugar		

Wash potatoes and boil 20 minutes or until very soft. Peel enough potatoes for 2¾ cups. Mix next 5 ingredients. In large bowl, combine sugars, margarine, and eggs. Beat together until light and fluffy. Add sweet potatoes and mix well. Add flour alternately with orange juice. Stir in pecans and orange peel. Pour into greased and floured bundt pan. Bake at 350° for 55-60 minutes. Cool in pan before removing. Serves 12.

Lillian Gips
Bruce Holmes '78 (son)
Jeffrey Broaddus '98 (grandson)

Baby Food Bars

3 eggs	1 (4-ounce) jar baby
2 cups sugar	food carrots
1¼ cups oil	2 cups flour
1 (4-ounce) jar baby	1 teaspoon baking soda
food apricots	1 teaspoon salt
1 (4-ounce) jar baby	½ teaspoon cinnamon
food applesauce	

FROSTING-

1 (3-ounce) package	2 cups powdered sugar
cream cheese	1 teaspoon vanilla
¾ stick soft butter	1 teaspoon milk

Mix eggs, sugar, oil, apricots, applesauce, carrots, flour, baking soda, salt, and cinnamon in order given. Bake at 350° for 30 minutes in large (10×15-inch) jelly roll pan. For frosting, combine cream cheese, butter, sugar, vanilla, and milk. Spread on warm bars. Enjoy! Makes 25 bars.

Kris Swanson Cox '95

Congo Squares

2¾ cups flour	3 eggs
2½ teaspoons baking powder	1 teaspoon vanilla
½ teaspoon salt	1 cup nuts
⅔ cup oil	1 cup semisweet chocolate chips
2¼ cups brown sugar	

Sift flour, baking powder, and salt. Set aside. Combine shortening and brown sugar. Mix well. Add eggs, one at a time beating well after each. Add vanilla. Add dry ingredients, nuts, and chocolate chips. (Mixture will be thick.) Bake at 350° for 25-30 minutes in a 10×15-inch pan. Cut into squares. Yield - 25 squares.

This recipe always turns out well.

Aggie Mom Friend

Speedy Iced Brownies

2 sticks margarine
2 cups sugar
1½ cups flour
Dash salt
4 eggs

½ cup cocoa
1 teaspoon vanilla
½ cup nuts
Miniature marshmallows

ICING-
½ stick margarine
2 tablespoons cocoa

½ teaspoon vanilla

Melt margarine in a large bowl or saucepan. Add remaining ingredients, except marshmallows and mix well. Cook in slightly greased 9×13-inch pan at 300° for 45 minutes or until brownies pull away from sides of pan. Sprinkle miniature marshmallows around over top of brownies and return to oven until marshmallows are soft. Spread until surface of brownies is covered with layer of marshmallows. Cool, then ice with icing and sprinkle additional nuts over icing.

For icing, melt and bring to boil, margarine, cocoa, and milk. Add sugar and vanilla. Mix with hand mixer or by hand until smooth. Spread over marshmallow layer on brownie.

Really quick, easy, and delicious.

Camille Dillard '68 (Don '64)
Danylle Dillard Leeds '91
Jason Leeds '92

Brownies

4 eggs
2 cups sugar
1 cup all-purpose flour
2 sticks margarine

2 squares unsweetened chocolate
1 teaspoon vanilla
2 cups pecans, chopped

Melt margarine and chocolate together and let cool. Beat eggs and add sugar and flour. Add chocolate mixture and vanilla. Stop beating and add nuts. Bake in 9×13-inch greased pan at 300° for 50 minutes. Sprinkle with powdered sugar and let cool prior to cutting.

Sandra Bruns
Frances Bruns Yoder '94
Charlotte Bruns Franta '96
John Yoder '93

Caramel Turtle Brownies

1 (14-ounce) bag caramels	6 tablespoons butter or
1 (5-ounce) can evaporated	margarine, melted
milk or ⅔ cup divided	1 (6-ounce) package semisweet
1 devil's food chocolate	chocolate chips
cake mix	Pecan halves for garnish
½ to 1 cup nuts, chopped	

Unwrap caramels (there are enough for the cook to sneak a few) and place in saucepan with 2 tablespoons evaporated milk. Set aside. In a mixing bowl, combine the remaining evaporated milk, dry cake mix, melted butter, and the nuts. Stir until well-blended. Spread half of this mixture in a greased 9×13-inch baking pan (mixture will form thin layer). Bake at 350° for 10 minutes ONLY. Meanwhile melt the caramels over low heat. Stir constantly. Be careful not to burn. Remove brownies from oven. Sprinkle with chocolate chips and drizzle melted caramels over the top. Cover evenly. Drop remaining cake mixture by teaspoons over all. Return to oven for 20 minutes. Do not overbake. Cut while warm, but do not remove from pan until completely cooled. They must "set up". Garnish with pecan halves if desired.

Nancy Bagwell
Lauren Bagwell '99
John Bagwell '03

Lemon Bars Deluxe

2¼ cups flour, divided	2 cups sugar
½ cup powdered sugar	⅓ cup lemon juice
1 cup margarine, softened	½ teaspoon baking powder
4 eggs, beaten	Powdered sugar

Sift together 2 cups flour and powdered sugar. Cut in margarine. Press in greased 9×13-inch pan. Bake at 350° for 25-30 minutes until slightly browned. Combine eggs, sugar, and lemon juice. Beat well by hand. Sift together ¼ cup flour and baking powder. Stir into egg mixture. Pour over crust and bake at 350° for 25-30 minutes. Sprinkle with powdered sugar. Cool and cut into bars. Makes 12 bars.

JaNahn Rodriguez, President ('97- '98)
David Rodriguez '94
Cindy Rodriguez '95
Dan Rodriguez '99

Down South Bars

2	tablespoons margarine	$1/_8$	teaspoon baking soda
1	cup brown sugar	1	cup pecans, chopped
5	tablespoons flour	1	teaspoon vanilla extract
2	eggs, beaten		Powdered sugar

Melt margarine in 8-inch square pan. Combine all ingredients, except powdered sugar, in separate bowl. Pour mixture over melted margarine - do not stir. Bake 350° for 20 minutes. Slightly cool. Cut while warm. Sprinkle with powdered sugar.

Cindy Etier
Emily Etier '01

Pecan Pie Bars

1	cup butter or margarine	1	teaspoon lemon rind, grated
½	cup powdered sugar	4	teaspoons lemon juice
2	cups flour	1	cup pecans, chopped
4	eggs	1	tablespoon cinnamon
2	cups sugar	½	cup powdered sugar
¼	cup flour		

Preheat oven to 350°. Mix butter, ½ cup powdered sugar, and 2 cups flour. Press into greased 9×13-inch pan. Bake 20 minutes. Beat eggs, sugar, and ½ cup flour. Then add lemon rind, juice, and pecans. Pour over baked layer. Bake 25-30 minutes. Sift ½ cup powdered sugar and cinnamon over top immediately. Cool, then cut into squares. Makes about 3 dozen.

Lillian Gips
Bruce Holmes '78 (son)
Jeffrey Broaddus '98 (grandson)

Luscious Pineapple Bars

2 eggs	2 cups flour
2 cups sugar	2 teaspoons baking soda
1 (20-ounce) can crushed pineapple, undrained	1 teaspoon vanilla
	½ cup nuts, chopped

FROSTING-

8 ounces cream cheese, softened	1¾ cups powdered sugar
	1 teaspoon vanilla
1 stick margarine, softened	½ cup nuts, chopped

Combine eggs, sugar, pineapple, flour, baking soda, and vanilla together and mix well. Add nuts and stir. Bake in a greased and floured 9×13-inch pan at 350° for 25-35 minutes. For Frosting, mix together all ingredients, except nuts, until creamy and spread on top. The nuts may be added to the frosting or sprinkled on top. Can be frozen. Makes 24-32 bars.

Mary Aasterud, President ('94-'95)
Valerie Aasterud McLaughlin '94

Texas Gold Bars

1 yellow cake mix (not pudding-style)	1 (8-ounce) package cream cheese, softened
1 stick margarine, melted	2 eggs
1 egg, beaten	1 pound powdered sugar
	1 teaspoon vanilla

Mix dry cake mix, margarine, and beaten egg. Press into a greased 9×13-inch pan. Mix cream cheese, eggs, sugar, and vanilla and pour on top of cake mix in pan. Bake at 300° for 1 hour. Serves 12.

Nancy Tong
Paul Tong '99

Pumpkin Bars

2 cups sugar	½ teaspoon nutmeg
2 cups flour	½ teaspoon salt
3 teaspoons baking powder	4 eggs
1 teaspoon soda	1 cup oil
2 teaspoons cinnamon	1 (16-ounce) can pumpkin

FROSTING-

4 teaspoons sugar	¼ cup shortening
4 teaspoons water	2 cups powdered sugar
Dash of salt	1 egg
¼ cup margarine	1 teaspoon vanilla

Bars: mix all dry ingredients in a mixing bowl. DO NOT use an electric mixer. Add eggs, oil, and pumpkin, and mix thoroughly. Pour into greased 11×17-inch pan and bake at 350° for 25-30 minutes. For frosting, mix all ingredients together and beat until smooth. Spread on cooled bars. Cut into 36 bars.

Sue Owen
Michael Owen '95

Grandma Bradfield's Toffee Squares

1 cup butter or margarine	¼ teaspoon salt
1 cup brown sugar	1 (12-ounce) package of
1 egg yolk	chocolate chips (melt while
1 teaspoon vanilla extract	other ingredients are baking)
2 cups flour (also good with	½ cup nuts (optional)
whole wheat pastry flour)	

Cream together first 4 ingredients. Slowly stir in flour and salt until well-blended. Pour into a greased 9×13-inch pan. Bake 20-25 minutes at 350° until brown. Texture will be soft. Remove from oven and pour melted chocolate chips on top. Let stand until set. Sprinkle with nuts. Cut into small squares while slightly warm. Enjoy!

Patricia Bradfield
Quisha Albert '00

Zucchini Bars

¾ cup margarine
½ cup brown sugar
½ cup granulated sugar
2 eggs
1 teaspoon vanilla
1¾ cups flour

1½ teaspoons baking powder
2 cups zucchini, unpared and shredded
1 cup coconut, shredded
¾ cup walnuts, chopped

CINNAMON FROSTING-
1 cup powdered sugar
2½ tablespoons milk
1½ tablespoons melted butter

1 teaspoon vanilla
½ teaspoon cinnamon

Cream margarine until fluffy. Beat in sugars gradually. Add eggs one at a time. Beat in vanilla. Stir in flour and baking powder. Stir in zucchini, coconut, and walnuts. Spread evenly in well greased 10×15-inch pan. Bake 40 minutes in 350° oven. Cool. For frosting, mix together all ingredients and spread over warm bars.

Aggie Mom

Boiled Cookies (No Baking!)

1 stick butter
4 cups sugar
½ cup cocoa
1 cup milk
Dash salt

6 cups quick oats
3 tablespoons vanilla
1 cup peanut butter
¾ cup pecans or walnuts, chopped

Mix butter, sugar, cocoa, milk, and salt. Bring to a boil and boil for 3 minutes. Mix quick oats, vanilla, peanut butter, and nuts. Stir into chocolate mixture. Drop by teaspoon onto buttered cookie sheets or spread in pans. Allow to cool and cut.

Debbie Cauthen
Christopher Cauthen '00

Many Way Butter Cookies

1 cup (2 sticks) butter	1½ cups all-purpose flour
¾ cup powdered sugar, sifted	1 teaspoon baking soda
1 egg	1 teaspoon cream of tartar
1 teaspoon vanilla extract	¼ teaspoon salt

In large bowl, cream butter. Gradually add sugar and beat until light and fluffy. Beat in egg and vanilla. Mix together flour, baking soda, cream of tartar, and salt. Gradually add creamed mixture. Chill dough for ease of handling. On lightly floured surface, roll dough to ⅛-inch thickness. With floured cookie cutters, cut desired shapes. Using wide spatula, transfer to baking sheet. Sprinkle with granulated sugar. Bake 6-8 minutes in preheated 400° oven. Remove immediately to wire rack to cool. Decorate before or after baking, if desired. Makes about 6 dozen cookies, depending on shape of cutters.

Very good tasting cookies.

Helen Moese
Linda Moese '97

Butterscotch Noodles

2 (6-ounce) packages butterscotch morsels	1 (6½-ounce) can cocktail peanuts
2 (3-ounce) cans chow mein noodles	

Melt morsels in top of double boiler. Add noodles and peanuts. Stir until coated. Drop by teaspoon onto wax paper to harden. Yield 54 cookies.

A Christmas tradition with my Aggies! Bet you can't eat just one!

Gail Stevenson
Jeff Rogers '97
Greg Rogers '99

Cheesecake Cookies

$^1/_3$ cup butter, melted
$^1/_3$ cup brown sugar
1 cup flour
$^1/_2$ cup nuts, chopped
$^1/_4$ cup sugar
1 (8-ounce) package
   cream cheese

1 tablespoon lemon juice
$^1/_2$ teaspoon vanilla
1 egg, beaten
2 tablespoons milk

Mix butter, brown sugar, and flour into crumbs. Add chopped nuts. Put half of mixture in bottom of 9-inch square pan. Bake at 350° for 10 minutes. Save remaining half for topping. Beat sugar, cream cheese, lemon juice, and vanilla until smooth. Add egg and milk. Pour cheese mixture over baked crumbs. Sprinkle remaining crumbs on top. Bake at 350° for 25 minutes. Cool. Store in refrigerator. Yield - 16 cookies

Betty Borsh
Aggie Mom Friend

Chewy Chocolate Chip/Oatmeal Cookies

1 cup oil
1 cup brown sugar
1 cup white sugar
2 eggs
1½ cups oatmeal
1 teaspoon vanilla

2 cups flour
1 teaspoon soda
1 teaspoon salt
1 (6-ounce) package
   chocolate chips
$^1/_2$ cup nuts

Preheat oven to 350°. In large bowl, by hand, mix oil, brown sugar, and white sugar until sugars are completely dissolved. Add 2 eggs and vanilla, and mix well. Then mix in oatmeal. In separate bowl, sift together flour, soda, and salt. Gradually stir into first mixture until thoroughly combined. Lastly, add chocolate chips and nuts. Use the one tablespoon ice cream scoop to drop dough on ungreased cookie sheet. Bake for 8 minutes. Cool on cookie sheet and remove. Makes 4 dozen.

This works well with raisins. I add about a cup of raisins. These are moist and chewy.

Eileen Buis
Josh Buis '97
Jordan Buis '99

Chocolate Puff Balls

½	cup margarine	2	teaspoons vanilla
2	cups sugar	2	teaspoons baking powder
4	squares chocolate, melted	2	cups flour
4	eggs		

Mix margarine and sugar together until well blended. Add eggs, one at a time. Add cooled melted chocolate. Add dry ingredients and vanilla. Chill dough. Roll into tablespoon-sized balls. Dip in powdered sugar. Bake in 345° oven for 12-15 minutes. Yield - 3-4 dozen. Delicious!

Thelma Maurer
Aggie Grandma

Coconut Macaroons

1½	cups coconut, grated	2	egg whites, beaten
½	cup sugar	½	teaspoon almond extract
½	teaspoon salt	1	jar of maraschino cherries
2	tablespoons flour		

Combine coconut, sugar, flour, and salt in bowl. Stir in beaten egg whites and almond extract. Mix well. Drop by teaspoon onto greased baking sheet. Press half of a cherry on each before baking. Bake at 325° for 15-20 minutes or until edges are brown. Remove from sheet at once. Makes about 1½ dozen cookies.

Beatrice Ray, Grandmother
Kristin Crawford '91
Julie Crawford '95

Date Nut Balls

½ cup flour
½ teaspoon baking powder
¼ teaspoon salt
1 cup pecans, chopped
1 cup dates, finely cut

2 eggs, beaten
1 cup sugar
1 teaspoon vanilla
Powdered sugar

Mix dry ingredients. Stir in dates and nuts. Beat sugar and vanilla into eggs. Add flour/date mixture. Blend. Spread into greased and floured 9×13-inch pan. Bake at 325° for 30 minutes. While warm, cut into squares and roll in ball. Roll crusty top towards center. Dust with powdered sugar. Store in tightly covered tin. Yield - 24.

Phyllis Williams
Aggie Aunt

Fruitcake Cookies

1 pound glazed cherries
1 pound glazed pineapple
1 pound raisins
6 cups pecans
½ cup margarine
4 eggs, separated
3 cups flour
1 teaspoon vanilla

1 teaspoon cinnamon
1 teaspoon nutmeg
1 teaspoon allspice
1 teaspoon baking soda
3 tablespoons buttermilk
4 ounces apple juice
1 cup brown sugar

Cream butter and sugar. Add egg yolk. Mix well. Put soda into buttermilk. Sift a little of the flour over fruit, nuts, and raisins. Sift spices with the rest of the flour. Add to butter, sugar, and egg mixture, alternately with buttermilk and baking soda, vanilla, and apple juice. Beat egg whites. Fold into mixture. Add fruits, nuts, and raisins. Mix well. Drop by teaspoon on greased cookie sheet and bake for 350° for 15 minutes.

This is the best cookie I have ever eaten!

Betty Pennington
Mitchell Lenamond '99
Shelley Guzman Lenamond '98 (granddaughter)

294

Ginger Snaps

¾ cup shortening	3 teaspoons ginger
1 cup sugar	2 teaspoons baking soda
1 egg	1 teaspoon cinnamon
¼ cup molasses	1 teaspoon salt
2 cups all-purpose flour	½ teaspoon ground cloves

Cream shortening and sugar. Beat in egg and molasses. Sift and add dry ingredients. Form into balls, roll in sugar. Bake at 350° for 12-15 minutes.

Sue Duncan
Nikki Duncan '97
Stephen Duncan '99

Graham Cracker Praline Cookies

24 (2½-inches square) graham crackers

ICING-

1 cup butter or margarine	1 cup pecans
1 cup brown sugar, firmly packed	1 teaspoon vanilla

FROSTING-

¼ cup margarine, softened	½ cup nuts, chopped
3 tablespoons half-and-half	1 cup powdered sugar
½ teaspoon vanilla	

Place 24 graham crackers side by side on a foil-lined cookie sheet. For icing, combine all ingredients and boil 2 minutes. Immediately pour over graham crackers. Bake in preheated 350° oven for 10 minutes. When cool, break into 48 small rectangular cookies. For frosting: mix all ingredients. Spread on cool cookies.

These keep in a tin in dormitory as long as it takes to eat them! They ship well too!

Dorothy Garland

Oatmeal-Coconut Thins

1 cup sugar	¼ teaspoon ground allspice
1 cup coconut, flaked	½ cup butter, melted
1 cup quick-cooking oats	1 tablespoon maple syrup
1 cup pecans, chopped	3 tablespoons orange juice
¾ cup all-purpose flour	1 teaspoon baking soda

Preheat oven to 300°. In a 3-quart bowl, combine sugar, coconut, oats, pecans, flour, and allspice. In small bowl or pan, combine melted butter, syrup, juice, and baking soda. Pour over dry ingredients. Stir by hand until well combined and mixture holds together. Mold into small 1-inch balls. Place 2-inches apart on greased cookie sheet. Bake near center of oven for 12-18 minutes or until golden brown. Cool 2-3 minutes before removing from baking sheet. Yield - 3 dozen.

Janie Wallace
Rachel Wallace '01

Spicy Oatmeal Crispies

1 cup shortening	3 teaspoons cinnamon
1 cup brown sugar	½ teaspoon ginger
1 cup granulated sugar	3 cups regular oats
2 eggs, beaten	1 teaspoon vanilla
1½ cups flour	1 (6-ounce) package chocolate
1 teaspoon salt	chips
1 teaspoon baking soda	

Cream sugars and shortening. Add eggs, then vanilla. Beat well. Add sifted dry ingredients, then oats, and chocolate chips. Place by teaspoonful on greased cookie sheet and bake at 350° for 10 minutes, or until golden brown. Makes 6 dozen.

Beverly Vespa
Jennifer Vespa '95

Peanut Blossoms

48 chocolate kisses, unwrapped	2 tablespoons milk
½ cup shortening	1¾ cups flour
½ cup sugar	½ teaspoon salt
½ cup brown sugar	1 egg
½ cup peanut butter	1 teaspoon vanilla
	1 teaspoon baking soda

Combine shortening, sugars, and peanut butter. Add egg, milk, flavorings, and dry ingredients. Shape into balls. Roll in granulated sugar. Bake on ungreased cookie sheet at 375° for 10-12 minutes. Remove from oven and immediately top each cookie with a chocolate kiss, pressing firmly enough to crack cookie edge.

JaNahn Rodriguez, President ('97-'98)
David Rodriguez '94
Cindy Rodriguez '95
Dan Rodriguez '99

Peanut Butter Balls

1 cup peanut butter	Dash of salt
2 cups powdered sugar	12 ounces chocolate chips
8 ounces margarine, softened	¾ stick paraffin
½ cup graham crackers, crushed	

Mix peanut butter, powdered sugar, margarine, graham crackers, and salt and form into balls. Place on cookie sheet. Melt chocolate chips and paraffin in top of double boiler. Dip peanut butter balls into chocolate mixture twice and put on waxed paper until set. Store in refrigerator.

Cindy Rodriguez '95

297

Peanut Butter Chocolate Balls

1½ cups graham cracker
    crumbs
1½ cups coconut, flaked
1½ cups nuts, chopped
16 ounces (3 cups)
    powdered sugar

12 ounces (1⅓ cups) crunchy
    peanut butter
1 teaspoon vanilla
1 cup butter, melted
½ bar paraffin
1 (6-ounce) package semisweet
    chocolate pieces

Combine first 7 ingredients, stirring well. Shape in 1-inch balls. Melt paraffin
in top of double boiler. Add chocolate morsels and heat until melted, stirring
constantly. Place several peanut butter balls in chocolate mixture, roll with
spoon to coat evenly. Remove from mixture with spoon and place on waxed
paper to cool. Reheat chocolate if it thickens during dipping. Yield -9 dozen.

Sue Duncan
Nikki Duncan '97
Stephen Duncan '99

Peanut Butter Cups

1 (10-ounce) roll refrigerated
    peanut butter cookie dough

36 bite-sized Reese's Peanut
    Butter Cups
    Cooking spray

Spray miniature muffin pans with cooking spray. Make 36 balls out of the
cookie dough, following the directions on the cookie package. Drop one cookie
ball in each muffin cup and bake at 350° for 10 minutes. While cookies bake,
remove wrappers from peanut butter cups. When cookies are removed from
the oven, they will fall. Immediately place a peanut butter cup in the middle
of each cookie. Press them down a little. Let cookies cool before removing
from pan. Yield - 36 cookies.

Laura Gonzalez

Pecan Tassies

2	(3-ounce) packages cream cheese	1½	cups chopped pecans
1	cup butter	1½	cups dark brown sugar
2	cups flour	2	tablespoons butter
2	eggs	2	teaspoons vanilla
			Dash of salt

Mix cream cheese, 1 cup butter, and flour. Form into 48 balls. Press into ungreased mini muffin tins. Make filling as follows. Beat eggs, then mix in pecans, brown sugar, 2 tablespoons butter, vanilla, and salt. Fill the unbaked tart shells. Bake at 350° for 25 minutes. Yield - 48.

Betty Pennington
Shelley Lenamond '98
Mitchell Lenamond '99

Also submitted by
Janis Andres
Monica Lynn Andres '98
Paul Leslie Andres '00

Sand Tarts

1	cup butter	2	teaspoons vanilla
½	cup powdered sugar	1½	cups nuts, chopped
2	cups sifted flour		

Cream butter and sugar. Gradually work flour into creamed mixture. Then stir in vanilla and nuts. Form into small balls. Bake on ungreased cookie sheet in 350° oven for 20 minutes. Cool slightly and roll in powdered sugar. Makes 5-6 dozen.

Anna Sheffield
Ann Sheffield Kuebler '97
Kevin Kuebler '97

Grandma Rose's Sugar Cookies

1   cup shortening
1¼ cups sugar
3   eggs
1   teaspoon vanilla

3   cups flour
1   teaspoon baking powder
¼   teaspoon salt

Cream shortening and sugar. Add eggs one at a time. Add vanilla. Slowly blend in flour, baking powder, and salt. Roll out on a well-floured board to ¼-inch thick. Cut out and place on cookie sheet. Sprinkle with sugar. Bake at 375° for 10 minutes. Do not overbake. Yield - about 4 dozen depending on cut-out size.

Ann Caronna
Ruth Caronna Schuman '89
Ken Schuman '88
Mark Caronna '96

Soft Sugar Cookies

2   cups sugar
4   cups flour
Pinch salt
1   teaspoon baking soda
3   teaspoons baking powder

1   cup shortening
3   eggs
1   teaspoon vanilla
½   cup milk

In bowl, mix dry ingredients. Mix in shortening as for pie dough. In separate bowl, beat together eggs, vanilla, and milk. Blend with dry ingredients. Drop on greased cookie sheet. Bake at 400° about 9-12 minutes.

Keep in covered container to keep soft.

Arlene Shea

Swedish Brune Brööd

1	cup butter at room temperature	1	teaspoon baking soda, dissolved in 1 egg yolk
1	cup sugar	2	cups flour
1	tablespoon molasses	½	teaspoon salt
1	tablespoon cinnamon	1	egg white

Cream butter and sugar. Mix in molasses and soda/egg yolk mixture. Stir in flour, cinnamon, and salt. Roll the dough into grape-sized balls. Beat egg white with fork. Dip balls into egg white and then sugar. Place on greased cookie sheet and bake at 350° for 10 minutes. Makes 3 dozen cookies.

Mary Aasterud, President ('94-'95)
Valerie Aasterud McLaughlin '94

Vanilla Nut Cookies

4	cups flour	2	cups granulated sugar
3	teaspoons baking powder	2	eggs, well beaten
¼	teaspoon salt	1	tablespoon vanilla
1	cup butter	1	cup nuts, chopped
½	cup brown sugar		

Sift dry ingredients. Cream butter. Add sugars gradually creaming together until light and fluffy. Add eggs and vanilla. Add flour gradually, mixing well. Fold in nuts. The mixture will be stiff. Divide the dough into 4-6 balls and shape into rolls 1½-inches in diameter. Place rolls in wax paper and chill (or freeze) overnight. Cut into 1/8-inch slices. Bake on greased baking sheet at 425° for 5 minutes or until light golden brown. Makes 6 dozen.

Allie Goodson
Buddy Goodson '69
Greg Myers '92 (grandson)
Cindy Myers Crook '96 (granddaughter)

Apple Pie

1½	tablespoons tapioca	2	tablespoons butter
⅛	teaspoon salt	1	(20-ounce) can sliced apples
¾	cup sugar (brown OR white		OR 5 cups apples, peeled,
	OR half of each)		cored, and thinly sliced
¾	teaspoon cinnamon	2	pie crusts
¼	teaspoon nutmeg		

Mix everything together in a large bowl. Fill prepared pie crust. Dot with a little butter. Place top crust on pie and pierce. Bake at 425° for 55 minutes or until syrup boils with heavy bubbles that do not burst. You may need to put foil around the pie crust edges to keep them from getting too brown. Makes 1 9-inch pie.

Sue Owen
Michael Owen '95

Apricot Cream Pie (Sugar Free)

1	baked 9-inch pie crust	1	package fresh dried apricots
1	(8-ounce) carton Cool Whip		(from produce section)
	Lite	1	package sugar-free cook and
			serve vanilla pudding mix

Cover apricots with water and cook slowly until apricots are soft and mushy, adding more water if necessary. Drain off water. Set aside to cool. Prepare pudding mix as directed on package. Pour apricot mixture in pie shell. Top with pudding. Cover with plastic wrap and chill. Serve with Cool Whip Lite.

Anna Sheffield
Ann Sheffield Kuebler '97
Kevin Kuebler '97

Blueberry Pie

FOR CANNED BERRIES-

3½ tablespoons Minute tapioca
¼ cup granulated sugar
¼ cup brown sugar
Dash salt
Dash cinnamon

2 (15-ounce) cans blueberries, drained
1⅓ cups juice from canned berries
2 tablespoons lemon juice

FOR FRESH OR FROZEN BERRIES-

3 tablespoons Minute tapioca
¾ - 1 cup sugar (white, brown, or half and half)
¼ teaspoon salt
2 pie crusts (top and bottom)

4 cups blueberries
1 tablespoon lemon juice
1 tablespoon butter

Mix all ingredients in a large bowl. Pour into unbaked pie shell. Dot with butter. Cover with top crust. Crimp edges and put several slits in crust. Bake at 425° for 45 minutes. Makes 1 9-inch pie. Serves 8.

Sue Owen
Michael Owen '95

Blueberry-Banana Pie

1 pie crust (lower half only)
1 banana
1 cup sugar
1 (8-ounce) carton Cool Whip

1 (8-ounce) package cream cheese
1 can blueberry pie filling

Bake bottom pie crust 9-11 minutes at 450°. Let cool. Layer sliced banana on pie crust. Mix together softened cream cheese, Cool Whip, and sugar. Pour over bananas into pie crust. Top with blueberry pie filling. Refrigerate for 1 hour. Serves 8.

Nancy Tong
Paul Tong '99

Blueberry Cream Pie

2	packages Dream Whip	1	(8-ounce) package softened cream cheese
2	9-inch pie shells, baked	1	cup sugar
3	bananas	1	can blueberry pie filling

Beat Dream Whip according to directions. Mix sugar with cream cheese in a separate bowl. Combine Dream Whip and cream cheese mixture. Slice bananas into baked pie shells. Pour ½ cream mixture in each pie shell over bananas. Chill 15 minutes. Spread ½ can blueberries over each pie. Refrigerate.

Enjoy!

Marion Crawford (Don '64)
Kristin Crawford '91
Julie Crawford '95

Butterscotch Pie

1	cup brown sugar	1¼	cups milk
3	heaping tablespoons flour	1	teaspoon butter
¼	teaspoon salt	1	teaspoon vanilla
¼	cup milk	1	9-inch pie shell, baked
3	egg yolks		

MERINGUE-

3	egg whites, room temperature	¼	teaspoon cream of tartar
		3	tablespoons sugar

Mix brown sugar and flour in a bowl. Add salt and ¼ cup milk. Separate eggs and stir in one egg yolk at a time. Heat 1¼ cups milk in top of double boiler. Add sugar mixture to milk. Stir and cook until very thick. Remove from heat. Add butter and vanilla. When cool, place in baked pie shell. For meringue - Beat egg whites until frothy. Add cream of tartar. Add sugar one tablespoon at a time. Beat until stiff peaks form. Spread on top of pie. Be sure to seal meringue to edges. Bake at 350° for 15 minutes.

Ann Caronna
Ruth Caronna Schumann '89
Ken Schumann '88
Mark Caronna '96

SENIOR BOOTS

Boots have been an important tradition at Texas A&M since the University's beginning in 1876. Senior boots became a hallmark at A&M in the early days. They were made in Europe until the 1920's when they became available locally. The engineer's boots pictured are circa 1915. They are part of an impressive collection of Corps memorabilia and Aggie history housed in the Sam Houston Sanders Corps Center on campus. The lace-up boots were a forerunner of the tall, sleek, pull-on, cavalry-style boots worn today.

Boots may be worn only by senior Corps members who often call for a Fish (freshman) to assist in removing them. Final Review marks the last time for outgoing seniors to wear their boots and the first time for incoming seniors. Boot Dance, a formal affair held that evening culminates the day. These well-loved boots are always treated with respect and are often used in household Aggie decor after college days are over.

"Old Army" Boots Photo
By
Richard Korcyznski

Cherry-Berry Pie

1	can pie cherries (NOT cherry pie filling)	2	tablespoons Quick Cook Tapioca
1	(10-ounce) package frozen strawberries, thawed	2	tablespoons cornstarch
1	cup sugar	1	teaspoon lemon juice
¼	teaspoon salt	2	prepared pie crusts, unbaked

Drain strawberries and reserve juice. Drain cherries and reserve juice. Combine juices, sugar, salt, tapioca, and cornstarch in medium-sized heavy saucepan. Cook over medium heat until thick and clear. Remove from heat and stir in lemon juice and drained fruit. Pour into bottom of pie crust. Lay top crust over and seal edges. Make slits for vents. Bake at 450° for 25-30 minutes. Cool before serving.

This is Beth's Grandfather's favorite pie!

Cindie Deasey
Beth Williamson '02

Grandma's Cherry Pie

1	(21-ounce) can cherry pie filling	1	teaspoon vanilla
1	graham cracker crust	½	cup milk
1	package Dream Whip	4	ounces cream cheese
		1	cup powdered sugar

Combine Dream Whip, vanilla, and milk in large mixing bowl. Set aside. Combine cream cheese and sugar in a small mixing bowl. Add small mixing bowl mixture to large bowl and combine well. Pour into a graham cracker crust. Top with a can of prepared cherry (or berry) pie filling. Chill for 2 hours before serving. Makes 1 pie. Serves 6.

June Siphon, Grandmother
Jennifer Luffy '00
Brian Luffy '02

No Bake Cherry Confetti Pie

1 (14-ounce) can sweetened condensed milk	½ cup coconut, flaked
1 (8-ounce) can crushed pineapple, undrained	½ cup pecans, chopped
	1 (8-ounce) container frozen whipped topping, thawed
1½ cups miniature marshmallows	1 (21-ounce) can cherry pie filling
	2 9-inch pie shells, baked

Mix together all ingredients (except pie shells). Pour into pie shells. Chill 1 hour before serving. Makes 2 pies. Serves 12-16.

Lanelle Boldt, Grandmother
Laura Boldt '94
David Boldt '97

Aunt Jewel's Chocolate Pie

1 9-inch pie shell, baked	2 rounded tablespoons cocoa
3 eggs, separated	2 cups milk
1 cup sugar	2 tablespoons butter or margarine
2 rounded tablespoons flour	1 teaspoon vanilla

Separate eggs. Put yolks, sugar, flour, and cocoa in saucepan. Add milk gradually, mixing well. Stir constantly until thickened. Remove from heat and add butter and vanilla. Pour into baked single pie crust. Beat egg whites until stiff. Add 3 tablespoons sugar and spread over pie filling. Bake at 325° until brown.

Julie Thedford (Marvin '65)
Mary Helen Ramsey '93
Clay Ramsey '93
Katherine Thedford '98

Chocolate Cheese Pie

1 cup sugar
3 (8-ounce) packages cream cheese
5 eggs

1 tablespoon vanilla
1 tablespoon lemon juice
1 (4-ounce) package German sweet chocolate, melted and cooled

Add sugar to cheese and blend well. Beat in eggs, one at a time. Add vanilla. Measure 2 cups of the cheese mixture, fold in chocolate. Add lemon juice to remaining cheese mixture and pour into buttered 10-inch pie pan. Top with chocolate mixture. Bake at 350° for 40-45 minutes. Chill. Garnish with whipped cream and chocolate curls, if desired. Serves 8.

Martha Tucker
Jennifer Tucker '97

Chocolate Chip Pecan Pie

1 pie shell, unbaked
2 eggs
½ cup flour
½ cup granulated sugar
½ cup brown sugar

¾ cup butter, melted
1 teaspoon vanilla
1 cup chocolate chips
1 cup pecans, chopped

Beat eggs until foamy. Add flour and sugars. Blend in melted butter and vanilla. Stir in chocolate chips and nuts. Pour into pie shell. Bake at 325° for 1 hour. Watch carefully. To prevent over browning, cover edge of pastry with foil the last 20 minutes.

Anna Sheffield
Ann Sheffield Kuebler '97
Kevin Kuebler '97

Easy Homemade
Chocolate Ice Cream Pie

1 can Eagle Brand milk	1 pint whipping cream, whipped
²/₃ cup chocolate syrup	2 graham cracker crusts

Stir together milk and chocolate syrup. Fold in whipped cream and pour into pie crusts. Freeze until firm. Makes 2 pies, each serving 6-8.

Susie Donahue
Megan Donahue '99
Ryan Donahue '02

Fudge Pie

1 cup sugar	2 eggs, beaten
½ cup flour	1 teaspoon vanilla
8 tablespoons butter or	½ cup pecans, chopped
margarine, melted	Peppermint ice cream (optional)
1 square unsweetened	
chocolate, melted	

Mix together sugar and flour. Add butter and chocolate and mix. Add eggs, vanilla, and pecans and blend well. Pour into 9-inch greased pie pan. Bake at 300° about 30 minutes. Serve with scoop of peppermint ice cream.

These make good brownies by increasing flour to 1¾ cups.

Gladys Heaton, President ('83-'84)
Patti Heaton '81
Mary Ann Heaton '85
Bill Heaton, Jr. '89

Hershey Pie

1 (8-ounce) Hershey's	1 (8-ounce) carton Cool Whip
Chocolate bar	Graham cracker crust
¼ cup water	

Melt Hershey bar. Add water and Cool Whip. Pour into graham cracker crust. Freeze for 8 hours before serving.

Cindy Etier
Emily Etier '01

Hershey-Almond Bar Pie

22 large marshmallows
½ cup milk
6 (1.55 ounce) Hershey's Milk Chocolate Almond bars
1 teaspoon vanilla
½ pint whipping cream
1 9-inch pie shell, baked

Combine all ingredients except cream. Heat over boiling water until melted. Cool. Whip and fold in whipped cream. Pour into baked pie shell and chill. Serve with ice cream and slivered, toasted almonds.

Debbie Cauthen
Christopher Cauthen '00

Hershey-Mocha/Almond Candy Bar Pie

CRUST-
1²/₃ cups coconut, shredded
4 tablespoons butter or margarine, melted

FILLING-
1 heaping teaspoon instant coffee
2 tablespoons warm water
½ pound Hershey Milk Chocolate bar with Almonds
8 ounces frozen whipped dessert topping

CRUST-
Mix coconut with melted butter and press in a 9-inch pie plate. Bake in 325° oven for 8 minutes until crust is slightly browned on edges. Cool well.

FILLING-
Dissolve coffee in the water in top of double boiler. Add to this the candy bar broken into pieces and melt in double boiler. (May cut almonds into smaller pieces). Cool. Fold candy mixture into thawed whipped topping. Pour into pie shell and freeze until shortly before serving.

Lynne Charbonneau
Scott Charbonneau '98
Mark Charbonneau '01

Nearly Fat-Free, Nearly Sugar-Free, No-Bake Lemon Pie

1   small box sugar-free lemon
    gelatin
¾   cup hot water
1   (12-ounce) carton Lite
    Cool Whip
2   teaspoons OR 9 packets of
    Equal Sugar Substitute

2   tablespoons lemon juice
1   (8-ounce) package fat-free
    cream cheese
2   reduced fat graham cracker
    crusts

Dissolve gelatin in the hot water and let cool. Mix cream cheese with the cooled gelatin. Add sugar substitute and lemon juice. Blend well. Stir Cool Whip into the mixture. Pour mixture into pie crusts. Refrigerate at least 1 hour.

Patricia Perez
Jose Perez '99

Grandma's Favorite Open Face Fresh Fruit Pie

PEACH PIE-
5-6 large peaches, peeled and
    sliced
1   cup sugar
3   tablespoons flour

⅛   teaspoon nutmeg
¼   teaspoon almond flavoring
1   10-inch pie shell

APPLE PIE-
5-6 Granny Smith apples,
    peeled and sliced
1   cup sugar
3   tablespoons flour

⅛   teaspoon nutmeg
¼   teaspoon almond flavoring
1   teaspoon cinnamon
1   10-inch pie shell

Pour into unbaked pie shell. Dot with butter. Bake 450° for 10 minutes, then 350° for 30 minutes until fruit is tender.

Thelma Maurer, Grandmother
David Rodriguez '94
Cindy Rodriguez '95
Dan Rodriguez '99

Peach Praline Pie

CRUST-

½ cup butter

¼ cup brown sugar, firmly
    packed

1 cup flour, sifted

½ cup pecans, chopped

FILLING-

1 quart vanilla ice cream,
   softened slightly

1- 1½ pounds fresh peaches
   OR 1 (16-ounce) package
   frozen peaches

¾ cup sugar

½ pint whipping cream, whipped

PRALINED PECAN HALVES-

1 cup sugar

½ teaspoon baking soda

½ cup half-and-half

1 tablespoon butter

1½ cups pecan halves

CRUST-

Mix together butter, sugar, and flour. Add nuts. Press into 9×13-inch pan. Bake at 400° for 7-9 minutes or until brown. Remove from oven and stir immediately. Reserve ¼ of mixture for topping. Press remainder in 9-inch pie pan. Cool.

FILLING-

Peel and slice fresh peaches. Sprinkle sugar over peaches and let set. Use blender or mixer on low speed and mash peaches (don't pureé them). Fold peaches and whipped cream into softened ice cream. Don't let ice cream soften too much. Spoon over pie crust. Sprinkle with reserved crumbs. Cover with foil and freeze several hours or overnight. Let thaw about 15-20 minutes before serving. Don't let pie melt. When ready to serve, garnish with whipped cream, fresh peaches and pralined pecan halves.

PRALINED PECANS-

Combine sugar and baking soda in deep saucepan. Add half & half, and stir well. Cook over medium heat to 234° (soft ball stage), stirring constantly. Remove from heat. Stir in butter and pecan halves. Beat until pecans are well coated and mixture thickens. Pour pecans onto buttered aluminum foil. Quickly separate each pecan with a spoon. Cool.

Mary Lou Laden, President ('80-'81)
Gary Laden '81

Peach Pie

2 pie crusts for top and bottom

CANNED PEACHES-

4 tablespoons tapioca
²/₃ cup granulated or brown
   sugar
¼ teaspoon salt
¹/₈ teaspoon mace

4 cups sliced peaches, drained
1¼ cups juice from canned peaches
2 tablespoons lemon juice
1 tablespoon butter

FRESH OR FROZEN PEACHES-

1½ tablespoons Minute tapioca
¼ cup granulated sugar
¼ cup brown sugar
¹/₈ teaspoon mace

4 cups peaches, peeled and sliced
2 tablespoons butter
2 tablespoons lemon juice

Mix everything together in large bowl. Pour into prepared unbaked crust. Dot
with butter. Add top crust. Crimp edges and slit top. Bake at 425° for 45
minutes. Makes 1 9-inch pie, or 1 8-inch square deep dish pie. Serves 8.

Sue Owen
Michael Owen '95

Chocolate Pecan Pie

3 eggs, slightly beaten
1 cup light or dark corn syrup
½ cup sugar
½ cup (3-ounces) semisweet
   chocolate chips

2 tablespoons margarine, melted
1 teaspoon vanilla
1½ cups pecan halves
1 9-inch pastry shell, unbaked

In large bowl, stir eggs, syrup, sugar, chocolate, butter, and vanilla until well
blended. Stir in pecans. Pour into pastry shell. Bake at 350° for 50-60 minutes. Serves 6-8.

Phyllis Condit
Matthew Clifton '01

Honey Crunch Pecan Pie

CRUST-
1¹/₃ cups flour
½ teaspoon salt

½ cup shortening
3-4 tablespoons cold water

PECAN FILLING-
4 eggs, slightly beaten
¼ cup sugar
¼ cup brown sugar
1 cup light corn syrup
½ teaspoon salt

1 teaspoon vanilla
1 tablespoon bourbon
2 tablespoons melted butter
1 cup pecans, chopped

CRUNCH TOPPING-
¹/₃ cup brown sugar
3 tablespoons honey

3 tablespoons butter
1½ cups pecan halves

Preheat oven to 350°. For crust, combine flour and salt in mixing bowl. Cut in shortening with pastry blender until mixture is uniform. Sprinkle with water, 1 tablespoon at a time, mixing until dough begins to form a ball. Roll out to ¹/₈-inch thickness. Line 10-inch pie shell.

FILLING-
Combine eggs, sugars, corn syrup, salt, vanilla, bourbon, and melted butter. Mix well. Fold in chopped pecans and spoon filling into unbaked pastry shell. Bake at 350° for 40 minutes. During the last 20 minutes of baking, cover the edge of pastry shell with aluminum foil to prevent burning.

TOPPING-
Combine sugar, honey, and butter in medium saucepan. Cook over medium heat until sugar dissolves, about 2-3 minutes. Stir constantly. Add pecans. Stir until nuts are well coated. Spread evenly over top of pie. Return pie to oven for additional 10-12 minutes or until topping is bubbly and golden brown.

A special occasion pecan pie!

JaNahn Rodriguez, President ('97-'98)
David Rodriguez '94
Cindy Rodriguez '95
Dan Rodriguez '99

Slim's Brown Sugar Pecan Pie

¾ cup brown sugar
2 tablespoons flour
1 teaspoon salt
1 cup light corn syrup
2 eggs

½ cup evaporated milk
1 cup pecans
¾ teaspoon vanilla
1 9-inch pie crust, unbaked

Mix all ingredients together and pour into pie crust. Bake at 375° for 50 minutes. Ingredients can be mixed without pecans and poured into pie crust. Pecans can then be arranged on top in any desired design.

Suzanne Blaney
Erin Blaney '01

Southern Pecan Pie

²/₃ cup sugar
²/₃ cup light corn syrup
3 large OR 4 medium eggs
4 tablespoons butter, melted

1 teaspoon vanilla
1½ cups pecan halves
1 pie pastry shell

Preheat oven to 425°. Beat together sugar, syrup, and eggs. Stir in butter, vanilla, and pecans. Pour into prepared pie shell. Bake for 5 minutes. Reduce heat to 350°. Bake 20-25 minutes until puffed in center. Serves 6-8.

Mary Cope, Grandmother
Wes Gilpin '93
Katherine Gilpin '97

Pecan Pie

1 10-inch pie shell, unbaked
½ cup sugar
2 tablespoons butter
¼ teaspoon salt
1 teaspoon vanilla

2 eggs, beaten
2 tablespoons flour
1 cup white corn syrup
1 cup pecans, chopped

Cream butter and sugar. Add flour and salt. Mix well. Add eggs and vanilla, beating well. Mix in corn syrup and add pecans. Pour into unbaked pie crust. Bake 35-40 minutes in 350° oven.

Kay O'Jibway, Austin County A&M Mothers' Club
Jeff O'Jibway '99
Jay O'Jibway '01

Pumpkin Pie

1	(16-ounce) can pumpkin	1	cup cold milk
1	(6-ounce) box instant vanilla pudding	1	teaspoon pumpkin pie spice
1	cup whipped topping	1	9-inch pie shell, baked
		1	cup whipping cream, whipped

Mix together all ingredients and beat for 2 minutes. Pour into pie shell and refrigerate. Top with whipped cream and serve. Serves 8.

Wanda Lymenstull, President ('81-'82)
Debra Brown '82
T. J. Lymenstull '86

Frost on Bonnie's Pumpkin Pie

1½	cups gingersnaps, crushed	½	cup milk
¼	cup butter, melted	½	teaspoon salt
½	cup powdered sugar, sifted	½	teaspoon allspice
1	cup whipping cream	½	teaspoon ginger
1¼	cups powdered sugar, sifted	½	teaspoon nutmeg
½	teaspoon ground cinnamon	½	teaspoon cinnamon
½	teaspoon vanilla extract	2	envelopes unflavored gelatin
3	egg yolks	¼	cup cold water
⅓	cup sugar	3	egg whites
1¼	cups pumpkin, cooked and mashed	¼	cup powdered sugar, sifted

Mix crushed gingersnaps, butter, and powdered sugar. Press into a 10-inch pie pan. Bake at 325° for 10 minutes. Whip cream until it stands in peaks. Add sifted powdered sugar, cinnamon, and vanilla extract. Beat until stiff peaks form, and chill until ready to use. Beat egg yolks, add sugar, pumpkin, milk, salt, and spices. Mix well and cook over medium heat until it boils. Cook 2 minutes longer, stirring constantly. Remove from heat and add gelatin which has been dissolved in cold water. Cool. Beat egg whites until stiff. Fold in powdered sugar. Fold in the cooled pumpkin mixture. Fill crust with a layer of pumpkin mixture, a layer of whipped cream mixture (using ½ of it) and another layer of the pumpkin. Chill 2 hours to set. Before serving, top with remaining whipped cream. Yield - 8 servings.

Eileen Buis
Josh Buis '97
Jordan Buis '99

Pineapple Cream Cheese Icebox Pie

1   (14-ounce) can sweetened
    condensed milk
1   (3-ounce) package cream
    cheese, softened

½   cup lemon juice
¾   cup crushed pineapple, drained
½   cup pecans, chopped
1   graham cracker pie crust

Sprinkle pie crust with pecans and set aside. Mix together milk, cream cheese, lemon juice, and pineapple and pour into pie crust. Bake at 325° for 20 minutes. Chill and serve with whipped cream. Serves 8.

Susie Donahue
Megan Donahue '99
Ryan Donahue '02

Snickers Bar Pie

1   (3-ounce) package cream
    cheese, softened
¼   cup peanut butter (creamy
    or crunchy)
¾   cup powdered sugar

1   (8-ounce) carton frozen
    whipped topping, thawed
2   (3.07-ounce) Snickers bars,
    finely chopped
1   prepared chocolate pie crust

In a large mixing bowl, beat cream cheese, peanut butter, and powdered sugar until creamy. Fold in whipped topping and candy bars. Pour into crust and refrigerate overnight. Serves 6-8.

Marilyn McBride
Shannon McBride '98

Grandma Dottie's Fresh Strawberry Pie

1	9-inch pie shell, baked and cooled	¾	cup sugar
4	cups fresh strawberries, washed and hulled	2	tablespoons cornstarch
1¹/₃	cups water	1	(3-ounce) package strawberry gelatin

Slice strawberries and place in cooled pie shell. Combine water, sugar, and cornstarch. Cook over medium heat until mixture comes to a boil. Stir in one package of strawberry gelatin. Stir until gelatin is dissolved. Pour mixture over strawberries while it is still hot. Refrigerate and serve with a dollop of whipped cream.

Eileen Buis
Josh Buis '97
Jordan Buis '99

Blueberry Cobbler

3	pounds blueberries, washed	½	stick butter, melted
1½	cups sugar	¹/₃	cup water

PASTRY-

1½	cups Bisquick	½	cup milk
1	tablespoon sugar		

Place blueberries in 9×13-inch pan. Sprinkle 1 cup of sugar over the berries. Combine ½ cup of sugar with 2 tablespoons flour. Mix well and sprinkle over the berries. Pour melted butter evenly over berries. Add ¹/₃ cup of water, poured into corner of pan so as not to wash sugar off berries. Tilt pan so water is evenly distributed. Mix pastry, roll out, and make strips. Place on cobbler and brush top of pastry with more melted butter. Sprinkle small amount of sugar over pastry. Bake at 400° for 10 minutes and 375° for 30 minutes.

Anna Sheffield
Ann Sheffield Kuebler '97
Kevin Kuebler '97

Grandmother's Cherry Cobbler

2	(16-ounce) cans red tart pitted cherries	1	teaspoon baking powder
1	cup sugar	½	teaspoon salt
1	teaspoon butter	⅛	teaspoon baking soda
1	cup flour	2	tablespoons shortening
			Buttermilk

Put sugar and cherries with juice in saucepan and heat until sugar is dissolved. Let cool. Mix flour, baking powder, salt, and baking soda. Cut shortening into flour until mixture resembles coarse crumbs. Add enough buttermilk to make a soft dough. Roll out on floured board until very thin. Brush with melted butter and sugar. Put cooled cherries and juice in a 2-quart baking dish. Cut biscuit dough in strips and lay across top of cherries until the surface is entirely covered. Press the strips gently against the side of the dish to seal. Bake at 400° for a couple of minutes, then reduce heat to 350° and bake 30 minutes until brown. Serves 6-8.

Any fresh fruit can be substituted, such as peaches, blackberries, raspberries, etc.

Suzanne Blaney
Erin Blaney '01

Peach Cobbler

¾	stick margarine	2	teaspoons baking powder
½	cup sugar	3	cups peaches, sliced
½	cup milk	¾	cup sugar
¾	cup flour		

Melt margarine in casserole dish. Mix sugar, milk, flour, and baking powder together and pour over margarine, but do not stir. Mix peaches and ¾ cup of sugar together. Pour on top of flour mixture in casserole dish but do not stir. Bake at 350° for 1 hour. Other fruit can be substituted for peaches.

Sandra Bruns
Frances Bruns Yoder '94
Charlotte Bruns Franta '96
John Yoder '93

Mexican Cobbler

1 (21-ounce) can apple pie filling	1⅓ cups sugar
1 teaspoon cinnamon	1 cup water
10-12 flour tortillas	1 teaspoon cinnamon
	1 stick margarine or butter

Chop apples into small pieces. Add cinnamon, then place about 1 tablespoon of apples in each flour tortilla. Roll and place in baking dish (use toothpick to hold together if needed). Mix sugar and cinnamon and add to water. Melt butter and add to sugar mix and pour over tortillas. Refrigerate overnight. Bake 35 minutes at 350° and cool about 20 minutes before serving. Top with Cool Whip.

Linda Murphy
Kristina Murphy '91
Karin Murphy Harbour '93
Sean Harbour '92

Also submitted by -
Nina Cox, President ('96-'97)
Chris Cox '92

Quicky "Cobbler"

1 (8-ounce) can crushed pineapple	1 (18 ¼-ounce) box yellow cake mix
1 (21-ounce) can cherry pie filling	1 stick butter or margarine
	1½ cups pecans, chopped (optional)

Pour pineapple (juice too) into greased 9×13-inch pan. Distribute evenly. Pour pie filling on top of pineapple and distribute evenly. Pour dry cake mix on top of pie filling and spread evenly. Dot with pats of butter all over. Top with chopped pecans if desired. Bake 40-50 minutes at 375°. Serve warm topped with vanilla ice cream.

Always a hit! Ingredients can be kept on hand all the time for an emergency dessert.

Laura Boldt '94

Angel Food Cake Dessert

1   angel food cake, broken
    in pieces
1   can sweetened condensed
    milk
Juice of 2 lemons

1   cup sugar
1   pint heavy cream
Coconut (optional)
Nuts, broken, (optional)
1   pint strawberries

Whip together the lemon juice and milk. Add sugar and whipped cream. Layer ½ the cake pieces and ½ the cream mixture. Repeat layers. Top with coconut and nuts. Serves 10.

I add strawberries to middle layer and save some for garnish.

Helen Moese
Linda Moese '97

Cherry-Pistachio Angel Trifle

1   angel food cake, torn into
    bite-sized pieces
2   (3.4-ounce) packages
    pistachio pudding mix
6   cups cold milk
½   pint whipping cream, whipped,
    OR frozen whipped topping

½   cup almonds, chopped
1   jar red maraschino cherries,
    drained and halved
1   jar green maraschino cherries,
    drained and halved

Prepare pudding using milk, according to package directions. In 3-quart trifle bowl, layer ½ cake, ½ pudding, ½ nuts, ½ whipped cream, and ½ cherries. Repeat layers. Serves 8-10.

Pretty for Christmas. Good and easy!

Judy Boldt (Bob '68)
Laura Boldt '94
David Boldt '97

Chocolate Angel Dessert

1   (12-ounce) package   ½   pint whipping cream, whipped
    semisweet chocolate chips   6   eggs, separated
1   angel food cake (buy ready- ½   cup pecans, chopped
    made in grocery bakery)

Melt chips in microwave oven (or in double boiler). Add beaten egg yolks and mix well. Cool. When mixture has cooled, fold into stiffly beaten egg whites, then fold in whipped cream. Be sure mixture is blended well. Tear up cake into small pieces. Put a layer of cake in 9×13-inch pan and pour half of chocolate mixture over cake. Repeat. Sprinkle pecans on top. Serves 12 generously.

Martha Tucker
Jennifer Tucker '97

Apple Crumb Dessert

4   cups fresh apples, peeled,   1   cup flour
    cored, and sliced thin OR   1   cup sugar
2   (20-ounce) cans apple pie   ¾   to 1 whole stick butter or
    slices (NOT pie filling)   margarine
Cinnamon or allspice to taste

Arrange apples in 8- or 9-inch square pan. Sprinkle with cinnamon or allspice, if desired. Mix flour, sugar, and butter until blended. Mixture will be lumpy. Pour over apples. If using fresh apples, pour ¼ cup water over all. Bake at 350° for 20 minutes or until top starts to brown.

VARIATION-
substitute fresh pears for apples. Serves 4-6.

A good quick dessert for unexpected company if you keep a couple of cans of apples handy.

Sue Owen
Michael Owen '95

Fresh Apple Dessert

1 package super moist yellow cake mix	1 teaspoon ground cinnamon
½ cup margarine or butter, softened	2 large cooking apples, thinly sliced
¼ cup brown sugar, packed	1 cup sour cream
	1 egg

Preheat oven to 350°. Mix dry cake mix, margarine, brown sugar, and cinnamon until crumbly. Reserve ²/₃ cup crumbly mixture. Press remaining crumbly mixture in bottom of ungreased 9×13-inch pan. Arrange apple slices on mixture in pan. Beat sour cream and egg until blended. Spread over apples. Sprinkle with reserved crumbly mixture. Bake 30 minutes or until topping is light golden brown. Cool. Makes 16 servings.

Tilly Vogeli
Michael Vogeli '94

Gene's Apple-Coconut Delight

1½ cups flour	3 tablespoons flour
¹/₃ cup sugar	4 cups apples, peeled and diced
½ cup margarine	1 cup coconut
3 eggs, beaten	½ cup nuts, chopped
1½ cups sugar	¼ cup sugar
¼ teaspoon salt	½ teaspoon cinnamon
3 tablespoons evaporated milk	

Combine first 3 ingredients with pastry blender and put into 9×13-inch pan. Bake at 350° for 15 minutes. Place diced apples on hot crust. Mix eggs, sugar, salt, evaporated milk, and 3 tablespoons flour together. Drizzle egg mixture over apples. Combine coconut and chopped nuts, sprinkle over mixture. Combine sugar and cinnamon and sprinkle on last. Bake at 350° for 40-45 minutes.

JaNahn Rodriguez, President ('97-'98)
David Rodriguez '94
Cindy Rodriguez '95
Dan Rodriguez '99

Banana Pudding

4	eggs, separated	2	teaspoons vanilla
1½	cups sugar	3	bananas
4	tablespoons cornstarch		Vanilla wafers
	Dash salt	¼	teaspoon cream of tartar
2²/₃	cups milk		

Beat egg yolks. Combine 1 cup sugar, cornstarch, and salt. Stir in milk gradually. Microwave on high for 10-12 minutes, stirring every 3 minutes. When mixture begins to thicken, stir a small amount of hot liquid into egg yolks. Gradually add to hot mixture. Microwave on medium for 3-5 minutes, stirring each minute until thick. Stir in 1½ teaspoons vanilla. Line 2-quart dish with wafers. Cover with slices of bananas. Add layer of pudding. Repeat layers. Beat egg whites with cream of tartar and ½ teaspoon vanilla until soft peaks form. Gradually add ½ cup sugar, beating until stiff peaks form and all sugar is dissolved. Spread on pudding, sealing edges. Bake at 425° for 5 minutes until delicately browned. Cool slightly. Serves 8.

Pat Hardi, President ('93-'94)
Steven Hardi '91, '94

Cream Cheese/Banana Pudding

1	(8-ounce) package cream cheese, softened	1	(14-ounce) can sweetened condensed milk
1	(6-ounce) box instant vanilla pudding	1	(11-ounce) box vanilla wafers
2	cups milk	4	bananas, sliced
1	teaspoon vanilla	1	(8-ounce) carton whipped topping

Beat cream cheese. Add milk, condensed milk, and vanilla and blend well. Beat in pudding mix. Fold in half of whipped topping. Layer in 7×11-inch dish in this order - pudding mix, vanilla wafers, banana slices, and remaining whipped topping.

Nina Cox, President ('96-'97)
Chris Cox '92

Easy Banana Split Trifle

1 (3.4-ounce) package vanilla instant pudding mix
4 cups milk (divided)
60 vanilla wafers (divided)
1 pint fresh strawberries, sliced
3 bananas, sliced
6 tablespoons chocolate syrup (divided)
1 (15-ounce) can crushed pineapple, drained
1 (3.9-ounce) package chocolate instant pudding mix
1 (8-ounce) container frozen whipped topping, thawed
16 maraschino cherries, drained and halved
¼ cup pecans, chopped

Prepare vanilla pudding according to package directions, using 2 cups cold milk. Arrange 30 vanilla wafers in bottom of 3-quart trifle bowl. Top with sliced strawberries. Spoon vanilla pudding in next. Arrange sliced bananas on top of pudding. Drizzle bananas with 3 tablespoons chocolate syrup. Arrange remaining 30 wafers over bananas. Spoon pineapple evenly over wafers. Prepare chocolate pudding according to package directions, using remaining 2 cups cold milk. (Let stand 30 seconds to thicken.) Spoon pudding over pineapple. Spread whipped topping over chocolate pudding spreading to edges of bowl to seal. Cover with plastic wrap and refrigerate overnight, or at least 1 hour. Before serving, arrange cherries on top. Sprinkle with pecans. Drizzle remaining chocolate syrup over top. Serves 8-10.

Judy Boldt (Bob '68)
Laura Boldt '94
David Boldt '97

Layered Fruit/Angel Dessert

1 angel food cake, torn into chunks
1 (16-ounce) can cherry pie filling
1 (20-ounce) can pineapple chunks, drained
1 (8-ounce) can Mandarin oranges, drained
4 bananas, sliced
4 kiwi fruit, sliced
8 ounces non-dairy whipped topping

Layer in order given. Chill before serving.

Ann Miller

Berries and Bits

1	(14-ounce) can evaporated milk	¾	cup small semisweet chocolate pieces
1½	cups cold water	2	cups whipped cream
1	(3.4-ounce) package instant vanilla pudding mix	36	vanilla wafers
		1	quart strawberries, halved

In large bowl, combine milk and water. Add pudding mix, beat well. Chill 5 minutes. Fold in whipped cream. Spoon 2 cups pudding into a 3-quart serving bowl. Top with half the wafers and strawberries, ¼ cup chocolate pieces and 2 cups pudding. Repeat. Garnish with strawberries and ¼ cup chocolate pieces. Chill.

FRUIT SUBSTITUTES-
2 cups blueberries, sliced peaches, nectarines, plum halves, or grapes.

Julie Thedford (Marvin '65)
Mary Helen Ramsey '93
Clay Ramsey '93
Katherine Thedford '98

Quick Bread Pudding

1	(1-pound) loaf raisin bread	2	packages NON-instant vanilla pudding
6	cups milk (divided)	2	teaspoons vanilla flavoring

Cut bread into 1-inch cubes (can do about ⅓ loaf at a time). Put into greased 9×13-inch pan and mix with 2 cups milk. Mix 4 cups milk, 2 packages dry non-instant pudding mix, and vanilla flavoring. Pour over bread in pan and mix. Bake 1 hour at 350°.

Great with Blue Bell Homemade Vanilla Ice Cream and wonderful when they say, "Oh, Mom, can I bring a few friends with me when I come home tomorrow?"

Lillian Gips
Bruce Holmes '78 (son)
Jeffrey Broaddus '98 (grandson)

Aunt Peggy's Cheesecake

1 ²/₃ cups graham crackers, crushed	2 (8-ounce) packages cream cheese
1¼ cups sugar	¼ teaspoon salt
¼ cup butter	2 teaspoons vanilla
3 eggs, well beaten	½ teaspoon almond extract
1 cup sugar	2 cups sour cream

For crust, mix crushed graham crackers, sugar, and butter. Pat in bottom of 10-inch spring form pan. Beat together eggs, sugar, cream cheese, salt, vanilla, and almond extract. Beat till well mixed. Fold in sour cream by hand. Pour into crust. Bake at 375° for 35-45 minutes. Cool. Cover and chill. Serves 12-16.

Mary Beth Dennehy
Kerry Dennehy '99
Erin Dennehy '01

Chocolate Almond Cheesecake

1½ cups chocolate wafer crumbs	4 eggs
2 cups almonds, blanched, lightly toasted, and chopped	¹/₃ cup whipping cream, unwhipped
	¼ cup amaretto liqueur
¹/₃ cup sugar	1 teaspoon vanilla
¾ cup butter, softened	2 cups sour cream
3 (8-ounce) packages cream cheese, softened	1 tablespoon sugar
	1 teaspoon vanilla
1¼ cups sugar	

Combine chocolate wafer crumbs, 1½ cups almonds, sugar, and butter. Press on bottom and sides of 9½-inch buttered spring form pan. In large bowl, cream together cream cheese and sugar. Beat in eggs, one at a time, beating well after each addition. Add whipping cream, amaretto, and vanilla, and beat mixture until light. Pour batter into shell and bake in preheated 375° oven for 10 minutes. Reduce heat to 275° and bake 1 hour or more until cake is set in middle. Remove from oven and let set for 5 minutes. In bowl, combine sour cream, sugar, and vanilla. Spread mixture evenly on cake. Return to oven and bake 5 minutes more. Transfer to rack. Cool. Remove sides of pan and press ½ cup toasted almonds around edge and top.

Dorothy Starry
Sheree Starry Wagner '80

Susie's Cheesecake

CRUST-

2　cups graham cracker crumbs

1　teaspoon cinnamon

2　tablespoons sugar

6　ounces (1½ sticks) butter, melted

FILLING-

3　(8-ounce) packages cream cheese

¾- 1 cup sugar

4　eggs

1　tablespoon vanilla

TOPPING-

2　cups sour cream

3　tablespoons sugar

1　teaspoon vanilla

Preheat oven to 400°. Mix graham cracker crumbs, cinnamon, sugar, and butter. Put into bottom and up sides of spring form pan. For filling, mix cream cheese, sugar, eggs (1 at a time), and vanilla and beat until smooth. Bake 30-40 minutes. Cool 10 minutes. Should be firm at edges. For topping, mix sour cream, sugar, and vanilla and add to cooled cheesecake. Bake 5 minutes at 400°.

Delicious!

Sue Heflin
Rogge Heflin '98

Chocolate Mousse Torte

1¾ cups flour
1¾ cups sugar
1¼ teaspoons baking soda
1　teaspoon salt
¼　teaspoon baking powder
²/₃ cup soft type margarine

4　(1-ounce) squares Baker's
　　Unsweetened Chocolate
1¼ cups water
1　teaspoon vanilla
3　eggs

MOUSSE FROSTING/FILLING-
10 ounces semisweet
　　chocolate

1　cup heavy cream
1　quart heavy cream

Preheat oven to 350°. Grease and flour 4 9-inch cake pans. Melt and cool chocolate. Place flour, sugar, baking soda, salt, baking powder, margarine, chocolate, water, and vanilla into large mixing bowl. Beat at low speed to blend; then beat 2 minutes at medium speed, scraping sides and bottom of bowl frequently. Add eggs. Beat 2 minutes more. Pour ¼ of batter (approximately 1 cup) into each pan. Layers will be thin. Bake 15-18 minutes until done, but do not overbake. Cool slightly and remove from pans. Cool thoroughly. Stack, fill and frost with Mousse Frosting. For frosting, melt chocolate in double boiler. Bring 1 cup heavy cream to boil. Combine with chocolate in mixing bowl. Beat on low to medium for 5 minutes. Cool to soft pudding consistency. (May refrigerate and re-warm.) Whip 1 quart cream to form stiff peaks. Add chocolate mixture and beat quickly to blend. After placing on cake, garnish with chocolate curls, if desired.

Gloria Gilpin, President ('98-'99) (Bobby '62)
Wes Gilpin '93
Katherine Gilpin '97

Death by Chocolate

1 (1pound-6-ounce) box
  chocolate brownie mix
1 (12-ounce) carton Cool Whip
2 (2.8-ounce) packages
  chocolate mousse

1 (12-ounce) package Heath
  bar candy bits OR 8 Heath Bars,
  crumbled
Kahlua (optional)

Prepare recipe of chocolate brownies as directed on package. Cool and crumble. Prepare chocolate mousse as directed on the package. Put ½ crumbled brownies in trifle bowl (glass bowl 4-6 inches tall) and sprinkle with Kahlua. Spread ½ chocolate mousse and then ½ Cool Whip on top. Cover with ½ Heath bar bits. Repeat second layer with rest of ingredients. Refrigerate 8-24 hours before serving. Serves 8-10.

Shirley Tingley, Former Federation President (Buddy, '48)
Darrel Lowery '82
Sheryl Tingley French '90

Fruit Pizza

1 roll sugar cookie dough
1 (8-ounce) package cream
  cheese, softened
¼ cup sugar
1 teaspoon vanilla

Fruit of your choice (bananas,
  kiwi, strawberries, cherries,
  blueberries, etc.)
Fruit Fresh

Cut softened dough into slices and spread on pizza pan or cookie sheet. Bake at 350° 12-14 minutes. Cool. Cream together cream cheese, sugar, and vanilla. Spread over cooled cookie. Top with fruit. Sprinkle with Fruit Fresh. Chill.

This is a favorite snack/dessert with both my Aggies, as well as my future Aggie - 6-year old Tyler! It is decorative and easy to make.

Gail Stevenson
Jeff Rogers '97
Greg Rogers '99

Four Layer Chocolate Delight

CRUST-

1½ sticks margarine, melted   1 cup nuts, chopped

1½ cups flour

FIRST FILLING-

1 (8-ounce) package cream cheese   1 cup powdered sugar (divided)

1 (12-ounce) carton frozen whipped topping   1 teaspoon vanilla

SECOND FILLING-

3 cups milk   1 (5 ½-ounce) package instant vanilla pudding

1 (5 ½-ounce) package instant chocolate pudding   2 teaspoons vanilla

   1 Hershey's Milk Chocolate bar

THIRD FILLING-

Remainder of frozen whipped topping carton

Combine margarine, flour, and nuts. Press into a 9×13-inch pan. Bake 20 minutes at 350°. Cool. Combine cream cheese, powdered sugar, 1 cup whipped topping, and 1 teaspoon vanilla. Mix well. Spread over cooled crust. Combine 3 cups milk, chocolate and vanilla puddings, and vanilla. Mix according to pudding directions. Pour over cream cheese layer. Top with whipped topping. Grate or shave Hershey Bar. Sprinkle over top (in a block ATM). Refrigerate.

VARIATIONS I-

Use pistachio instant pudding instead of vanilla pudding.

Use butterscotch instant pudding instead of vanilla pudding.

Gail Stevenson
Jeff Rogers '97, Greg Rogers '99

VARIATION II-

PUMPKIN DELIGHT-

Combine margarine, flour, and nuts. Press into a 9×13-inch pan. Bake 20 minutes at 350°. Cool. Combine cream cheese, powdered sugar, and 1 cup whipped topping, Mix well. Spread over cooled crust. Combine and mix 1½ cups milk, 1 package of vanilla instant pudding and pie filling, and 1 cup canned pumpkin. (May use 2 cups if you want thicker layer of pumpkin.) Mix 1 teaspoon pumpkin pie spice and 1 cup whipped topping. Spread whipped topping on top. Sprinkle with chopped pecans (form the block ATM).

Great for Thanksgiving.

Dianne Mayfield, Federation Officer
Mitch Cogbill '93, Donna Cogbill '94

All Seasons Lemon Trifle

1	angel food cake	1	(8-ounce) carton Lite Cool Whip
1	(14-ounce) can Eagle Brand milk	1	cup fresh strawberries, sliced
2	teaspoons lemon rind	1	cup fresh blueberries, OR 1 cup blackberries, sliced
1/3	cup fresh lemon juice	1	cup fresh raspberries
1	(8-ounce) carton lemon non-fat yogurt	1/2	cup flaked coconut, lightly toasted

Cut or tear cake into pieces. Combine condensed milk, lemon juice, rind, and yogurt. Fold in 2 cups Cool Whip. Set aside. Place 1/3 cake pieces in 4-quart trifle bowl. Top with 1/3 of lemon mixture. Top with strawberries. Repeat layers using blueberries (or blackberries), and raspberries. Spread remaining Cool Whip on top and sprinkle with coconut. Cover and refrigerate for 8 hours. Makes 16-18 servings.

We serve this at lots of Church dinners. Also good if using on one type of fruit and leftover white or yellow cake, instead of angel food cake.

Shirley Tingley, Former Federation President, (Buddy, '48)
Darrel Lowery '82
Sheryl Tingley French '90

Pumpkin Logs

3	eggs	2/3	cup canned pumpkin (1 can makes 3 logs)
1/2	cup sugar		
1	teaspoon baking soda	3/4	cup flour

ICING-

1	cup powdered sugar	2	tablespoons margarine
1	(8-ounce) package cream cheese	1	cup nuts, chopped
		1	teaspoon vanilla

Mix ingredients for cake roll. Pour into a 10×15-inch cookie sheet lined generously with greased wax paper. Bake at 375° for 15 minutes. Invert into slightly dampened linen towel. Carefully remove wax paper. Immediately roll cake and towel together and cool in refrigerator while mixing icing. Mix ingredients for icing. Unroll cake; remove towel. Spread icing on cake. Roll up. Keep refrigerated. Wax paper will smoke while baking thin layer cake but it will not catch fire. Inverting cake onto slightly dampened towel reduces cracking of cake when rolled up.

Nancy Tong
Paul Tong '99

Pumpkin Roll

3 eggs	1 teaspoon lemon juice
1 cup sugar	2 teaspoons cinnamon
2/3 cup pumpkin	1/2 teaspoon ginger
3/4 cup flour	1/2 teaspoon salt
1/2 cup pecans, chopped	1/2 teaspoon nutmeg
1 teaspoon baking powder	

FILLING-

1 cup powdered sugar	1 (8-ounce) package cream cheese
2 tablespoons margarine	1/2 cup pecans, chopped
	1 teaspoon vanilla

Beat eggs 5 minutes. Gradually add sugar. Stir in pumpkin and lemon juice. Fold in dry ingredients. Grease 10×15-inch pan and line with waxed paper. Grease paper. Spread mixture evenly over paper. Bake 15 minutes at 375°. Turn out immediately on a cotton towel that has been sprinkled with powdered sugar. Peel off the waxed paper and roll up starting from the 10-inch side. Cool thoroughly, unroll and spread with filling. Then re-roll and refrigerate. Makes 1 roll. To make filling - mix softened cream cheese and margarine. Add other ingredients and beat until mixed. Serves 12.

My Sunday School has made and sold these for years. They freeze well, and they are perfect for holiday entertaining.

Martha Tucker
Jennifer Tucker '97

Swedish Creme

1 cup sugar	2 cups sour cream
2 cups heavy cream	2 tablespoons vanilla
2 teaspoons unflavored gelatin	Fresh strawberries
	Fresh blueberries

In a double boiler, combine the sugar, cream, and gelatin. Cook for at least 10 minutes, until the sugar has dissolved. Cool. Add and beat in the sour cream and vanilla. Pour the mixture into wine glasses 2/3 full. Top with fresh sliced fruit.

Bettyeann White (Glinn '53)
Julee White '80
Glinn White, Jr. '82

Strawberry Shortcake

1	small package frozen strawberries, thawed	1	cup boiling water
1	(3-ounce) package strawberry gelatin	1	cup ice, filled with water
		1	(13-inch) purchased angel food cake

Use a Tupperware Jel-Ring Mold. Put strawberries on bottom of jel-ring mold. Mix gelatin and boiling water until dissolved. Add ice and water, stirring until the ice melts. Pour ½ of gelatin over the strawberries. Fit the angel food cake on top, pushing down with spatula until firmly in place. Pour remaining gelatin over the cake. Seal and place in freezer for exactly 45 minutes (no longer). Unmold shortcake and serve with center of ring filled with whipped topping. Do not leave in the freezer longer than 1 hour. If made ahead, burp the seal and let jel overnight or 2-3 hours in the refrigerator. Serves 10.

Helen Moese
Linda Moese '97

Strawberry Mousse

1	pint frozen strawberries, thawed	¼	cup sugar
1	(3-ounce) package strawberry gelatin	2	cups whipping cream

Mash thawed strawberries. Drain, reserving liquid. Add enough water to juice to make 1½ cups liquid. Bring juice mixture to a boil. Add gelatin and stir until dissolved. Chill until consistency of unbeaten egg whites. Combine strawberry pulp and sugar. Mix well. Stir into gelatin mixture. Beat cream until soft peaks form. Fold into strawberry mixture. Spoon into lightly oiled 7-cup mold. Chill until set. Serve slices garnished with whipped cream and fresh strawberries.

Very pretty!

Maggie Jahn

Tiramisu

2	cups mascarpone Italian cheese	8	tablespoons amaretto
4	eggs, separated	1	cup VERY strong coffee
²/₃	cup sugar		Loffelbiscuits for Tiramisu
2	teaspoons unflavored gelatin		(Italian market)

Line pan with waxed paper if using a spring form pan. For regular pan or serving dish, spray lightly with cooking spray and just scoop out each serving. Beat egg yolks, vanilla, and sugar very well. Add mascarpone, 6 tablespoons of the amaretto, and gelatin. Beat thoroughly. In separate bowl, beat egg whites forming soft peaks. In another dish, add 2 tablespoons amaretto to coffee. Dip one side of biscuit in coffee, turn over, place in bottom of pan, lining entire pan with dipped biscuits. Add egg whites to mascarpone mixture, folding in. Spoon half over biscuits. Repeat biscuits, then remaining mixture. Refrigerate for several hours. Sprinkle with cocoa.

This recipe is from Anny Moulter of Mainz Weisenau, Germany.

Gloria Gilpin, President ('98-'99) (Bobby '62)
Wes Gilpin '93
Katherine Gilpin '97

Italian Tiramisu

1	(16-ounce) container mascarpone cheese	1½	cups whipping cream (divided)
½	cup powdered sugar, sifted	2	tablespoons water
⅓	cup plus 3 tablespoons Kahlua	2	teaspoons instant espresso coffee granules
2	(1-ounce) squares semisweet chocolate, coarsely grated	2	(3-4 ½-ounce) packages ladyfingers (unfilled)
1½	teaspoons vanilla (divided)	1	(1-ounce) square semisweet chocolate (for garnish)
½	teaspoon salt		

Combine mascarpone cheese, ½ cup powdered sugar, 3 tablespoons Kahlua, 2 ounces grated chocolate, 1 teaspoon vanilla, and salt. Stir well with wire whisk. Beat 1 cup whipping cream until soft peaks form. Gently fold whipped cream mixture into cheese mixture. Set aside. Combine remaining ⅓ cup Kahlua, water, espresso granules, and remaining ½ teaspoon vanilla. Stir well. Separate ladyfingers in half lengthwise. Line the bottom of a serving dish with ¼ ladyfingers. Brush with 2 tablespoons of the espresso mixture. Spoon ⅓ of the cheese mixture over saturated ladyfingers. Repeat layering procedure twice. Top with remaining ladyfingers. Brush with remaining espresso mixture. Beat remaining ½ cup whipping cream until foamy. Gradually add 2 tablespoons powdered sugar. Add enough Kahlua and a little bit of milk to thin mixture slightly. Spoon over top. Sprinkle with reserved grated chocolate and powdered sugar. Cover and chill at least 6 hours.

Patricia Bradfield
Quisha Albert '00

Chocolate Leaves

¼ cup of your choice of one of the following ingredients:

Semisweet chocolate morsels	**Butterscotch morsels**
Candy Melts	**White chocolate**

In a metal measuring cup with handle (½ cup is ideal), melt one of the above ingredients to spreading consistency (NOT liquid), while stirring over hot water. Dip container in hot water again as it cools. Wash leaves (such as rose, photinia, ligustrum, holly, etc.) and pat dry. Spread chocolate on underside of leaf in a thin layer using butter spreader, other small knife, or back of small spoon. Place on tray a few at a time. Freeze for 5 minutes. Peel leaf off gently, beginning at stem and you can usually use the leaf again. If the weather is hot, use ice cubes on your fingers to keep chocolate from melting. For fall leaves, do some in chocolate, butterscotch, and tinted Candy Melts. For Christmas leaves, use green Candy Melts. For more vivid color, add concentrated paste color, or liquid food coloring sparingly as more than a drop might destroy the consistency. Makes a beautiful garnish for desserts. If used for candy, make thicker layers.

Be creative. Who knows? You might be the one who comes up with a perfect Aggie Maroon!

Lillian Gips
Bruce Holmes '78 (son)
Jeffrey Broaddus '98 (grandson)

Easter Bird's Nest Treats

2 cups miniature marshmallows	1 (6-ounce) package chow mein noodles
¼ cup butter or margarine	1 (12-ounce) package small jelly beans

In 2-quart saucepan, combine marshmallows and butter. Cook over low heat, stirring occasionally, until melted, about 6-8 minutes. Stir in noodles until very well coated. With buttered fingers, press mixture on bottom and up sides of each cup of 12-cup (buttered) muffin pan. Refrigerate 2 hours or until firm. Remove nests and fill with jelly beans. Makes 12 treats.

Judy Boldt (Bob '68)
Laura Boldt '94
David Boldt '97

AGGIE SPIRIT

One thing Aggies do best is spread the Aggie Spirit. Aggies believe that anything worth having is worth "Aggie-izing", especially in maroon and white! Food, decorative accessories, clothing, jewelry, toys, stationery, luggage, lawns, pets, barns, cars...nothing escapes the Aggie Spirit!

Aggie Collection Photo
By
Richard Korcyznski

Cherry Almond Bits (Love That Microwave!)

1 cup brown sugar	½ cup candied cherries, chopped
⅓ cup evaporated milk	½ teaspoon almond extract
2 tablespoons corn syrup	1 cup slivered almonds, toasted
1 cup semisweet chocolate pieces	24 candied cherry halves

Place 24 foil mini cups on baking sheet. In 2-quart glass bowl, combine brown sugar, milk, and syrup. Microwave 4-6 minutes, or until thickened, stirring every 2 minutes. Stir in chocolate chips, chopped cherries, and almond extract. Stir until chocolate is melted and mix has thickened. Let stand 3 minutes. Drop by rounded teaspoons into foil cup. Press candied cherry halves over top. Refrigerate 30 minutes.

VARIATION-
Substitute ½ cup candied fruit for cherries and ½ teaspoon orange extract for almond extract. To toast almonds, spread in single layer in microwave-safe baking dish. Microwave on high for 2½-4 minutes, stirring every minute until nuts are browned.

Sue Owen
Michael Owen '95

Peanut Brittle (Microwave)

1 cup sugar	1 teaspoon butter or margarine
½ cup light corn syrup	1 teaspoon vanilla
1 cup peanuts	1 teaspoon baking soda

(If using raw, unsalted peanuts, add, for first microwave cycle, ⅛ teaspoon salt.) Combine syrup and sugar. Microwave on high for 4 minutes. Add roasted/salted peanuts. Microwave 3-5 minutes on high (900 watts for 3 minutes). Add margarine or butter. Add vanilla. Mix well 1-2 minutes. Add baking soda. Stir until light and foamy. Spread on well greased cookie sheet. Let cool for 1 hour. Break into small pieces.

Gloria Gilpin, President ('98-'99) (Bobby '62)
Wes Gilpin '93
Katherine Gilpin '97

Never Fail Peanut Brittle

3	cups sugar	1	tablespoon margarine
1	cup light corn syrup	1	teaspoon salt
½	cup water	2	teaspoons baking soda
3	cups raw Spanish peanuts		

Boil sugar, corn syrup, and water until thread spins. Add peanuts and cook slowly to 300° on candy thermometer. The mixture will have a brownish-gold color. Remove from heat and add margarine, salt, and baking soda. Pour onto 2 buttered cookie sheets. Spread as thin as possible. Cool completely. Break into pieces.

Peggy Erickson, President ('85-'86), President Federation ('95-'96)
Kelle Erickson '85
Traci Erickson Thomas '89
Ashlee Erickson '95

Wes's Peanut Butter Balls

32	ounces creamy peanut butter	1½	cups powdered sugar
2	cans Eagle Brand Milk	2	cups chocolate chips

Combine all ingredients, mixing thoroughly until well blended. Hand mixing works best. Roll into 1-inch balls. Stores well in sealed tins or zip bags. Using high quality ingredients assures a high quality product. Makes approximately 100 balls.

A Mother's Day party given by our third grade class was the beginning of these no-bake treats that have become a family favorite. It is just not Christmas until we all sit around the table rolling the sticky mixture in our palms, popping a few in our mouths as we go.

Wes Gilpin '93

Chewy Pralines

2	cups light corn syrup	2	cups whipping cream
2	cups dark brown sugar	2	teaspoons pure vanilla extract
1	pound (4 sticks) unsalted butter		7-10 cups (2-2½-pounds) pecans, chopped

Clamp a candy thermometer onto the side of a 4-5-quart saucepan with a heavy bottom. Over low-medium heat, cook together corn syrup and brown sugar until mixture reaches 250°. Remove from heat. Add butter (cut into 1 tablespoon-sized chunks) and stir until dissolved. Slowly stir in cream. Return to heat. Stirring constantly, cook until temperature on candy thermometer reaches 248° (maybe 30 minutes). Remove from heat. Stir in vanilla and pecans. Drop by tablespoon onto lightly buttered (or use cooking spray) sheets of foil. Makes 65 (2-inch) pralines. Recipe may be halved.

These are "to die for" rich!

Eileen Buis
Josh Buis '97
Jordan Buis '99

Martha Washington by Barge

2	boxes powdered sugar	1	pound pecans
1	can Eagle Brand milk	1	(8-ounce) package Baker's Semisweet Chocolate
2	teaspoons vanilla	1	bar paraffin
8	ounces butter, melted		
2	cans coconut, flaked		

Mix well powdered sugar, milk, vanilla, and butter in large bowl. Add coconut and pecans. Mix with hands. Roll into small balls. Mix semisweet chocolate and paraffin in top of double boiler. Dip balls with toothpicks. Place on buttered wax paper. Yield - 64

JaNahn Rodriguez, President ('97-'98)
David Rodriguez '94
Cindy Rodriguez '95
Dan Rodriguez '99

Orange Ice Cream

4 oranges (grate rind of some)	1 pint cream
Juice of 1 lemon	1½ quarts of milk
2½ cups sugar	

Combine all ingredients and freeze in ice cream freezer. Beat with electric mixer and re-freeze.

Ona Cook
Aggie Aunt

Peaches and Cream Ice Cream

¾ cup sugar	2 eggs, beaten
2 tablespoons cornstarch	1 cup whipping cream
1 teaspoon salt	2 cups peaches, pureed
3 cups milk	1 tablespoon lemon juice
¹/₃ cup light corn syrup	1 teaspoon vanilla

Stir together in 2-quart saucepan sugar, cornstarch, and salt. Add milk, corn syrup, and eggs. Stir constantly over low heat until mixture coats a spoon. Chill. Add cream, pureed peaches, lemon juice, and vanilla. Freeze in ice cream freezer. Makes 2 quarts. Can be doubled. Serves 16.

Sue Owen
Michael Owen '95

Maroon and White Wines

MAROON AND WHITE WINES

by Merrill Bonarrigo '75
Messina Hof Wine Cellars, Inc.

The Spirit of Aggieland is alive and well and flourishing at Messina Hof Winery. After all we only make maroon and white wines! I never dreamed when I graduated from Texas A&M in 1975 that I would be affiliated with a winery—right here in the Brazos Valley! My husband, Paul, and I have pursued the making of the perfect wine, and especially the perfect wine for food.

Wine does not come with a list of instructions, like how to read the label or how to pronounce the name. To help end some of this confusion, here are simple tips in "Wine for Aggies" nomenclature. First, in our country, wines are named for the types of grapes used to make that wine. In Europe, the wines are named after the geographical regions in which the grape was grown.

When reading the wine label be aware of these points: 1) the name of the winery producing and bottling the wine, 2) the brand name, 3) appelation of origin—where grapes are grown—must be 75 percent grown in the stated appelation, 4) wine varietal or fanciful name—must be 75 percent of the labeled variety, and 5) vintage year—date of harvest—95 percent of grapes used must have been harvested in the vintage year stated on the label.

One of the most intimidating aspects of wine is the pronunciation of its name. Here is a pronunciation chart so that you can at least sound like you know what you are talking about.

VARIETAL PRONUNCIATIONS

Chablis	Sha-blee
Pinot Blanc	Pea-no Blanh
Fume Blanc	Foo-may Blanh
Sauvignon Blanc	So-vee-nyanh Blanh
Riesling	Reez-ling
Traminer	Trah-mee-ner
Gewurztraminer	Gay-versh-trah-mee-ner
Charbono	Shar-bo-no
Pinot Noir	Pea-no-No-ahr
Cabernet Sauvignon	Kab-er-nay So-vee-nyonh
Muscat Canelli	Muss-cat Ka-nell-ee
Pinot Chardonnay	Pea-no Shar-doh-nay
Chenin Blanc	She-nahn Blanh
Sauterne	So-tairn
Semillon	Say-mee-hanh
Sylvaner	Sil-vah-ner

Cabernet Franc	Kab-ernay Franh
Zinfandel	Zin-fan-dell
Gamay	Gay-may
Red Pinot	Red Pea-no
Gamay Beaujolais	Gay-may Boh-sho-lay
Merlot	Murr-law

Once the purchase is made, how do you open the bottle? Place the bottle on the corner of the table. If the bottle has a foil capsule, cut the top of the foil at the upper edge neck. Remove the foil. If the bottle has the latest "B-Cap" or cork label which is just a foil disc on top of the cork, you may puncture it directly with the opener. Uncork with the wine. Wipe the top of the bottle to remove any remaining cork. Always pour your glass of wine first. Even if you use a good screwpull, you can occasionally get little pieces of cork floating on top of your wine. By pouring your wine first, you get the small cork pieces—not your guests.

When opening champagne, make sure the bottle is never aimed at a guest when opening it. Cover the cork with a side towel when removing it. Champagne should be served in a chilled stemmed tulip glass. It requires two pouring motions. Do not attempt to completely fill the glass with the first pouring motion.

Restaurant purchases are safer in that someone else is opening the wine for you. The wine steward (Sommelier) will hand the cork to the host and pour an ounce sample for the host's approval. The host should then feel and smell the cork. It should have a wine smell to it and should be wet to the touch on one end and dry on the other. Wine should be stored on its side in order to keep the cork moist thereby preventing air from touching the wine in the bottle. Then the host will swirl the wine in the glass, smell, and taste the wine. After the host approves the wine, the steward will pour for the guests.

When tasting the wine, hold the glass by the stem so as not to warm the bowl of the glass. As you practice the technique, learn to swirl the wine to the left and then to the right. (When you get really good, you can put one hand in your pocket while swirling.) Use these generally accepted wine terms when describing the wines you are tasting.

WINE TERMS

Big — A wine strong of flavor and high in alcohol and acidity

Body — The feeling of weight in the mouth distinguishes heavy from light wines

Character — Complexity in a wine that shows unmistakable and distinctive features

Delicate — A light and agreeable balance of flavor and quality

Depth — Subtle richness giving a feeling of many flavor-layers

Dry — Complete absence of sweetness

Earthy — A mineral or organic taste of the soil or terrain

Flinty — The smell of struck flint, typical of certain austere dry wines from high mineral soil, metallic

Fruity — A pleasantly ripe, but not necessarily grapy, smell

Full-bodied — Thick in the tactile sense

Grapy — A rich, sweet aroma produced by certain grape varieties

Luscious — All the balance qualities of softness, sweetness, fruitiness, and ripeness

Tannin — Very dry wine which when sipped tends to make the mouth pucker

VARIETAL TERMS

Whites —

Chardonnay — Apple, lemon, pineapple, peach, vanilla, buttery, oaky

Sauvignon Blanc — Grass, hay, herbs, citrus, woody, vegetal

Riesling — Pear, peach, citrus, floral, honey, apricots

Gwurztraminer — Melon, peach, apricot, cloves

Chenin Blanc — Spicy, floral, fruity, apples, pears, peaches

Muscat Canelli — Floral, nectary, apricot

Reds —

Cabernet Sauvignon — Black current, cassis, herbal, mint, eucalyptus, green pepper

Merlot — Cassis, Black cherry

Pinot Noir — Black cherry, plum, raisin, grapy, earthy

Gamay — Strawberry jam

Zinfandel — Raspberry, spicy, black pepper

Lenoir — Wood, blackberry, chocolate, raspberry

Wine is a totally natural beverage that does not require the hand of man to make. Yeast live naturally on the skin of the grape and any puncture in the skin will permit the yeast to enter the fruit and initiate the fermentation process.

The winemaker takes that natural process and manages it to make sure the end product is of commercial quality. This includes using specially prepared yeasts instead of the natural wild yeasts. These yeasts possess unique characteristics of flavor and aroma which are imparted to the wine. There are hundreds of decisions made by the winemaker that can change the resulting wine.

Unlike beer and iced tea with PH over 4.0, wine has a PH of 2.95 - 3.65 which makes it the perfect food beverage. The lower PH cleanses the palate preparing the tongue for each bite of food. The last bite tastes as flavorful as the first.

Food and wine pairing is one of the most fun and challenging hobbies that lasts a lifetime. Every meal is a new experience. Tastes, flavors, textures, and aromas are all elements that affect the combinations of food and wine. Have you ever been to a restaurant and experienced a fabulous meal with a wonderful wine and then gone back to that same restaurant and ordered the same bottle of wine with a different dish expecting the previous WOW only to be disappointed? The wine most likely did not change. The variable was the food.

High acid foods such as tomatoes, citrus, and vinegar are best suited to high-acid wines, such as Riesling, Gewurztraminer, or Chenin Blanc.

Sweetness masks bitterness and saltiness. So if you accidentally add too much salt, serve a sweeter wine like the Muscat Canelli, Riesling, or blush/rose wines.

Rich fatty foods such as cheese, oil based sauced, fatty meats, and paté match best with crisp more acidic wines that will cut through the oily texture to cleanse the palate. Buttery or oily wines will tend to coat the mouth.

Foods with sweetness are best paired with wines of the same sweetness. If the food is sweeter than the wine, it will make the wine taste dry or more tart than it tastes on its own.

Dishes prepared with the same wine to accompany the meal are better married to that wine in flavor.

Food should never overwhelm the wine, and wine should never overwhelm the food. You are looking for balance.

Wines with crisp acidity, dry or slightly sweet, light or medium body, low to moderate alcohol, smooth tannins, and neutral flavor are more likely to combine well with foods.

Once you have achieved the thickness you desire in your sauce, you may add more wine to enrich the flavor of the sauce and better pair the like flavors.

So remember, the most important rule is to drink those maroon and white wines you most enjoy with foods you most enjoy!

Kitchen Hints from the 12th Mom

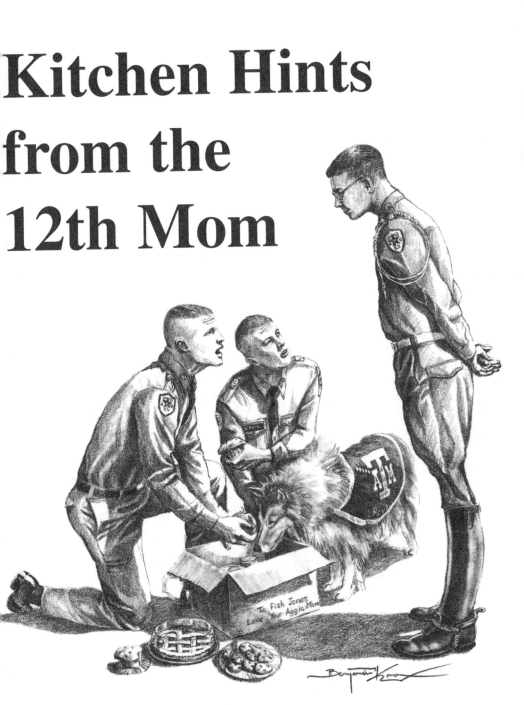

INGREDIENT MEASURES

Ingredient	Amount	Approximate Measure
Apples	1 medium apple	1 cup, sliced
	1 pound	3 cups peeled, sliced, or diced
Bananas	3-4 medium	2 cups, sliced
	3-4 medium	1¾ cups, mashed
Bread Crumbs	1 slice fresh	½ cup soft crumbs
	1 slice dry	⅓ cup dry crumbs
Celery	1 medium stalk	½ cup chopped or diced
Cheese	1 pound	4 cups, grated or shredded
	1 pound	2⅔ cups, cubed
Coconut	3½ ounces flaked	1⅓ cups
	1 pound shredded	5⅔ cups
Cracker crumbs	28 soda crackers	1 cup
	15 graham crackers	1 cup
Eggs	1 egg	4 tablespoons liquid
	4-5 whole eggs	1 cup
	7-9 egg whites	1 cup
Flour	1 pound all-purpose	3 cups, sifted
	1 pound cake flour	4½ cups
Lemons	1 lemon	1 tablespoon grated rind
	1 medium	2-3 tablespoons juice
	5-8 medium	1 cup juice
Mushrooms	1 pound	5-6 cups, sliced
Nuts	¼ pound chopped	1 cup
	1 pound	4 cups halves
Onions	1 medium	½ cup, chopped
	1 medium	1 tablespoon minced, dried onion
Oranges	3-4 medium oranges	1 cup
	1 orange	2 tablespoons grated rind
Shortening or margarine	1 pound = 3 cups	1 stick butter or margarine = ½cup

Sugar	1 pound brown	2½ cups
	1 pound granulated	2 cups
	1 pound powdered	3½ cups
Yeast, active dry	¼ ounce package	1 scant tablespoon, or 1 (6-ounce) cake, compressed, fresh yeast

SUBSTITUTIONS

Butter	1 cup	1 cup margarine or ⅞ cup vegetable shortening.
Buttermilk or sour milk	1 cup	1 cup plain yogurt, or 1 tablespoon lemon juice or vinegar plus enough milk to equal 1 cup (let stand 5 minutes), or 1¾ teaspoons cream of tartar plus 1 cup milk.
Chocolate, semisweet	1 ounce	½ ounce unsweetened chocolate plus 1 tablespoon sugar.
Chocolate, semisweet	6 ounces chips	½ cup plus 1 tablespoon cocoa plus 7 tablespoons sugar plus 3 tablespoons butter or margarine.
Chocolate, unsweetened	1 ounce	3 tablespoons cocoa plus 1 tablespoon butter or margarine.
Cornstarch	1 tablespoon	2 tablespoons all-purpose flour.
Cream, half-and-half	1 cup	1½ tablespoons butter plus whole milk to equal 1 cup, or ½ cup light cream plus ½ cup whole milk.

Cream, sour	1 cup	1 cup plain yogurt, or ¾ cup sour milk, buttermilk, or plain yogurt, plus ⅓ cup butter, or 1 tablespoon lemon juice plus enough evaporated whole milk to equal 1 cup.
Cream, whipping	1 cup	¾ cup whole milk plus ⅓ cup butter.
Flour	1 cup sifted cake	1 cup minus 2 tablespoons sifted all-purpose flour.
Flour	1 cup self-rising	1 cup sifted all-purpose flour plus 1½ teaspoons baking powder and ⅛ teaspoon salt.
Fresh Herbs	1 tablespoon	1 teaspoon dried herbs, crushed.
Honey	1 cup	1¼ cups granulated sugar plus ¼ cup liquid (any liquid the recipe calls for).
Sugar, granulated	1 cup	1¾ cups powdered sugar, or 1 cup packed light brown sugar, or 1 cup superfine sugar, or ½ cup honey and reduce the amount of liquid by ½ cup.
Sugar, powdered	1 cup	⅛ cup plus 1 tablespoon granulated sugar.
Tomatoes	1 16-ounce can, cut-up	3 fresh medium tomatoes, cut-up.
Vanilla extract		Grated lemon or orange rind for flavoring, or try a little cinnamon or nutmeg.

Index

Index

INDEX

INDEX

INDEX

INDEX

HULLABALOO IN THE KITCHEN II

Dallas County A&M University Mothers' Club
P. O. Box 796212
Dallas, Texas 75379-6212

Please send _____ copies of Hullabaloo In The Kitchen II $19.95 each   _____

Postage and Handling $3.50 each   _____

Tax (Texas residents) $1.93 each   _____

                                                    (Total — $25.38 each)

                                                    Total enclosed   _____

Name _____

Address _____

City _____ State _____ Zip _____

Make checks payable to **Dallas County A&M University Mothers' Club**
All proceeds from the sale of the cookbook will be returned to Texas A&M University for
scholarships and student activities.

HULLABALOO IN THE KITCHEN II

Dallas County A&M University Mothers' Club
P. O. Box 796212
Dallas, Texas 75379-6212

Please send _____ copies of Hullabaloo In The Kitchen II $19.95 each   _____

Postage and Handling $3.50 each   _____

Tax (Texas residents) $1.93 each   _____

                                                    (Total — $25.38 each)

                                                    Total enclosed   _____

Name _____

Address _____

City _____ State _____ Zip _____

Make checks payable to **Dallas County A&M University Mothers' Club**
All proceeds from the sale of the cookbook will be returned to Texas A&M University for
scholarships and student activities.